D1317888

WHEN ILLNESS STRIKES THE LEADER

WHEN ILLNESS STRIKES THE LEADER
THE DILEMMA OF THE CAPTIVE KING

JERROLD M. POST, M.D.

ROBERT S. ROBINS

YALE UNIVERSITY PRESS   NEW HAVEN AND LONDON

Published with assistance from the foundation established in memory of
Philip Hamilton McMillan of the Class of 1894, Yale College.

Designed by Sonia L. Scanlon.
Set in Bembo type by The Composing Room of Michigan, Inc.,
Grand Rapids, Michigan.
Printed in the United States of America by Vail-Ballou Press, Binghamton, New York.
The following publishers have generously given permission to use quotations from
copyrighted works: From "As Time Goes By" (Herman Hupfeld) © 1931 (Renewed)
Warner Bros. Inc., Bienstock Publishing Company, and Redwood Music Ltd. All rights
for the U.S. controlled by Warner Bros. Inc. All rights reserved. Used by permission.
From *The Complete Greek Tragedies,* edited by David Grene and Richmond Lattimore,
Oedipus at Colonus, trans. Robert Fitzgerald, © 1941 by Harcourt, Brace, & Co.

Library of Congress Cataloging-in-Publication Data

Post, Jerrold M.
When illness strikes the leader : the dilemma of the
captive king / Jerrold M. Post, Robert S. Robins.
p.   cm.
Includes bibliographical references and index.
ISBN 0-300-05683-4 (alk. paper)
1. Public administration—Decision making—
Psychological aspects.   2. Heads of state—Mental
health.   3. Heads of state—Drug use.
4. Diseases and history.   5. Political leadership—
Psychological aspects.   I. Robins, Robert S.
II. Title.   [DNLM: 1. Decision Making.
2. Leadership.   3. Mental Disorders—
psychology.   4. Politics.   5. Sick Role.
6. Substance Abuse—psychology. BF 637.L4 P857w]
JF1525.D4P68   1993
351.007'25'019—dc20
DNLM/DLC
for Library of Congress   92-25302
CIP

British Library Cataloguing in Publication Data
A catalogue record for this book is available from the British Library.

The paper in this book meets the guidelines for permanence and durability
of the Committee on Production Guidelines for Book Longevity
of the Council on Library Resources.

10 9 8 7 6 5 4 3 2 1

In loving memory of
Jack and Lillian Post
and
Robert Thaddeus Robins

CONTENTS

Contents

ACKNOWLEDGMENTS

We are particularly indebted to Alexander George, Hugh L'Etang, and Bert Park for their encouragements throughout this project and for their critical reading of the manuscript. We have been greatly helped by colleagues and students, family and friends, with whom we discoursed, often vigorously, about the book. All cannot be thanked, but we do wish to express our gratitude to Henry Rothschild, M.D., Allen Johnson, Jr., of the New Orleans *Gambit*, Frederick Sheehan, Viola Sheehan, Mark Smith, M.D., and Vamik Volkan, M.D. We are grateful to our wives, Carolyn Post and Marjorie McGann Robins, for their support and constructive criticism.

Special thanks to Gladys Topkis, senior editor at Yale University Press, for her sense of vision, vigorous critical intellect, and patience; to Laura Dooley, whose editorial gifts were embellished by her knowledge of history; and to Mary Louise Mesquita, graduate research assistant extraordinaire, whose scholarly diligence and perseverance were of immeasurable importance in bringing this project to conclusion.

The Carnegie Corporation of New York provided generous support to the leadership research of Jerrold Post. In 1987–88, Robert Robins was a visiting scientist at the Tavistock Clinic, London, which provided a stimulating intellectual haven during an important phase of work on this book.

Introduction

The towering stature of America's first president has usually obscured the fact that the United States narrowly averted having an impaired leader in office at the beginnings of its history. In 1792, as he neared the end of his first term as America's "elected monarch," George Washington, sixty years old, hesitated whether to seek reelection. Conscientious and decisive throughout his public career, he feared that he was losing his mental powers. In a letter to Thomas Jefferson he noted that his memory was getting worse and that his mind was showing a general decay.[1]

We know now that Washington's fears were justified and that he had accurately identified a progressive dementia. His mental abilities, especially his emotional stability and capacity to evaluate reality, were in evident decline before his second term ended in 1797. They became severely compromised soon after he left office, as exemplified by a conflict with President John Adams in September 1798 over how to counter a threat from the French. In that clash Washington was emotionally intemperate, confused, and out of touch with reality, reactions that grew more and more prominent as he became increasingly senile after leaving office.

Washington was unusual; the early symptoms of senile deterioration typically are least—and last—recognized by the victim, a circumstance that can have serious consequences for the political system. What is not unusual, however, is the onset of mental deterioration during the later years of a popular leader's career.

We should not be surprised when leaders are afflicted by serious illness. Political leaders tend to achieve high status in late middle age and even old age; indeed, some societies confer the wreath of leadership only upon the aged. Having aspired to high office throughout a lifetime, leaders are often reluctant to relinquish power. But time is an implacable and ultimately victorious foe. Although the decline of old age may strike some as early as their fifties, others not until their eighties, such decline inevitably occurs. Arteriosclerosis, cancer, stroke, and uremia as well as the end stages of alcohol abuse are far more common in this age group than in any other. Not only are leaders prey to the illnesses that afflict us all, but for some the pressures of high office exact a special toll. Even excluding the assassinated presidents, American chief executives have had a substantially lower life expectancy than their fellow citizens of the same age. Aging, ailing leaders are not a rare exception—illness and disability are frequently guests and occasionally permanent residents in the throne room.

Curiously, however, studies of political leadership characteristically assume that the leader is healthy in mind and body. The topic of a mentally imbalanced or physically impaired leader is not seriously considered in the 446 pages of James McGregor Burns's *Leadership* (1978), winner of both the Pulitzer Prize and the National Book Award. Neither "illness" nor "disability" appears in the index of Glenn Paige's otherwise comprehensive *Scientific Study of Political Leadership* (1977). What literature does exist on health and politics is spotty, most of it individual case histories. Few scholars have attempted systematically to survey the effects of illness on leadership. Important exceptions are the pathbreaking works of Hugh L'Etang, *The Pathology of Leadership* (1970) and *Fit to Lead?* (1980), Arno Karlen's provocatively titled *Napoleon's Glands: And Other Essays in Biohistory* (1984), and the recent study by the neurosurgeon Bert Park, *The Impact of Illness on World Leaders* (1986). These well-documented and perceptive studies address the effects of physical and mental impairment on individual leaders. The authors approach the subject as medical historian-detectives. Their principal interest is to diagnose retrospectively and describe events in a narrative context rather than to consider systematically the effects of illness in high office on leadership and governmental functioning. They have not focused on the effects of the disabled leader's illness on the government's decision-making, the consequences of the illness for the group-based struggle for power, and the relationship between the disabled leader and the inner circle.* Yet every leader's decisions and actions are mediated by that inner circle through which information and feedback are filtered and decisions implemented. Nor have they addressed

---

*Both L'Etang, *Pathology of Leadership,* and Park, *Impact of Illness on World Leaders,* have illustrated how illness affected the decision-making of several important leaders—Hitler, Churchill, Roosevelt, and Wilson. They have also examined the role of a key member of the inner circle—the leader's physician.

the mediating role of the leader's personality, which significantly affects the impact of illness upon the leader and the manner in which the ailing leader interacts with his leadership circle.

Concern about the relationship between a malleable ruler and his inner circle is certainly not new. A leader on a string manipulated by uncertain and unknown masters, one of the worst forms of government, has often been seen as worse than tyranny. As the English reformer William Tyndale pronounced: "Yea, and it is better to have a tyrant [as] thy king than a shadow; a passive king who does nought himself, but suffereth others to do with him what they will, and to lead him whither they list. For a tyrant, though he do wrong unto the good, yet he punisheth the vil, and maketh all men obey, neither suffering any man to poll but himself only. [A passive king] shall be much more grievous unto his realm than a right tyrant."[2]

The leader rendered incompetent and manipulable by illness is a special case of the shadow king, *Rex Inutilis,* as Tyndale so graphically characterized it early in the sixteenth century. The medically disabled shadow king has played an important role throughout history and is richly represented in the twentieth century. What was the effect of the decision-making paralysis associated with three aging, ailing leaders in the Soviet Union—Leonid Brezhnev, Yuri Andropov, and Konstantin Chernenko—in setting the stage for the vigorous transformational leadership of Mikhail Gorbachev? How did Ferdinand Marcos's terminal kidney disease affect his political judgment and pave the way for Cory Aquino's "People Power revolution"? How much did the rigidity of old age contribute to the decision by the eighty-five-year-old Deng Xiaoping, previously known as a liberal reformer, to unleash the violent repression of Tiananmen Square? As events moved rapidly in East Germany during the summer of 1989, the aged autocrat Erich Honecker was incapacitated by a serious gastrointestinal disease, and the Wall came tumbling down.

Can anyone doubt that the decisions—or indecision—of these leaders contributed to the march of history? Yet the analysis of the transformational events of their tenure has almost entirely ignored the influence of illness and the encroachments of old age on the leaders' flawed decision-making. Why is it that scholars have largely overlooked the effects of illness and disability on leadership? To some extent this oversight is undoubtedly a reflection of the impersonalist point of view that has dominated Western intellectual history since at least the mid-nineteenth century. If individuals matter little in politics, their health will matter even less.

The neglect probably also results from the lack of a general theory relating health to political events and of the interdisciplinary training necessary to address this domain. If a scholar has neither the conceptual framework nor the methodological training to evaluate a phenomenon, he or she is not likely to consider it.

Another obstacle is the paucity of data. Reliable, which is to say intimate, personal and confidential data on health are extremely difficult to acquire. This, however, may be less a question of the unavailability of health data than of the lack of the specialized perspective and training necessary to identify critical health issues. Medically naive political analysts may insufficiently appreciate the degree to which leadership decisions can be influenced and distorted not only by the early stages of illness but also by medical treatment. Most political scientists lack the medical knowledge and clinical experience required to provide sophisticated differential diagnoses at a distance and to evaluate the effects of an ailing body on a leader's mind and decision-making.

By the same token, it is a rare physician who has been able to supplement a medical education with graduate training in political science, international affairs, and history. Studies of medically disabled leaders by politically unsophisticated physicians often attribute to illness behaviors that may in fact be determined by the complexities of the political system. In addition to the impersonalist point of view, the absence of a general theory, and the complexities of interdisciplinary analysis, there is probably an important psycho-political reason for the lack of attention to the impact of illness on political leadership. The optimistic assumption of the leader's health probably reflects our common wish for leaders to be omnipotent, omniscient, and immortal. When the crown of leadership is placed on the monarch, prime minister, or president, that leader becomes the repository of the followers' hopes and dreams. And it is unthinkable that this symbol of strength and wisdom can be afflicted with mortal ailments.

The previously able leader rendered incompetent by illness, and the politics surrounding that illness, are the subjects of this study. Because of the majesty conferred upon the chief of state by his followers, be he emperor or king, prime minister or president, we have employed the language and metaphor of royalty throughout this book. To avoid both the pitfalls and the burdens of highly specialized training in multiple disciplines, we—a physician trained in psychiatry who has devoted his career to the study of political leadership, and a political scientist with a career-long interest in the disabled political leader—have endeavored to bring an interdisciplinary perspective to bear on the complex problems of the medically disabled political leader and the effects of leader illness on the political system.

The politics surrounding the illness of a leader often require that the disabled leader remain in office, for the old cliché that an evil known is preferable to one unknown too often holds true, especially in closed societies. During the last years of Mao Zedong's rule, when he was suffering from senile megalomania,[3] those in the leadership circle who differed or would not cooperate were destroyed. The leader and his inner circle became locked in a fatal embrace, each dependent upon the other for survival. The cases of Mao Zedong, Joseph Stalin, and Ferdinand Marcos suggest that in closed societies and when there is no clear mechanism of succession, the intricate relationship between the ailing leader and the inner circle will be crucial. Because of this circumstance of secret and malignant interdependence, here we have called such leaders "captive kings."

Disease always comes as an uninvited guest, at the table of the great as in the lives of lesser mortals, profoundly affecting the political equilibrium. In reviewing more than a hundred cases to identify patterns and themes associated with the effect of illness upon the relationship among the leader, inner circle, followers, and political system itself, we have identified a number of broad issues. Of critical importance is the nature of the illness and how it presents itself. The argument of this book has been organized in terms of these issues: the nature of the illness and its effects on decision-making; the possibility of masking illness in high office; the effects of prescribed drugs and substance abuse on leadership behavior; the complexities of the medical treatment of the ailing VIP; the effects of old age and mortal illness on political behavior and the interaction of personality and style with age and illness; and the relation between the nature of the political system and illness in high office. We shall examine the manner in which the demands of high office compromise the quality of medical care and illustrate with examples from contemporary history that being a VIP can be dangerous not only for the health of the leader but also for the well-being of the nation.

We shall illustrate the principal themes with examples from past and contemporary history, sometimes revisiting the same leader to illustrate different points. For expository purposes, these factors are described separately. But the course of the illness, the relationship between the disabled leader and the inner circle, and their relationship with the polity are of course constantly interacting and changing.

The initially mildly impaired leader, able to work fully in concert with the inner circle, will over time become progressively impaired. What first was a circumstance in which he and the inner circle were managing the public may change to one in which he is being managed by the inner circle. Should the illness be characterized by increasing irritability and rigidity, with wide fluctuations in the leader's ability to function, the moderate members of the inner circle who attempt to counter his excesses may be ousted, to be replaced by more compliant sycophants. Especially in a closed society, where the alternative to power may be death, the mortally wounded king and desperate court increasingly become locked into a mutual dependency in which neither trusts the other but each needs the other to survive—the syndrome of "the captive king and his captive court."

WHEN ILLNESS STRIKES THE LEADER

1

WHEN THE THRONE ROOM
BECOMES THE SICK ROOM

For God's sake, let us sit upon the ground
And tell sad stories of the death of kings
For within the hollow crown
That rounds the mortal temples of a king
Keeps Death his court.
—Shakespeare, *Richard II*

Is the fate of the world—our fate—in the hands
of sick men?
—Burnet Hershey, *The Nation,* June 1949

When illness strikes the leader, even if he is quaran-
tined behind a wall of secrecy, the political equation
is fundamentally altered, for when illness infects the
royal chamber, the entire palace—indeed, the entire
political system—is affected. How illness enters the
palace has significant consequences for the conduct of
government. Does illness come in by the front gate,
announcing its arrival dramatically and undeniably, or
does it enter quietly and unobtrusively through the
back door? The stealthy invader, the disease with a
gradual and insidious onset, is easiest to conceal yet, if
undisclosed, may have catastrophic consequences for
the nation.

If the disease leaves his mental capacities undamaged,
the leader, at least initially, can participate in decisions
that will affect how the country will be governed during his illness. The leader and his inner circle can meet,
as they did before illness struck, and decide whether,
when, and how to present the facts to the public.
Though ill, the king still rules; not only can he decide
his present fate, but he may be able to maintain some
control over the future. The leader can be instrumental
in devising contingency plans and in setting in motion
temporary or definitive arrangements for succession.

Concealing the Disease

With the active support of the inner circle, the leader may decide to conceal the illness, for a host of reasons. Concealment may be a function of the leader's own denial of his failing health. The leader and the inner circle may rationalize that the country is in a crisis and that the public would be thrown into a panic if it became known that its leader was ill. But in fact the inner circle may well recognize that to acknowledge the leader's illness would be to lose power.

The insidiousness with which the illness presents itself may aid this endeavor to conceal it. Subtle signs of early illness are easily overlooked, so that those outside the inner circle who are in a position to evaluate the leader's health and decision-making may tend to ignore early warning signs, especially if the inner circle assists in the deception.

The Shah of Iran's Hidden Cancer

No case better illustrates the feasibility and the profound political consequences of a chief of state's attempting to lead his country while burdened with a hidden illness than that of Mohammed Reza, shah of Iran. History may well record that the reactions of the shah and his inner circle to his hidden cancer played a major role in paving the way for the Ayatollah Khomeini's Islamic revolution in 1978–79.

Throughout his reign, the shah sought to modernize Iran by increasing the influence of science and technology, decreasing the role of religious authority, and in general aspiring to establish a social and economic pattern more like that of Western Europe than of Third World countries. The absolute ruler of Iran, the shah was attempting a revolutionary reform of the nation from the top down—what he called his White Revolution—and by all accounts he seemed to be succeeding. Although Western liberals believed that liberal reforms were not taking place fast enough, they generally approved of the shah's program and believed that he was following a constructive and well-conceived plan of development.

In the early 1970s, at the height of the White Revolution, the shah was still a relatively young man, in his forties. His son and heir was just a teenager. Firmly ensconced on the Peacock Throne, the shah believed that by applying himself with patience and persistence over the next several decades, he would have more than enough time to make his dreams a reality and bring Iran into the twentieth century. His Western allies shared his belief. The autocratic shah was very much in charge and determined to accomplish his own personal vision.

But illness invaded the throne room and transformed the political equation. In 1973 the shah first fell ill, although the diagnosis of malignancy

2

was not established until the next year.* In April 1974 two French hematologists visited Iran and made the provisional diagnosis that the shah was suffering from lymphocytic leukemia, a form of cancer of the white blood cells that, though usually fatal in the elderly, is compatible with many years of survival. Admonished by the shah's personal physician not to use the word *cancer* to him, the French physicians told the patient that he was suffering from Waldenstrom's macroglobulinemia, the technical name for a rare and mild form of cancer of the blood and lymphatic system. Even with this diagnostic soft-pedaling, the shah had been confronted with the painful reality of his mortality. The gravity of his illness made it clear to him that he would not have time to modernize Iran patiently and systematically.

Malignancies that affect the blood and lymphatic system follow a variable course. For some, such as chronic lymphocytic leukemia and a number of the lymphomas, the disease has a slow development with many remissions, marked until its final stages by no evident symptoms except increasing fatigue and weight loss. With sophisticated chemotherapy, appropriate supportive treatment, and careful control of the victim's schedule it is possible to hide the illness for an extended time.

The shah was able to conceal his grave malady from public view until 1979, when he fled to Mexico before the onslaught of the Iranian revolution. He then sought to enter the United States for treatment at the Sloan-Kettering Institute, the first stop on a painful terminal odyssey. We now know that the shah was waging a prolonged battle with cancer from 1973 until 1979, when he fled Iran and was forced to reveal his illness. He suffered debility not only from the disease itself but also from chemotherapy, which was administered intermittently from February 1975 on. Powerful psychoactive drugs were reportedly also employed to alleviate his anxiety and depression. In addition to dulling the faculties and interfering with mental acuity, some of these drugs have major effects on mood and could have distorted the shah's judgment. Steroids, a frequent treatment for

---

*Material bearing on the timing and specific diagnosis of the shah's illness is somewhat contradictory. It would appear that he was experiencing non-specific gastrointestinal distress during the latter part of 1973, but it was not until the Iranian New Year on March 21, 1974, that the shah discovered a swelling under his rib cage (Zonis, *Majestic Failure,* 154–55). His physicians sought consultation from the eminent French hematologist Jean Bernard, who made the provisional diagnosis of lymphocytic leukemia, cancer of the white blood cells. Reports from the Sloan-Kettering Institute indicate that the shah was early on diagnosed as suffering from lymphoma, cancer of the lymph glands. The details of his medical diagnosis and later medical treatment can be found in Breo, "Shah's Physician Relates Story of Intrigue, Duplicity," and in Shawcross, *The Shah's Last Ride.*

leukemias and lymphomas, can produce both euphoria, with attendant overoptimism, and depression, with feelings of hopelessness and despair.*

In later chapters we shall note the effects of the shah's reaction to his cancer and its treatment on his political program and his ability to cope with the rising tide of religiously led opposition. Our purpose here is to examine how well the shah managed to keep his illness a secret from others—family, friends, and enemies alike. Who knew of the shah's disease, and how and when did they learn of it? Almost certainly he confided in someone in his immediate circle whose support was needed to facilitate his medical treatment. The nature of the chronic leukemias and lymphomas is such that close associates must have noticed their leader's failing health. Nonetheless, the shah successfully determined to shield Empress Farah from the dread news; she was not informed until 1977.

That the Hippocratic requirements of medical confidentiality prevented the shah's French physicians from informing their government strains credulity; initial approaches to the French medical establishment were probably made through diplomatic channels. In any event, French intelligence would have had a lively interest in the shah's health and probably would have made it a central task to discover the diagnosis. The generosity of the French in granting asylum to the shah's bitterest enemy, Ayatollah Khomeini, when the rest of world thought the shah was healthy and looking forward to a long rule could be explained in part by their knowledge that the shah's mortal illness would soon end his reign.

It would seem reasonable to assume that not long after the diagnosis had been established Washington or the U.S. embassy in Tehran would have learned of the shah's illness from the French. If the French government knew, however, it apparently chose not to inform its NATO allies, something that will not surprise observers of the so-called Western alliance. The public evidence suggests that the grave nature of the shah's malignant illness was not recognized by the American government until just months before the shah fled Iran. It was in November 1978, fully five years after the diagnosis was established, that President Jimmy Carter's secretary of the Treasury, Michael Blumenthal, visited the shah and brought back a disturbing report of his passivity, introspection, and withdrawal despite the increasingly dangerous political situation that surrounded him.

If not from the French, might it not have been expected, in view of the large U.S. diplomatic, military, and intelligence presence in Iran, that the U.S. mission in Iran could have penetrated the veil of secrecy early on?

---

*According to Breo, it was not until 1979, when the shah sought refuge in the Bahamas, that Prednisone was added to the powerful cancer chemotherapy drugs that were being administered to him ("Shah's Physician Relates Story of Intrigue, Duplicity").

Given his background in intelligence, as well as his long-standing relationship with and frequent opportunities for personal observations of the shah, it is puzzling that Ambassador Richard Helms did not become aware of the shah's fatal illness. Early in his tour of duty Helms found the shah drawn, haggard, and appearing ill. He also observed him swallowing pills. Helms says that he spent the rest of his time in Iran trying to determine the nature of the shah's illness and what medication he was taking, but to no avail. Apparently these concerns were not reported to Washington, for Blumenthal's report in 1978 shook the Carter administration.

Why was Washington so late in receiving information about the shah's ill health and in determining not only the gravity of his illness but also the implications for his political leadership and the future of Iran? Several factors appeared to be operating:

- The disease was of a nature that could be hidden. In its earliest stages it appeared to be nothing more than fatigue and some weight loss in a man who had always been very slim;
- The strain that showed on the shah's face and in his demeanor could be ascribed to the deteriorating political situation in Iran; and
- The shah had to show himself only when he chose to. When he was in pain or extremely debilitated, he could remain out of sight.

In addition, some American political analysts were not convinced of the central importance of the shah's role in Iran and hence were insensitive to observations that he might be ill. It was believed that the forces of modernization that had been set in motion were irreversible, certainly unstoppable by an obscure religious leader. If the shah was an inconsequential player, they reasoned, then the state of his health was irrelevant. Yet Ambassador Helms surely did not make this assumption. It may be that the very importance he ascribed to the shah's leadership contributed to his decision not to report his concerns over the shah's health to Washington. The former director of Central Intelligence, a man deeply concerned with secrecy, Helms may have concluded that such a report would probably have leaked, further weakening the shah's power base. A strong pro-Western Iran was considered crucial to U.S. strategic interests in the Persian Gulf.

For a number of senior American officials, in fact, an Iran without the shah was unthinkable. They felt the shah's leadership to be crucial and were not psychologically disposed to see him as weak, either physically or emotionally. In the past, they reasoned, the shah had always risen to a crisis and, *other things being equal,* he would undoubtedly do so again.

But other things were not equal, and as we now know, the shah was mortally ill. The diminished stamina experienced by cancer victims, especially when undergoing chemotherapy, can obviously have major adverse effects on their political effectiveness. Can anyone doubt that the shah's fight to survive the ravages of cancer diminished his ability to lead Iran? In retrospect, his weakened physical and emotional condition and faltering leadership contributed to the success of the Islamic revolution, which in turn forced the cancer into the open. Had the illness not coincided with the Islamic challenge, it would probably have remained secret even longer. But as we shall demonstrate later, the Islamic challenge was not a coincidence, for the aberrant and inconsistent leadership behavior prompted by the shah's reactions to his cancer may well have helped precipitate the Islamic challenge.

A number of questions beg to be asked and answered. Had the U.S. government penetrated the shah's veil of secrecy and learned of his terminal illness in 1973, would it have reposed full confidence in the shah's leadership and ability to withstand the challenge to his rule? Knowing that the shah was fighting for his life as he was fighting for his political survival, would the United States not have made contingency plans, reached out to possible moderate successors? With differing American postures toward the shah himself and toward possible moderate successors, might Khomeini's drive to supplant the shah have failed?

It seems possible that another moderate leader might have assumed the shah's mission for his country, with a still modernizing Iran remaining in the Western camp. The United States, moreover, could have assumed a lower profile and been less prominently supportive of the shah, to avoid the resultant hostility should Khomeini succeed in overthrowing the shah. Although one could argue that this softening might have accelerated the shah's fall, placing sole reliance on the efficacy of the shah's leadership left the United States inevitably in the position of succeeding him as the prime object of hatred in the Iranian mind, of becoming "the Great Satan." Had the Carter administration assessed more accurately the likelihood of Khomeini's replacing a dying shah, might it have been able to soften the antagonism of the Shiite clerics, perhaps avoiding the Iranian hostage crisis? Without this crisis, how differently would the Carter presidency—and subsequent elections—have played out? Could the tide of Khomeini's Islamic revolution have been stemmed? Would hostage taking have won such popularity as a tactic for advancing the cause of radical Islam? Would Irangate have occurred? The questions multiply.

The answers to these rhetorical questions cannot be determined, but it is probably not too great an exaggeration to assert that the shah's successful concealment of his mortal illness contributed to the success of the Islamic revolution, profoundly altering the history of the Middle East and the course of international relations.

Western readers will be tempted to believe that "it can't happen here," that the closed nature of the political system in Iran and the shah's controlling, autocratic leadership permitted him to keep his condition secret for so long. To be sure, a cover-up of disability is more difficult to accomplish in a society that has an aggressive press and a vigorous opposition, but in fact illness and disability have frequently been concealed in democratic societies when the government wants to do so *and the nature of the illness permits*.

President Cleveland's Carcinoma of the Mouth

Like the shah of Iran, President Grover Cleveland also suffered from a gradually developing malignancy. But unlike the progressive cancer that afflicted the shah and ultimately caused his death, Cleveland suffered from a form of cancer that was amenable to definitive surgical treatment.

In June 1893, at the beginning of Cleveland's second term in office, two events—one medical, one political—occurred almost simultaneously. President Cleveland became aware of a growth about the size of a quarter on his upper palate. Examination soon revealed that the growth had invaded the underlying bone of the upper jaw. Cleveland's serious medical condition could not have occurred at a less propitious time. Strenuous efforts were being waged by opponents of the gold standard to introduce silver as a means of exchange. (The struggle was later immortalized by William Jennings Bryan at the Democratic National Convention of 1896: "You shall not press down upon the brow of labor this crown of thorns, you shall not crucify mankind upon a cross of gold.") Those who favored the introduction of silver felt that reliance on gold placed rigid constraints on the economic system, while opponents felt that passage of the Sherman Silver Act would be destabilizing and inflationary. The skillful and determined opposition of President Cleveland was the primary force in thwarting the introduction of silver.

Cleveland was opposed in these efforts by his vice president, Adlai Stevenson. Any sign that Stevenson might replace Cleveland would create an uncertainty that would probably cause panic in the financial markets. Cleveland accepted the advice of his consulting surgeon, Dr. Joseph D. Bryant, to have the growth removed. Because of the delicacy of the political situation he also determined to keep his condition a secret, not an easy thing to do. The press in the late nineteenth century was as active as any today, and the Republican opposition to Cleveland was vigorous and vigilant. Then as now there were major concerns over the possibility of a leak, so it was determined to restrict the details of the president's condition and the planned operation to as small a group as possible. Only the necessary health personnel, the First Lady, and Secretary of War Daniel S.

Lamont and his wife would know the true story. For reasons outlined above, the vice president was explicitly excluded from this select circle.

A false name was used in processing Cleveland's laboratory tests and even in the assembling of the medical team. The White House physician, Dr. Robert O'Reilly, secretly and rapidly organized a team of four doctors and a dentist skilled in anesthesia. Secrecy would have been impossible if the operation were carried out in a hospital, so the team hit upon the remarkable expedient of claiming that Cleveland would be taking a pleasure cruise up the Hudson River and then to his summer residence at Buzzards Bay. The salon of a large private yacht, the *Oneida*, would be transformed into an operating theater.

On June 30 the president and his entourage weighed anchor. Bryant publicly accompanied the presidential group to the yacht. The rest of the medical team had secretly been brought on board earlier and were kept out of sight. On July 1, while under way,

> Mr. Cleveland was propped up on a chair against the ship's mast and administration of the anesthetic was begun. At first nitrous oxide was used; later, when the patient had become unconscious, a switch to ether was made. Satisfactory anesthesia was obtained only after some difficulty. Dr. Hasbrouk then extracted the two left upper bicuspid teeth, following which Dr. Bryant began excision of the growth. He worked rapidly and with great skill, and thirty-one minutes after its beginning, the operation was completed. Most of the upper jaw was removed, but the orbital plate—the lower wall of the bony cavity containing the eyeball—was left intact. Nor was an external incision necessary. With the fitting of a prosthesis (artificial part) the contour of the face and the characteristic features would be restored.[1]

Two days later the president was ambulatory. On the Fourth of July Cleveland walked off the yacht to go to Grey Gables, his summer home in Buzzards Bay. Visitors noted that he seemed somewhat changed in appearance, lethargic and depressed. The evident problem with his mouth was blamed on a severe toothache followed by a difficult extraction. On September 1, two months after the operation, Dr. Bryant declared the wound healed and his patient able to resume normal activities. An improved prosthesis of vulcanized rubber had been fitted that gave his voice and appearance their former character.

Nevertheless, the cover-up was challenged. Just three days before Cleveland was pronounced recovered, a detailed account of the operation appeared in the Philadelphia *Press*. Those who knew the story to be true stonewalled and successfully maintained that it was false. In the meantime the crisis over silver had been resolved with the repeal of the Sherman Silver Act.

Cleveland lived for another fifteen years, dying from a cause unrelated to the earlier cancer. The full story of the cancer operation was not revealed until 1928, when Dr. W. W. Keen, a member of the medical team, published an account of the illness. And not until March 1980 was the precise nature of the tumor described.[2]

It was remarkable that the diagnosis and operation were carried out in such secrecy, a secrecy that along with skillful medical technique and excellent prostheses permitted a credible denial even in the face of a detailed leak. Such secrecy was possible only because the disease, verrucous carcinoma, though malignant, behaves less vigorously than other oral cancers. Yet this story does demonstrate that a diagnosis and operation for cancer can be successfully concealed despite an enterprising press, a strong opposition, and extreme political pressure. It should also be noted that the cover-up apparently did not detract from the president's leadership.

President Pompidou's Multiple Myeloma

A contemporary example of an undisclosed progressive malignancy in a leader of a Western society with a free press and a vigorous opposition is the case of President Georges Pompidou of France, a powerful and highly visible leader. In this case, the disease was strongly suspected but not confirmed, and the ailing leader continued to rule despite severe and public disability.

Pompidou first held political office when, at age fifty, he was named prime minister in 1962. In June 1969 he was elected the second president of the Fifth Republic. During the spring and summer of 1972, Pompidou had been feeling spent and drained of energy. He often spent weekends at his country retreat in Carjac to refresh his spirits. That August he felt exhausted, rarely leaving the house and spending most of his time in an armchair. Concerned about his health, Pompidou called his personal physician, Dr. Jean Vignalou. He acknowledged that foreign relations trips abroad, which he had always found stimulating, tired him. Moreover, he felt weak simply when standing and was drained by walking even the length of his office. Vignalou set up a comprehensive medical examination, including a battery of X-rays and blood tests. The preliminary findings of a markedly depressed white blood cell count led to further tests, including a bone marrow examination and radiologic examination of the bones.[3] The tests confirmed the diagnosis of multiple myeloma, a slowly progressive cancer of the bone marrow.

Making it clear that he knew this was a fatal illness, Pompidou detailed his wishes for a simple interment. The decision was made to conceal the nature—indeed, the existence—of this serious illness from public view. Pompidou also shielded his wife from the knowledge of his cancer; she did not learn of it for more than a year.

Like the leukemia that afflicted the shah of Iran, multiple myeloma is very variable, with periods of remission, and often responds to chemotherapy. But cancer chemotherapy can be debilitating, and it renders the patient susceptible to infection. In the sixteen months after his diagnosis in August 1972, Pompidou had a number of absences from public view. The terminal nature of his illness was denied to the very end, his team of French physicians attributing his brief absences and hospitalizations to minor ailments, such as flu, and to minor surgery for hemorrhoids.

- At a tree-lighting ceremony on December 8, 1972, Pompidou did not remain long with his young guests. He excused himself for not approaching the school children in attendance by saying he had "a bit of the flu." He joked with the attendees, "If work is health, then the implication is that I do not work a great deal, given I have the flu."
- In the following January and February he repeatedly canceled appointments and avoided other duties owing to "flu."
- In April, May, and June, colleagues noted Pompidou's ill appearance. He continued to cancel official duties, claiming relapses of the flu. His temper began to grow short. Exiting from Mass, he snapped quite uncharacteristically at reporters, "If I do not go out since my arrival, it is because of you. You bother me."
- In July, Pompidou took a two-week vacation in Fouesnant, then visited the official summer residence at Brégançon for another two weeks, and in mid-August left for another two-week holiday at his country home at Carjac.[4]

By now the reduction in Pompidou's official appearances and his apparent physical changes had led to widespread rumors that he was seriously ill, with either a blood disease or cancer. His weight had fluctuated significantly. Sometimes he appeared gaunt, but at other times he appeared to have sustained a twenty-pound weight gain, with an obviously bloated face, a frequent side effect of treatment with adrenal steroids, such as cortisone, often prescribed for multiple myeloma.

That summer Henry Kissinger visited Pompidou, who said bitterly, "Each time someone shakes my hand, I get the impression they're taking my pulse. . . . Nixon? Ah, believe me, he has his problems, he has Watergate. But me, I am dying! That's the most serious of problems, don't you think?"[5] Kissinger observed Pompidou's intellectual acuity and opined that the president's conduct of state affairs was in no way compromised by his illness.

It was only after a trip to China in 1973 frequently interrupted by medical problems that Pompidou told his wife he was dying of cancer. He began to spend more time away from Paris in order to rest. The medical reports still spoke of "viral infections." His appearance continued to decline. A series of cancellations of official functions ensued in March 1974: the inauguration of the new terminal at the airport in Roissy-en-France, a meeting with Leonid Brezhnev on the Black Sea, and an annual dinner for the diplomatic corps. Meetings scheduled for April in Japan and Germany were "indefinitely postponed."[6]

Pompidou experienced sufficient pain one evening in late March to prevent his attendance at one of the most important diplomatic dinners of the year. He told his wife on her return from the reception that he did not believe such pain was possible.[7] He was now in the end stages of his disease. He could walk only with great discomfort, presumably from a cancerous lesion in the bone. His appearances were reduced to a minimum, and for the most part he confined himself to his apartment.

After presiding over a meeting of the Council of Ministers on March 27, Pompidou returned to his Paris apartment, where he spent the weekend. He did not leave the apartment and did not receive Premier Pierre Messmer for their usual Monday morning meeting. The next day, April 2, Pompidou was expected at the Elysée Palace for the official reception of President Habyarimana of Rwanda but did not arrive. It was announced first that Premier Messmer would take his place, then that Pompidou had canceled for health reasons. Finally at 10 P.M. came the official announcement that Pompidou had died an hour earlier.[8]

Although political commentators have observed that Pompidou apparently functioned with full effectiveness to the very end, with no apparent weakening in the acuity of his judgment and political decision-making, can this really be? Can a leader face his impending death without it affecting his decision making? Assuredly there were effects. By informing only those senior government officials of whose loyalty he was confident, Pompidou contributed to a political crisis. He had not designated a successor, and the French constitution does not provide for a vice president. Accordingly, Pompidou's death precipitated a succession crisis, and decisions were made on an emergency basis that could have been made after judicious consideration. What other decisions were influenced is unclear.

In spite of the swirling rumors, the medical denials of serious illness never weakened. The press was only able to report rumors and guesses. The veil of medical confidence was never penetrated. In this respect, illness is unlike other political secrets. As long as the ailing leader makes some effort to maintain his routine and is supported in his deception and denials by his physicians, rumors of his illness will not be confirmed.

Distorting and Minimizing Public Illness: The Attempted Assassination of President Reagan

We have seen how cancer of the blood and lymphatic system, oral cancer and associated surgery, and multiple myeloma could all be hidden or substantially obscured from public view. Certain medical conditions, however, appear to insist on publicity. But this is only appearance. In illness, as in so many things, the devil is in the details. The crucial details of even the most public of illnesses may be kept secret.

The age of television virtually guarantees that an assassination attempt against a chief of state will be instantly transmitted not only throughout the country but around the world. In a free society, the omnipresent television also guarantees that details of the assassination victim's medical recovery will be faithfully recorded—or so it seems.

When John W. Hinckley, Jr., fired at Ronald Reagan audiences throughout the world saw the televised assassination attempt and then watched with amazement the extraordinary recovery of the seventy-year-old president. The nightly news regularly featured film-clips of Reagan, apparently vigorous, alert, and in good spirits. But the moments recorded by television were carefully chosen, and showed brief and unrepresentative intervals of lucidity and vigor in an otherwise disabled president. Members of the Reagan White House staff have substantially confirmed the details of the following excerpt, from Bob Woodward's *Veil:*

> Reagan's closest advisers soon learned it was an act. [The morning after Reagan's first, and reassuring, public appearance] the president limped from his bedroom to an adjoining room in the upstairs residence of the White House. He emerged slowly, walking with the hesitant steps of an old man. He was pale, and disoriented. Those who observed him were frightened. Reagan hobbled to a seat in the Yellow Oval Room, started to sit down and fell the rest of the way, collapsing into his chair.
>
> He spoke a few words in a raspy whisper and then had to stop to catch his breath. He looked lost. The pause wasn't enough and his hands reached for

an inhaler, a large mask-like breathing device next to his chair. As he sucked in oxygen, the room was filled with a wheezing sound.

Reagan could concentrate for only a few minutes at a time, then he faded mentally and physically, his wounded lung dependent on the inhaler. During the following days he was able to work or remain attentive only an hour or so a day.

The few who were granted access to the president were gravely concerned. This was supposed to be the beginning of the Reagan presidency, but at moments it seemed the end of the Reagan they knew. At times the president was overcome with pain; he seemed in constant discomfort. His hearty, reassuring voice sounded permanently injured, his words gravelly and uncertain. His aides began to consider that his was going to be a crippled presidency—that it would, at its very beginning devolve into something similar to Woodrow Wilson's at the end, a caretaker presidency, and that they would be reduced, or elevated, to a team of Mrs. Reagan's.

The senior aides were intent on protecting this terrible secret and their own uncertainty, at least until the prognosis was clearer.[9]

Physicians at the George Washington University Medical Center, where Reagan was hospitalized, dispute Woodward's characterization, maintaining that the image of the president as vigorous and alert was accurate. A senior member of the Reagan White House, however, confirms the main thrust of Woodward's characterization and indicates that Reagan did not regain his former stamina until perhaps six months after leaving the hospital. Although the degree of Reagan's impairment is disputed, the important point here is the discrepancy between reality and the image conveyed to the public. In a fluctuant disability, controlled access to the press and careful selection of media images can convey the impression that the leader is much healthier than he really is.

An important consequence of public illness is the effect on the leader's psyche. Anyone who comes close to death and then escapes it is always in some way changed; it is typical to feel the "renewed" life as even more precious, to be used and enjoyed with greater intensity. Some people experience a sense of guilt that they were spared while others died or were seriously wounded. Sometimes, for a person who occupies a position of historic responsibility, escaping death can seem to be a message of grace from a higher power. Michael Deaver, Reagan's deputy chief of staff, stated in a television interview soon after Reagan's term of office ended that as a consequence of his surviving the assassination attempt Reagan believed he had been specially saved. Thereafter, according to Deaver, Reagan was less willing to take advice or direction.

The Course of the Illness and Its Political Effects: President Eisenhower's Myocardial Infarction

The nature and course of the illness will significantly influence the degree to which the disability can be concealed and its political effects. Insidious illness, such as the progressive malignancies suffered by the shah of Iran and President Pompidou, is the easiest to conceal, whether in a closed or an open society. In a closed society, the ability to conceal is obviously much greater, but had the shah of Iran had a major coronary or suffered some disabling injury, his illness could not have been hidden for five years, regardless of his control over the Iranian press.

Illness with a dramatic onset is much harder to conceal, although, as Woodrow Wilson's stroke, discussed in chapter 4, exemplifies, even in an open society the circle around the president can do much to conceal the gravity of the condition. Even an acute illness such as a heart attack can be covered up, as the initial handling of President Dwight David Eisenhower's heart attack in 1955, just a year and a half into his presidency, attests.

On Saturday evening, September 24, 1955, Vice President Richard Nixon noted in passing a brief item in the Washington *Evening Star* to the effect that President Eisenhower, then at the summer White House in Denver, was suffering from a slight case of indigestion. Shortly afterward he received a call from Press Secretary Jim Hagerty informing him that the president had had a coronary. The nation learned several hours later that the president had suffered a "mild" coronary thrombosis and was hospitalized in Fitzsimmons Army Hospital.

Reconstructing the events from the report made by the president's physician, Major General Howard Snyder, and from Nixon's memoirs,[10] it is clear that there was significant deception early on, not only of the nation but of senior government officials, including the vice president. Indeed, the manner in which this critical illness was treated provides powerful support for one theme we develop in this book: being a VIP can be dangerous to one's health.

The pace of Eisenhower's day on September 23 would have taxed most mortals. He had risen at 5 A.M. while on a fishing trip with friends in the Rockies. After an eighty-two-mile drive back to Denver, he tackled two hours of paperwork before moving on to his favorite recreation, golf. He played twenty-seven holes of golf, ending the day by having a roast lamb dinner with friends.

At 2:30 A.M. on Saturday, September 24, he awoke experiencing severe chest pain. At his request, Mamie Eisenhower called his doctor and personal friend, Major General Snyder, who arrived at 3 A.M. Snyder immediately recognized that Eisenhower had suffered a heart attack—an occlusion of a coronary artery—and required emergency treatment. He administered three injections—a coronary dilator, an anticoagulant to thin the blood and keep the clot from extending, and morphine for pain. He decided not to summon help, not wishing to upset Mamie Eisenhower and believing that the excitement that would inevitably follow on his call for assistance could adversely affect the president's chances for recovery. He thus assumed the immense responsibility of not sharing the information concerning the gravity of the president's condition and watching over him personally until morning. He administered a further dose of morphine at 3:45 A.M. and sat by Eisenhower's bedside as the president slept.

Prolonging the individual assumption of responsibility, but now adding the additional element of deception, at 7 A.M. Dr. Snyder informed the press secretary that the president was suffering from indigestion and would not be keeping his morning appointments. That morning's press briefing became the basis for the story Nixon later read. When the president awakened at 12:30 P.M., Dr. Snyder ordered that an electrocardiograph be brought from Fitzsimmons Army Hospital to the private home in which the Eisenhowers were staying. The cardiogram, taken at 2 P.M., confirmed Dr. Snyder's diagnosis, and the decision was finally made to transport the president to Fitzsimmons for hospital treatment of his now-confirmed coronary. There the president was placed in an oxygen tent, and treatment with anticoagulants, sedation, and pain medication continued. Only after Eisenhower had been hospitalized did Major General Snyder call the assistant press secretary to inform him of the true nature of the president's illness. Several hours more elapsed before official Washington and the world at large learned that Eisenhower had been hospitalized for a heart attack.

General Snyder's report to the White House, as cited by Nixon, is revealing:

> It was difficult for me to assume the responsibility of refraining from making public immediately the diagnosis of coronary thrombosis. I postponed public announcement because I wished the president to benefit from the rest and quiet induced by the sedation, incident to combating the initial manifestations. This decision also spared him, his wife, and his mother-in-law emotional upset upon too precipitant announcement of such serious import. This action, I believe, limited the heart damage to a minimum and enabled us to confirm this diagnosis by cardiogram and make an unhurried transference from home to hospital.

In assessing Dr. Snyder's emergency medical response and his initial decision to withhold an announcement and manage the coronary at home, Nixon asserts: "I believe most would agree that Dr. Snyder met the crisis of his career with skill and courage and that he deserves the commendation of his medical colleagues in the country."[11]

Without in any way questioning the skill that Dr. Snyder brought to the medical care of his charge, serious questions must be raised concerning his decision against immediately hospitalizing his very important patient. The line between being courageous and foolhardy is often narrow, and many physicians would consider that Dr. Snyder crossed that line. The interval immediately after a coronary is the most critical, and should Eisenhower have suffered a major complication of an early coronary occlusion, such as a rhythm disturbance, congestive failure, or shock, Dr. Snyder would not have had the requisite medical facilities and assistance. The decision to maintain President Eisenhower at home could have been fatal.

Would the physician have made the same decision for someone not of the president's status—for example, for a member of the White House staff? Probably not. Thus we have the ironic situation that because of the president's high status, he received what many would consider insufficient and potentially life-threatening treatment.

This case also illustrates another motivation for deception; namely, protection of the very important patient. In this case, the doctor's concern was solely for the medical welfare of his patient and the well-being of his family. But because of the public role of his patient, he estimated—no doubt accurately—that a public announcement would precipitate commotion and draw major public attention, upsetting the president's family and becoming a source of stress for the ailing president, which in turn could be detrimental to his health. Major General Snyder may not have considered the political consequences of this deception. What would have happened if an international crisis had occurred during that period of medical isolation?

The first hours brought anxiety about the future. Sherman Adams, Eisenhower's chief of staff, heard the news in Prestwick, Scotland. An inner circle cover-up was not contemplated:

> Obviously some temporary direction had to be arranged for co-ordination. Who was going to be boss? If I knew Nixon, he would be wary of appearing to assume presidential prerogatives before he became constitutionally eligible for them. . . . I thought that perhaps the necessary actions of importance could be made by the Cabinet acting as a body, with matters of secondary concern being handled, as had been the habitual practice, by the White House staff. I hoped that no emergency would arise during the president's early convalescence that would require his personal action.[12]

Fortunately there was no crisis. Congress was out of session, and the government coasted for two weeks. Eisenhower first met with some of the Cabinet on October 11. White House staff consulted Attorney General

Herbert Brownell about formally delegating presidential responsibility to a governing council during Eisenhower's period of incapacity, but he advised against it. Instead, a group was established which, though never formally designated as a governing council, nevertheless in a restrained manner acted very much like one. It consisted of Vice President Nixon, Attorney General Brownell, Secretary of the Treasury George Humphrey, Eisenhower's long-time aide and personal friend Major General Wilton Persons, and Chief White House Assistant Sherman Adams.

The president recovered—as it was evident he would after the first few days. There was little temptation for a cover-up (after the first few days) because the disability was predictably limited in time, thereby minimizing the uncertainty. Detailed and accurate medical information was eventually made public.

In the case of Eisenhower's heart attack, the initial decision to engage in deception was reversed because the nature of the illness required that the president be medically sequestered, which would have to be explained. But in fact, on the basis of his initial reasoning, wishing to spare the president stress, Dr. Snyder might well have opted to continue the deception and create a medical facility in the western White House. The attack, a left anterior myocardial infarction, was serious, but the president had already survived the most critical initial period and there was every reason to believe that with rest and reduced activity he would be able to return to fully effective leadership in four to six weeks. If Eisenhower's absence from public functions had been explained as indisposition caused by a "flu," as Pompidou's physicians did, and by managing public appearances and the media, as the Reagan White House staff apparently did, an extended deception might well have been carried out.

President Eisenhower's Stroke: The Possibility of Public Panic

President Eisenhower's heart attack had a minimal effect on him and his political position. In contrast, his later stroke created serious problems. Two years after the myocardial infarction, in November 1957, Eisenhower suffered a cerebral vascular accident—a "stroke"—which affected his speech. The disorder passed in a few days, although Eisenhower at one point told his close aides he was thinking of resigning. The inner circle disclosed much less of this episode to the public than they had for Eisenhower's heart attack. Why was this?

The public looks to the leader for wisdom, for judgment, for decisiveness. With Eisenhower's heart attack, there was a public perception that with rest and proper medical treatment their wise leader would fully recover. But the stroke raised the possibility that Eisenhower's mental abilities would be affected and that he would no longer be able to think clearly and make decisions or communicate with the nation. The full disclosure of this possibility, in the judgment of the circle surrounding the president, might have precipitated public panic. If Eisenhower had not shown rapid signs of recovery or had the disease's course appeared uncertain, a situation like that of Woodrow Wilson, in which the president was under the unacknowledged control of the inner circle, could have arisen.

This makes an important point. An illness that affects the mental functioning of the leader is especially difficult for the circle of leaders to manage and is most likely to lead to attempts to conceal the nature or degree of the disability. Physical illnesses that affect the central nervous system and produce mental impairment, such as the strokes of Wilson and Eisenhower, can be expected to have a major impact on the decision-making of the leader. If such illnesses come to light, they can be expected to have a negative impact on the perceptions and confidence of the populace. They are accordingly much more complicated for the inner circle to manage. Especially serious are neurological conditions that adversely affect the mental processes by producing an organic brain syndrome. This group of conditions includes strokes and brain tumors that damage the dominant hemisphere, as well as progressive cerebral degenerations, such as cerebral arteriosclerosis (hardening of the arteries of the brain) and Alzheimer's disease, which produce senile or pre-senile dementias.

Each of the following psychological manifestations of organic brain syndromes can have significant political consequences:[13]

- The afflicted individual is unaware of the degree of impairment.
- Intellectual capacities generally decline. Afflicted individuals suffer a progressive impairment in their capacity to think abstractly. Thinking becomes more concrete, rigid, and inflexible, with a tendency to see things in black-and-white terms.
- Responses to stimuli become less flexible and more stereotyped; it becomes difficult to change a mindset, and afflicted individuals are seen as becoming more stubborn. Concentration and memory, particularly recent memory, are usually especially affected.
- Judgment is impaired. Impulses that earlier had been checked may now be more easily expressed. An individual may behave more aggressively or be more easily provoked.
- Emotional reactions in general become less well controlled. Afflicted individuals are irritable, easily provoked to anger, tears, or euphoria, and more sensitive to slight. Depressive reactions are common.
- Earlier personality traits tend to flower. As with the normal aging

individual, the basic personality and life style remain intact. But even more than in an older person without organic problems, longstanding attitudes and drives are expressed in an exaggerated way. The characteristically distrustful person may become frankly paranoid. A significant example is the flowering of Stalin's paranoia in his later years.

- The course of cerebral degeneration is characterized by wide fluctuations but is invariably downhill. Reliable reports of the leader's excellent health thus should not lead to a discounting of other reports of his failing health.

Individuals can fully recover from isolated strokes, but cerebral degenerations are another matter. Only rarely can primary neurological diseases be fully treated and the organic brain syndrome described above reversed. And once medical decline is evident, the political dynamics are almost always set irrevocably in motion. Not uncommonly, the inner circle will initially attempt to cope with the leader's labile moods and variable abilities on a day-to-day basis, then rule in his name, and finally be compelled to replace the leader.

In such circumstances, the leadership circle will find a fluctuant disability especially vexing. During the early phases of such dementing diseases as cerebral arteriosclerosis and Alzheimer's disease, the individual may function with apparently full or only slightly diminished effectiveness at some times and be significantly impaired at others. Changes may occur when there is a supervening illness. Thus if a leader has diminished blood flow to the brain, so that even under optimal conditions there is barely sufficient cerebral oxygenation, an illness such as pneumonia, which further reduces oxygen to the brain, could produce confusion and irrationality, from which the leader might recover when the pulmonary illness has cleared. Thus the severe case of bronchitis from which Franklin Delano Roosevelt suffered during the Tehran meeting in 1943 may have seriously compromised his already impaired cerebral oxygenation and affected his mental functioning.

Such changes can occur in the span of a single day. It is not uncommon for an individual to be alert in the morning and have dulled capacities in the afternoon. Moreover, when the afflicted individual is alert, he will often not recognize how impaired his functioning had been.

In contrast to the stroke suffered by Eisenhower, acute and dramatic in onset, illnesses affecting mental faculties often have an insidious onset that may not be noticed at first, especially by those outside the individual's immediate circle. Such illnesses lend themselves to concealment. Winston Churchill's progressive cerebral arteriosclerosis illustrates the point.

Winston Churchill's Progressive Arteriosclerotic Dementia: Propping up a Figurehead

At the beginning of World War II, Winston Churchill was a healthy man of sixty-four.* By the end of that conflict the natural process of aging, six years of hard work under tension, heavy drinking, and the frequent use of sedatives had taken their physical toll. His physician, Charles, Lord Moran, named 1944 as the year Churchill's mental and physical health began to wane. In his diaries Sir Francis Alan Brooke, Churchill's chief of the Imperial General Staff, observed on March 24, 1944, "He seems quite incapable of concentrating for a few minutes on end, and keeps wandering continuously."[14]

Nor was Churchill free of the symptoms of emotional illness. A tendency to severe depression (what Churchill called his "black dog") had troubled him throughout his life and continued to plague him. His rejection by the British people in the first postwar election, for example, precipitated a major depression. At age seventy, Winston Churchill was a sick old man.

His physical decline accelerated. In 1949, he suffered the first in a succession of cerebrovascular accidents; the stroke affected sensation in both his right arm and leg. In 1950 and 1951 he suffered two attacks as a consequence of temporarily inadequate blood flow to the brain; these, however, did not progress to full strokes.

In 1951, at the age of seventy-six, Churchill was a virtual walking textbook of pathology. Scarcely an organ system remained unaffected. He had significant illnesses affecting his heart, brain, lungs, gastrointestinal tract, skin, and eyes. His medical history included several attacks of pneumonia, a heart attack, a major stroke, two episodes of cerebral ischemia, diverticulitis, inflammation affecting the eyes, eczema, and intermittent severe depression. On October 27, 1951, this aged, ailing leader was once again elected prime minister by a slim majority of seventeen.

Because Winston Churchill is one of the central figures in modern British history, little in his life has remained unexamined. His health problems have been richly documented in a diary kept by his physician, Lord Moran. Churchill will serve as a useful example at many points in this book, but here we wish to emphasize the political effects of progressive cerebral arteriosclerosis as well as to demonstrate the capacity of the British parliamentary system to tolerate a cover-up of the extended disability of a leader.

---

*Both L'Etang (*The Pathology of Leadership* and *Fit to Lead?*) and Park (*The Impact of Illness on World Leaders*) have made major contributions to the medical historiography of Churchill. This section is informed by their analyses.

Churchill's physician had recognized his patient's failing powers several years before his victory in 1951. Lord Moran noted in his diary as early as 1947 that Churchill's mind was no longer fertile. Even though Lord Moran expressed "doubt whether he is up to the job,"[15] in September 1951 he wrote that his duty as a doctor was to see that Churchill stayed in politics and stayed in office as long as possible—an interesting interpretation of the Hippocratic oath! Lord Moran warned his patient neither of the dangers facing him nor their likely effects on his leadership of the nation.

The inner circle noted Churchill's rapid decline soon after the election. On some days he was nearly his old self, but more often than not he was unable to cope. The private secretary to the queen reported that Churchill often could not follow the trend of a conversation.[16] At one point he even forgot that the electric power industry had been nationalized. He was frequently unable to contain his emotions, often irritable and short of temper, at other times breaking into tears or becoming extremely maudlin. He also suffered from delusions of grandiosity, believing that only he could prevent a third world war.

This situation was difficult but tolerable. Churchill's excesses were blunted by the inner circle, and Foreign Secretary Anthony Eden, the number two person in the Conservative party and Churchill's heir apparent, compensated for Churchill's lapses by providing quiet but firm leadership behind the scenes.* In the spring of 1953 this delicate political equilibrium was disrupted when Eden fell seriously ill with obstructive jaundice. Two operations were carried out in London, without success. The reputation of Harvard medicine had crossed the Atlantic, and it was decided to attempt a third operation in Boston. An obstruction of the bile duct was successfully treated, but Eden required an extended period of convalescence and was unable to return to his duties until October 1953.

In late June 1953, at about the time that Eden was about to undergo the third operation, Churchill suffered a second major stroke, which affected the left side of his body. That the two strokes in concert affected both sides of his body indicates arteriosclerotic involvement throughout his brain. This serious illness created a delicate political situation. The inner circle believed that Eden should succeed Churchill, but even putting aside the question whether Churchill would step down, this would be impossible given Eden's own uncertain health. If the prime ministership went to the next man in line, R. A. Butler, Eden might never have his opportunity. A

---

*The relationship between Churchill and Eden was not an easy one; managing Churchill from behind the scenes was extremely stressful for Eden and probably contributed to his reliance on psychoactive medication. The tension between Churchill and Eden also magnified Churchill's later reluctance to yield the reins of power.

full knowledge of Churchill's condition would create pressure from Butler's supporters, among others, for a prompt succession. Butler was in effect made acting prime minister, but on the condition that his authority extend no further.

The decision was made to deceive those outside the inner circle. Lord Moran, in concert with Dr. Dennis Brain, a leading neurologist, drew up a medical bulletin referring to the difficulties in Churchill's cerebral circulation, which read: "For a long time the Prime Minister has had no respite from his arduous duties and a disturbance of the cerebral circulation has developed, resulting in attacks of giddiness." Two senior Cabinet ministers, R. A. Butler and Lord Salisbury, subsequently decided to omit language indicating that Churchill was ill and redrafted the statement to read as follows: "The prime minister has had no respite for a long time from his very arduous duties and is in need of a complete rest."[17] They then persuaded Churchill to sign the sanitized statement. Butler, who became acting prime minister, even kept the news from his ministerial colleagues.

The cover-up worked. Five days after the stroke, Churchill's press secretary stated that there was no medical evidence to indicate that the prime minister was suffering from any particular ailment. It is not surprising that Moran supported the medical cover-up, for he had earlier noted in his diary, "My first care must be not to put sharp weapons into hands of anyone who might use them to hurt him." Yet he was uncomfortable with the deception. "This may well be right, that is if he comes through. For if he recovers and wants to carry on as Prime Minister, then the less we say about a stroke, the better for him. But will anyone who knows the P.M. credit that he is willing to take a month's rest merely because his doctors thought he was overdoing things? And besides, if he died in the next few days will Lord Salisbury think his change in the bulletin was wise? It is a gamble."[18] Moreover, Moran believed that only he recognized the gravity of the situation, for his own diagnosis and prognosis, quite accurate, was never communicated to others in the official surround.

It is strange that no one around the P.M. seems able to grasp what is the exact nature of his disability. This is not an acute illness from which he may recover completely. He will never again be the same man he was before the stroke, because the clot in the artery has cut off some of the blood which went to his brain and was the ultimate source of all his activities. So his brain is always a little aenemic, and when the circulation flags a little, then he has no zest for work and cannot face detail, or his leg twitches, or something of the kind. He is really living on a volcano, and he may get another stroke at any time.[19]

22

For those in the inner circle, Churchill's continuing decline after the 1953 stroke was alarming. Harold Macmillan believed that Churchill's refusal to step down was unfair to Anthony Eden. Many also recognized that Churchill was killing himself by overwork. Others, however, resented his standing in their way. Some were principally concerned with the effect of his fluctuant incapacity on the country's well-being. As Norman Stone noted in the London *Times* in May 1988, this became the worst government Britain had experienced since World War II: "It did virtually nothing to redress the imbalances created in 1945—imbalances that sensible people on the Labour side well appreciated. Taxation and nationalization were still grotesque." Health and education policy drifted, trade union monopoly was not faced, there was too great a concern for a disappearing empire. Why? "[The government] was endlessly preoccupied, almost from the start, with the issue of succession. Churchill was needed, but he was not wanted. . . . By 1954 he had become an endearing embarrassment. Yet he would not go. On the contrary, he resisted retirement up to the moment when he received an invitation to his retirement from his would-be successor, Anthony Eden."[20]

Yet many, including Churchill himself, preferred Churchill in power even though ailing to a healthy alternative. For some time various plans had been suggested to ease Churchill out. The most ingenious was that Churchill should remain prime minister but move to the House of Lords and that Anthony Eden would become leader of the Commons. None of these suggestions, often made through Churchill's personal secretary, Jock Colville, or through Churchill's wife, Clementine, was successful in convincing him to relinquish power. Churchill illustrates one of the most politically troublesome characteristics of cerebral deteriorations—the victim is often the last to recognize the gravity of the condition and the magnitude of the incapacity. Churchill was approached several times by friends and family about his possible retirement, but he declared his intention to remain in power until "either things become much better or I become much worse."[21]

Churchill, always a showman, kept much of the criticism at bay by his continuing, though less frequent, personal flamboyance. Harold Macmillan, the most open and persistent of those in the inner circle who tried to get Churchill to resign, tells of visiting Churchill one morning by invitation and finding him in bed "with a little green budgerigar sitting on his head . . . a cigar in his hand and whisky and soda by his side, from which the little bird took sips from time to time . . . while Gibbonesque sentences were rolling from the maestro's mouth about the Bomb. From time to time the bird said a few words in a husky kind of voice like an

American actress."[22] This was not senility but self-confident eccentricity in the grand manner.

Eventually the press began to comment on the extent of Churchill's disability. Even he began to acknowledge it. On August 29, 1954, he said to his doctor, "I have become so stupid, Charles. Cannot you do anything for me?" Six weeks later, however, he boasted, "If they try to get me out I will resist."[23] In March 1955 he spent much of his time depressed and staring vacantly ahead.

Already ill when he entered office, from the time he suffered his second major stroke in 1953 Churchill was completely unable to carry out his duties. The progressive dementia was amplified by his vulnerability to depression. Churchill's success was based upon his intellectual grasp and strength of will. To see both sapped by age—and his occasional periods of lucidity permitted him to recognize his deterioration—was profoundly depressing.

On April 6, 1955, after six months of almost total inactivity, he finally succumbed to the persuasion of his friends and the pressure of his adversaries and left 10 Downing Street. Having learned painfully the folly of confronting the magnitude of Churchill's disability directly, the inner circle based its most effective arguments not on a criticism of Churchill's poor health and impaired leadership but on the positive state of the nation. They argued that he had fulfilled his promises to the people about improving housing, stabilizing prices, reducing taxation, ending rationing, creating a balance of payments surplus, and increasing the rate of growth.[24] Parliament had been sitting for four years, and now was a good time for an election. Churchill was told that he could finish on a note of triumph. Otherwise he would have to undergo an election campaign. Ever mindful of the judgments of history, Churchill yielded. Contrary to Lord Moran's prediction, he did not die soon after but lived for another decade in declining health.

The deception surrounding Churchill's disability was as fluctuant as the disability itself. The inner circle never kept his inadequacies completely secret, as was the case with the shah and President Cleveland. The deception resembled that surrounding President Wilson's stroke in that not the fact of the disability was concealed but the degree. Many suspected that Churchill was not as healthy as an effective chief executive should be, but his near total disability was disguised. We shall return to Churchill to address his depressive illness, his relation to his doctor, and his abuse of drugs and alcohol. As we will see, Churchill's medical problems were greatly aggravated by his proclivity to depression and his substance abuse. But he was able to cope with these problems. It was cerebral arteriosclerosis that destroyed his ability to function as prime minister.

President Roosevelt's Mental and Physical Decline

Much as Lord Moran played a key role in obscuring the degree of Churchill's incapacity, so a decade earlier Dr. Ross McIntire had actively distorted and suppressed the gravity of Franklin D. Roosevelt's failing health and impaired cognitive capacity. And just as Churchill probably would not have regained the prime ministership had the degree of his disability been known, so Roosevelt would almost certainly not have been chosen to run for an unprecedented fourth term if the extent of his illness had not been concealed.

Understanding the effects of an illness requires knowing not only the personality of the sufferer but also the patient's previous experience with and reactions to illness and disability. Roosevelt, of course, suffered from the disabling consequences of poliomyelitis almost all his political life. As Hugh Gallagher, himself a polio victim, asserts in *FDR's Splendid Deception* (1985), the effect of polio on its victims is always traumatic; it becomes a central event in their lives. The disease strikes unexpectedly, cutting down the young and the healthy and reducing those who do not recover to physical dependence. It profoundly alters its victims' self-reliance; they have lost control not only of their bodies but also of their lives.

For the politician, polio adds the special difficulties of public image. Pity is deadly to a politician; people do not like to identify with the infirm. They want their leaders to be strong and in command. Recognizing this, Roosevelt drew the press into a denial: newsreels never showed him being carried or wheeled about. Of the 35,000 still photographs at the Roosevelt Presidential Library, only two show him in a wheelchair.

Roosevelt even managed somewhat to convert his handicap into a political virtue, a mark of courage and perseverance. During the campaign of 1928, Frances Perkins, later designated secretary of labor, observed, "The handicap and the very presence of wheelchair and braces worked to the President's advantage."[25] Before he was stricken with polio, Roosevelt's upper-class elegance and hauteur conveyed an aloofness, an emotional inaccessibility to the polity, but his affliction softened his patrician edges.

Roosevelt must have taken great pride in overcoming his disability. It was a spur to him, a barrier to overcome in achieving greatness. But if this special sense of self helped him surmount his disability, it also led him to incorporate leading despite impaired health as a core element of his political personality. This central value and special sense of self contributed to his remaining in office and running for a fourth term despite grave illness.

At the Yalta Conference in February 1945, Roosevelt's decision-making capacity was obviously impaired from a combination of hypertension, diffuse atherosclerosis, and congestive heart failure secondary to hypertension and chronic pulmonary disease. He suffered prolonged episodes of clouded consciousness. Churchill's physician observed the extent of Roosevelt's physical deterioration and its effect on his leadership. He was highly critical of the denial by the Americans—including the medical staff—of the gravity of Roosevelt's condition:

> The President looked old and thin and drawn; he had a cape shawl over his shoulders and appeared shrunken; he sat looking straight ahead with his mouth open, as if he were not taking things in. Everyone was shaken by his appearance and gabbled about it afterwards.
>
> Everyone seemed to agree that the President had gone to bits physically. . . . It was not only his physical deterioration that had caught their attention. He intervened very little in discussions, sitting with his mouth open. . . . I doubt, from what I have seen, whether he is fit for his job here.
>
> He [the President] has all the symptoms of hardening of the arteries of the brain in an advanced stage, that I give him only a few months to live. But . . . the Americans cannot bring themselves to believe that he is finished. His daughter thinks he is not really ill, and his doctor backs her up.[26]

Lord Moran was not alone in noting Roosevelt's deteriorated condition at Yalta. Indeed, his seriously compromised health was evident in the weeks preceding the crucial diplomatic mission. On Inauguration Day, 1945, John Gunther wrote: "I was terrified when I saw the President's face. I felt certain he was going to die. . . . It was gray, gaunt and sagging, and the muscles controlling the lips seemed to have lost part of their function."[27] Roosevelt died just a few months later, in April 1945.

James Farley, former chairman of the Democratic National Committee, had expressed serious concern on the eve of the Yalta summit: "Cordell Hull and I agreed that he was a sick man . . . and should not be called upon to make decisions affecting this country and the world."[28] Ambassador William Bullitt observed: "Roosevelt, indeed, was more than tired. He was ill. Little was left of the physical and mental vigor that had been his when he entered the White House in 1933. Frequently he had difficulty in formulating his thoughts, and greater difficulty in expressing them consecutively."[29]

When Roosevelt addressed Congress on his return from Yalta, his physical decline was obvious. "Roosevelt's voice was strangely thick and blurred as he told Congress about Yalta. . . . At times his face and words flamed with the old eloquence [only] to ebb away. Thus it was constantly in the final weeks. . . . His gray-blue eyes clouded, his face went slack, his head hunched over. Then suddenly, miraculously, the old gayness and vitality would return."[30] Nevertheless, White House physician Dr. Ross T. McIntire denied that Roosevelt's health was sufficiently compromised to warrant reducing his work load.[31] Roosevelt's son James later remarked bitterly, "I have never been reconciled to the fact that father's physicians did not flatly forbid him to run [in 1944]. . . . The fourth-term race in 1944 was Father's death warrant. I realized with awful irrevocable certainty [during the campaign and on Inauguration Day] that we were going to lose him."[32]

In fact, the serious decline in Roosevelt's health was obvious as early as December 1943, when on his return from the Tehran conference, the president appeared "bone tired" and his characteristic spark and vitality were missing.[33] At the family's insistence, he entered Bethesda Naval Hospital in March 1944 for a thorough medical evaluation. A specialist in cardiology, Dr. Howard Bruenn, conducted the examination.

Bruenn found the president's health seriously compromised. Roosevelt was breathing with difficulty and could not lie flat without discomfort. His face was ashen and his lips were blue, evidence of inadequate oxygenation deriving from cardiac insufficiency. Bruenn found not only a significantly elevated blood pressure (186/108) but, on examination of the blood vessels of the retina, the classic signs of long-standing hypertension. Roosevelt was suffering from congestive heart failure; his left ventricle was enlarged, showing that the heart was consistently working against resistance. His heart, in other words, was failing because of long-standing hypertension. Bruenn's main diagnoses were "hypertension, hypertensive heart disease, failure of the left ventricle of the heart, and acute bronchitis."[34] Moreover, in addition to the acute bronchitis, which was responsible for Roosevelt's persistent cough, there were signs of long-standing pulmonary disease. Severe anemia, first discovered in 1941, was still present.

Despite the gravity of Dr. Bruenn's findings, they were suppressed and a bland and reassuring medical communiqué was issued by the White House physician. A U.S. Navy commander, Dr. Bruenn was subordinate in rank to Admiral McIntire. McIntire tightly controlled access to Bruenn's evaluation and conveyed the following "findings" to the family: "The results show a moderate degree of arteriosclerosis, although no more than normal for a man his age; some changes in the cardiac tracing; cloudiness in his sinuses; and bronchial irritation." In the press conference that followed, he was reassuring: "I can say to you that the checkup is satisfactory. When we got through, we decided that for a man of sixty-two we had very little to argue about, with the exception that we have had to combat the influenza plus the respiratory complications that come along afterward."[35] McIntire asked Bruenn to stay on as attending physician, but under his command. Commenting on the relationship of McIntire and Bruenn, Roosevelt's biographer Jim Bishop has observed:

The Admiral remained the physician-in-residence . . . . he pounced on Bruenn's daily reports, but he hid or destroyed them. As a physician, McIntire understood the situation but denied it. His daily reports from Bruenn became Navy secrets. The Admiral's dominance was complete. McIntire could have revealed the President's grave condition to FDR in April 1944. If this had not stopped Roosevelt from running for the fourth term, the Admiral, as a physician of integrity, could have retired or requested other duty. . . . McIntire was lying—not only to the world but to the President himself.[36]

The blanket of military discipline continued to cover Dr. Bruenn's findings and their implications. Beyond not making his findings public, he was ordered not to discuss his evaluation with the president, and his access to the president's family was restricted. This situation persisted as Roosevelt's clinical condition deteriorated further. In April his blood pressure readings were consistently at a dangerous level, running between 210/110 and 230/130. In September 1944 a reading of 240/130 was obtained. These are the values of malignant hypertension, a medical emergency usually requiring hospitalization. Blood pressure at these levels would interfere with normal brain functioning, producing "hypertensive encephalopathy," creating problems with alertness and concentration and interfering with intellectual functioning. Roosevelt's secretary Grace Tully has written, "It was in the last year that I found the Boss occasionally nodding over his mail or dozing a moment during dictation." As the frequency of these episodes increased, Tully became "seriously alarmed."[37]

John Flynn's description of Roosevelt's behavior at a July 1944 meeting with Douglas MacArthur in Hawaii is striking in regard to the president's impaired mental functioning: "He faltered and paused, his eyes became glassy, and consciousness drifted from him. The man at his side nudged him, shook him a little, pointed to the place in the manuscript at which he broke off and said: 'Here, Mr. President, is your place.'"[38] Speechwriter Robert Sherwood saw Roosevelt in September 1944 and was "shocked by his appearance. . . . I had heard that he had lost a lot of weight, but I was unprepared for the almost ravaged appearance of his face. He had his coat off and his shirt collar seemed several sizes too large for his emaciated neck."[39]

Although Dr. Bruenn did not comment on Roosevelt's neurologic status, Dr. Bert Park, a neurosurgeon who has painstakingly researched the medical histories of several important twentieth-century leaders, has observed that the illnesses from which Roosevelt was suffering—hypertension, anemia, chronic obstructive pulmonary disease, and congestive heart failure—in concert almost certainly would have severely impaired his mental functioning. In particular, Park believes that Roosevelt was suffering from "sub-acute chronic diffuse hypoxia of the brain"—chronic insufficient oxygenation of the brain.[40] This is a very reasonable explanation for the drowsiness, problems in concentrating, and episodes of semi-stupor that affected Roosevelt during his last two years of life. Yet despite the obviously increasing impairment of Roosevelt's leadership capacity, Dr. McIntire continued to reassure the president, his family, and the public that Roosevelt was in good health for a man of his age.

In 1946, in response to stories that Roosevelt had been ill at Yalta and widespread criticism of his medical treatment, McIntire defended his treatment of the president in *White House Physician*. In it he asserted that the president "never had a serious heart condition," reported Roosevelt's blood pressure to be "well within a most satisfying range," and stated unequivocally, "Never once was there a loss of vigor or clarity. Had he been 'dying on his feet' at Yalta, I, as one bound by his professional oath, could not and would not have permitted the President to have poured out his energies in day and night sessions."[41]

This rosy picture stood in vivid contrast to the observations of others close to Roosevelt. His biographer Jim Bishop was most graphic, describing "wide vacillation, within hours, of peak form alternating with periods of apparent incomprehension. His signature became indecipherable, and he often lost the train of thought midway through a sentence. All had agreed that Franklin Roosevelt 'looked dead on his return from Yalta.'"[42]

In 1970, Dr. Bruenn finally felt able to correct the self-serving distortions in McIntire's book. His detailed account, "Clinical Notes," is the basis for the medical findings reported here. Interestingly, Bruenn reports that Roosevelt's medical record has disappeared from the files of Bethesda Naval Hospital.

It is difficult to penetrate Admiral McIntire's motives for stubbornly insisting on Roosevelt's good health, denying the gravity of his health problems, and not declaring that Roosevelt was medically unfit to run for a fourth term. The most charitable interpretation would be that he believed Roosevelt was essential at that critical moment in history and that it was his job to keep the president going. Yet McIntire must have realized that his credentials were not the strongest. His training as an ear, nose, and throat specialist was not well suited to Roosevelt's cardiopulmonary problems. Indeed, he had been made White House physician not for his professional attainments but for his social connections. McIntire was nominated for his position by none other than Cary Grayson, Woodrow Wilson's physician, primarily because of their shared belief that presidential illnesses should *not* be divulged. Perhaps McIntire was deceiving not only the president and the nation but also himself. After all, his patient's health had suffered serious deterioration under his very eyes. To acknowledge the extent of Roosevelt's deterioration meant facing his own professional failings.

What of Dr. Bruenn's reluctance to break the silence? Surely his conflict was profound, for he was bound by the code of military discipline. Yet in effect, he participated in a conspiracy to misrepresent the president's health status to the president, his family, and the nation. As we have noted, Jim Bishop asserted that Dr. McIntire had an obligation in April 1944 to confront Roosevelt with the gravity of his condition and to recommend strongly that he not run for a fourth term. If overridden, Admiral McIntire had the professional obligation to resign or to request another assignment.

We believe that the ethical and professional responsibility bearing on Dr. Bruenn was of equal weight—that he should not have permitted Dr. McIntire's assessment to be the last word when he knew it to be in error but should have pushed further within the chain of command of military medicine. If that route was not successful, he too should have resigned or requested a change of assignment, for he was knowingly complicit in a medical cover-up. But as the only physician on the team with a clear grasp of the seriousness of the president's health problems and the requisite training to deal with them, he may well have concluded that his continuing presence was critical to the president's survival, a judgment difficult to fault.

On the basis of our review of the record, we fully concur with Dr. Park's conclusion that "Franklin Roosevelt was a very ill and dying man during his last year in office."[43] The gravity of his medical condition was known to a few. Terminally ill, he should never have been permitted to run for a fourth term. The president who represented the United States at the crucial negotiations in Yalta was seriously impaired and just months away from death. He was present at those negotiations because of a major medical cover-up, and his situation demonstrates many elements of the syndrome of "the captive king."

When the throne room becomes the sick room, the effects spread throughout the kingdom. There may simply be drift, with opportunities lost, as with Wilson and Churchill in his later years. Or the disease may contribute to disaster, as with the shah of Iran. Especially when the onset is insidious, the disability is subtle, and the monarch's diminished reasoning and leadership capacities are evident only to his inner circle, the king and his court may be held captive by the illness. In turn, the nation may unwittingly be held in thralldom. And if this is true when the king becomes physically ill, it is especially the case when madness strikes the king.

2

THE MAD KING

MENTAL ILLNESS
AMONG THE MIGHTY

As death makes no distinctions in his visits between
the poor man's hut and the prince's palace,
so insanity is equally impartial in her dealings
with her subjects.
—The Reverend Dr. Francis Willis,
mad-doctor to King George III, 1798

We are not ourselves
When nature, being oppress'd, commands the mind
To suffer with the body.
—Shakespeare, *King Lear*

The subjects of the throne accord a reverential awe to
the king. Before the coronation, he is viewed as flesh
and blood, but once crowned, he becomes the object
of veneration. Similarly, when the intense deliberations to select a pope from among competing cardinals
are completed and the puff of white smoke finally
emerges from the Vatican, the new Vicar of Christ is
accorded holy veneration.

The same aura that surrounds kings and pontiffs
rests on the shoulders of the democratically elected.
During the Nixon-Kennedy election campaign of
1960, an extremely close camaraderie developed between John F. Kennedy and his advisers, a tightly knit
group of political professionals working together on a
first-name basis. But when, early in the morning after
a long, uncertain night, it finally became clear that
Kennedy had won a razor-thin victory and he entered
the hotel suite, his staff stood as one and intoned, "Mr.
President." Kennedy's relationship with his key advisers had fundamentally changed. They now ac-

corded him a special reverence. The American public now looked to him to be omniscient and omnipotent.

The role transcends the individual. There is a wish, an expectation, of ultimate wisdom that followers accord their designated leaders, especially at times of crisis. In a sense the leader is the creation of the followers, the embodiment of their collective wish to be cared for, led, and directed. It is the power of these collective needs reposed in the leadership role that makes the specter of illness in the throne room so threatening and contributes to the wish to deny, the impulse to conceal.

As we observed in the preceding chapter, when the king is struck by physical illness, the degree to which his leadership capacities are manifestly weakened is crucial to his ability to provide the symbolic strength his followers require. Thus physical illness that does not affect the leader's mental functioning is not nearly so threatening as that which does. A heart attack can be viewed as a temporarily disabling external event that has happened to the leader, who will be returned to full effectiveness after the requisite treatment. It is of concern to his political following, but it is not devastating.

Leaders carry out two functions in society. First, they represent the authority of the state and the community ideal of its members. This is their symbolic function. Second, leaders develop policies, select those who will execute the policies, and oversee this process. This is their instrumental function. Mental disorders interfere with both roles.

Accordingly, impressions of a dysfunctional, confused leader can be very disturbing to the political following. It is particularly troubling when the leader's mental acuity and decision-making ability are *primarily* affected by illness. When the physical illness affects brain functioning, when the leader's thinking and judgment are manifestly impaired, the followers' need for their leader to be all knowing and all wise is threatened. Arteriosclerosis that affects the brain and produces a disabling stroke or progressive dementia is thus much more threatening to the polity than arteriosclerosis that affects the heart.

Most threatening of all is illness that affects the leader's state of mind. Mental illness is perceived as striking at one's very core. The very essence of the individual is disturbed. Out of touch with reality, with peculiar thinking and distorted emotions, the mentally ill individual inspires feelings of discomfort and alienation. When madness strikes the king, his followers are cast adrift without the mandated symbol of strength in the palace.*

---

*Although our principal argument here is the devastating negative impact of mental illness in the leader upon his followers, this has not always been the case. Under extraordinary circumstances, particularly in times of social disaster when other means

Indeed, the prospect of a mentally unstable leader is so threatening to political followers that even a hint of emotional illness or a past history of psychiatric treatment can have serious consequences. Capitalizing on the rumor that 1988 presidential candidate Michael Dukakis had sought counseling for depression following the death of his brother and his loss of the governorship of Massachusetts, President Reagan called Dukakis "an invalid" and raised questions about his emotional stability. How unfortunate that the stigma of mental illness is so strong that an aspiring politician must eschew the potential benefits of psychiatric treatment in the face of life's reverses lest his or her career be damaged.

The disclosure of a leader's psychiatric illness may even be a political death warrant. The revelations during the 1972 campaign that vice presidential candidate Thomas Eagleton had undergone psychiatric treatment for severe depression was to cost him and his party dearly.

Thomas Eagleton: Position Denied Owing to Mental Illness

In 1972 the Democratic party selected George McGovern to be its standard-bearer. He chose Senator Eagleton of Missouri as his running mate. Ten days after the Democratic convention, probably as a result of a series of articles prepared by the Knight newspaper chain, Eagleton publicly acknowledged that in his twenties he had voluntarily entered a psychiatric clinic for a series of electroshock treatments for debilitating depression. This highly effective therapy unfortunately had a particularly frightening place in the public mind, a fear magnified by Ken Kesey's book (later a play and an Oscar-winning film) *One Flew over the Cuckoo's Nest,* in which the protagonist is subjected to "shock therapy."

Eagleton emphasized that his treatment for depression had taken place more than twenty years earlier and that the treatment has been fully successful—there had been no recurrences. Nevertheless, the response to these revelations was devastating. Polls revealed that the public could not tolerate the prospect of electing someone who might succeed to the high-

---

for coping with societal problems have failed or when a strong tradition of such legitimation exists, royal madness, rather than being troubling, can actually attract popular support. There are a number of interesting historical examples of psychiatrically impaired leaders whose impairment was valued and interpreted as a virtue, a form of legitimation—holy madness. In these circumstances, there will not be a captive king, but the society will make itself the captive of its defective ruler. Two cases of such "holy madness" legitimated—Saul the Prophet and Hung Siu-Tshuen—are described in appendix A.

est office with a history of serious mental illness—which might recur. Democratic leaders felt they had no choice but to remove Eagleton from the ticket. McGovern's selection of Eagleton now created the widespread perception that he was an ineffective leader. McGovern and his new running mate, Sargent Shriver, lost the election to Richard Nixon and Spiro Agnew by a wide margin.

Yet this affair had no lasting effect on Eagleton's subsequent senatorial reelection or on his career. The public apparently recognizes that the duties of legislators and the power they exercise permit them to cope with impairments that would disable an executive, especially a chief executive. If one of the two senators from Missouri fell into a severe depression, the nation would not be affected, nor would the consequences be great for the state.

But there is no tolerance for mental illness in the chief of state, from whom we expect wisdom, clarity of decision-making, and total control of his reactions. The prospect of a mentally ill chief of state fills the polity with dread. And because of this, there is a collective wish to deny that mental illness can ever affect our leaders. This "mental health mythology," as Arnold Rogow calls it, holds that "Very Important Persons do not become mentally ill . . . that VIPs never experience anything more than 'exhaustion' and the exhaustion, of course, reflects the fact that they overworked themselves in the nation's service."[1]

Once the leader is hospitalized for psychiatric illness, however, the potential for political damage is minimal. The political system has identified him as mad and has thrown up its defenses against him. The more obvious a mental illness is, the less likely it is to have political consequences. Full-blown mental illness is usually blatant and can be expected to be "managed" in one way or another by the system. It is the subtle mental illness and the early manifestations of severe illness that is most difficult to detect and diagnose, especially by laypersons. Undetected and undiagnosed mental illness is the most damaging because the political system has not yet implemented measures to contain or limit aberrant leadership behavior.

Royal Madness

Let us begin with real monarchs before we describe their democratic and authoritarian counterparts. In societies where the choice of ruler is determined by heredity and not by public favor or individual ambition, we can see how the political system has coped with both subtle and overt mental disorder.

Mad King Ludwig of Bavaria

The exemplar of madness in high places, from whom this chapter takes its title, is Ludwig II of Bavaria, popularly known as the Mad King, who ruled from 1864 to 1886. He displayed delusions of persecution and grandiosity and was intermittently paranoid, depressed, or manic throughout his reign. In later years his paranoid tendencies dominated.

The Royal House of Wittelsbach, rulers of Bavaria, had a reputation for mental imbalance, probably as a consequence of inbreeding over generations. Many of its members and their close relatives suffered from mental illness. Ludwig's grandfather Prince Wilhelm Karl feared all his life that he would die penniless and was exceedingly shy and misanthropic. Countess Hessen-Hamburg, his grandmother, claimed to have seen a ghost and for many years went to sleep only in the morning and made her entire court follow her schedule. His aunt Princess Alexandra was an intelligent and talented woman who suffered from the fixed idea that she had a glass piano inside her.[2] Ludwig's brother Otto suffered from delusions and outbreaks of violence that led to his psychiatric hospitalization.

During his persecutory phase, fearing assassination plots, Ludwig would become reclusive and withdrawn. In contrast, during his megalomanic phase, he was prone to frenzied hyperactivity and excitement, resembling the manic phase of manic-depressive psychosis. These megalomanic phases are responsible for the fanciful castles that have become such a tourist attraction but threatened to bankrupt Ludwig's Bavaria. The intensity of the manic phases, of the emotional or affective component of his illness, suggests that Ludwig was suffering from a mixed schizophrenic and affective disorder, what today would be termed schizo-affective schizophrenia.

The first hint that Ludwig was going mad was in 1866.[3] Ludwig suffered increasingly from sleeplessness and headaches. The culture of the victim often shapes the expression of mental illness. Many nineteenth-century Europeans believed the moon to have mystic powers to drive people mad, and Ludwig increasingly behaved like a "lunatic." He became obsessed with the moon and took to driving all night when the moon was out. One observer noted, "He often does not go to bed for forty-eight hours; he did not take off his boots for eight weeks, behaves like a madman, makes terrible faces, barks like a dog, and at times says the most indecorous things; and then again he is quite normal for a while."[4] Ludwig seemed to realize that his mental state was degenerating and, probably echoing his physicians, blamed his condition on his homosexuality. Letters indicate constant efforts, "oaths," to control his sexual appetites.

Had Ludwig quietly withdrawn into his own world, he would have been much less of a problem for his court and for the nation. But when he was in his megalomanic phase, the intensity of his manic drive in concert with his delusional preoccupations and obsessions impelled him to make consequential political decisions that almost destroyed Bavaria. No mere figurehead, King Ludwig translated his delusional preoccupations into political activity. Ludwig was obsessed with German culture. Overruling his advisers in 1870, he brought Bavaria into the Franco-Prussian War on the side of Prussia, which led to the loss of Bavarian influence and the creation of the German empire. The nobility of the German people extolled in Richard Wagner's operas—as well as a sexual attraction to the composer— led Ludwig not only to patronize Wagner but to make him a political adviser, an action that angered his more conventional advisers.

On the other side of the emotional mountain of Ludwig's grandiose expansion and preoccupation with German ideals was the valley of depression and persecution. Reversals convinced Ludwig that he was the object of conspiracies. In his despair he considered suicide. Seeing disloyalty at every turn, he ordered the expulsion or extreme punishment of suspected traitors in his leadership circle, a step that perpetuated unctuous sycophancy. Eventually, Ludwig's circle of political supporters narrowed to a small group who were exploiting him for their own financial ends. He also began to spend his family patrimony. Responsible political leaders and family members called in a group of "mad-doctors." They declared Ludwig unfit to exercise authority and recommended that he be sent to a nearby sanitorium. Ludwig was removed from the throne and soon afterward apparently murdered his psychiatrist and committed suicide.

Ludwig's insanity damaged the reputation of the monarchy, perhaps a benefit for the country in the long run. It also resulted in the extravagant waste of public money, although some of his "follies" are now profitable tourist attractions. Had Ludwig had the power to have his casual decrees of execution and torture carried out (none was), these manifestations of his paranoid phases could have done great damage. Ivan IV (The Terrible) of Russia exercised such power, creating a state of terror and inflicting great damage on the nation. The pattern is typical: depression and mania do limited harm and are generally managed by the system. As we shall see, it is uncontrolled aggressive paranoia that presents the greatest danger.

The Short, Unhappy Reign of King Talal of Jordan

King Abdullah of Transjordan, the second son of King Hussein of the Hejaz, was a man of immense ability. In 1922 he was persuaded by Winston Churchill, then secretary of the Colonies, to restrain his expansionist ambitions. In return Great Britain granted him the emirate of Transjordan. Emir Abdullah assumed the title of king of Jordan in 1946.

During the Middle East war of 1948, with the aid of the Arab Legion, Jordan occupied central and eastern Palestine, including the Old City of Jerusalem. Abdullah hoped to dominate a greater Syria, a vast expanse of territory that included Syria, Lebanon, and Jordan.

Abdullah's politico-military success stood in stark contrast to the infirmity within the royal family. As a boy, his son Talal, the putative heir to the throne of Jordan, showed signs of weakness and emotional instability. Abdullah treated Talal with contempt and made no effort to groom him for the throne, considering him irredeemably weak. Talal's psychological infirmity eventually became manifest, and he was sent to sanitariums in Europe for psychiatric treatment. Subject to withdrawal and fits of violence, he was diagnosed as suffering from dementia praecox (schizophrenia). Nevertheless, Talal married and fathered five children.

The undisguised revulsion King Abdullah felt toward Talal was matched by the love he felt for Talal's oldest son, Hussein. Abdullah showered affection on young Hussein and inculcated in him a mission of leadership. Hussein was by his grandfather's side on the steps of the Omar Mosque in Jerusalem on June 21, 1951, when King Abdullah, at the height of his power, was felled by an assassin's bullet. The sixteen-year-old Hussein miraculously escaped injury, which imbued him further with a sense of destiny and fatalism.

Talal, at the time being treated in Switzerland for another schizophrenic decompensation, was brought back to Amman and officially crowned in September 1951. He reigned for less than a year. The contrast with his predecessor could not have been starker. Anyone would have had difficulty in filling the shoes of the charismatic Abdullah, but for Talal, weak, indecisive, subject to psychological withdrawal, and manifestly peculiar in his behavior, the stress was overwhelming. At the beginning of Talal's rule, Egypt urged him to break with Great Britain and denounce the Anglo-Jordan treaty. He declined, and Jordan's political isolation from its Arab neighbors was the result.

During the following months, King Talal required several long periods of psychiatric treatment in a Swiss sanitarium. By May 1952 a crown council was established to rule in his absence; because of Talal's continuing mental infirmity, the council recommended that he be removed from power. On August 11, 1952, the Jordanian parliament proclaimed Hussein king of Jordan. Talal spent the rest of his years in political-medical exile, hospitalized in Cyprus for chronic schizophrenia. His effective replacement by a group of experienced court advisers—some of them British—and the gradual accession of King Hussein to full powers served Jordan well.

Overt mental illness like Talal's schizophrenia harms the polity principally by acts of omission rather than those of commission. The advantages a vigorous leader can provide are foregone. Government tends to drift. In a crisis, this can be catastrophic, as it nearly was in Jordan after Abdullah was assassinated. Very often, as in Jordan, other leaders step in to prevent the ship of state from foundering. The obviously schizophrenic patient cannot hide his disease and lacks the ability to prevent his replacement. Rulers like Talal are more a problem than a danger to the state.

Sometimes the consequences of mental illness have a major effect on the state, sometimes they do not—much depends on the nature and severity of the illness and the political environment. Overt diseases are easier to deal with than covert ones. Mental illness is dynamic, and the borderline between sanity and madness, between eccentricity and psychosis, is not always easy to discern. When the illness is blatant, as with King Talal, the system can usually manage it. In developed polities and even in some less developed political systems, responsible and courageous individuals will step in to cope with a leader's madness.

Depression, which is characterized by inactivity and indeciseiveness, is considerably easier to manage than such active illnesses as mania and aggressive paranoia. As we shall see in the cases of Cromwell, Castlereagh, Churchill, and Begin, only with Cromwell was the state hurt by the leader's depressive personality. When the leader is depressed, the system usually can compensate.

Depression: Destroyer of Confidence and Will

You may my glories and my state depose,
But not my griefs; still am I king of those.
—Shakespeare, *Richard II*

He looks on himself as a man whom the Gods hate
and pursue with their anger. A far worse lot is before
him; he dares not employ any means of averting or
of remedying the evil, lest he be found fighting
against the gods. The physician, the consoling
friend, are driven away. "Leave me," says the
wretched man, "me, the impious, the accursed,
hated of the gods, to suffer my punishment." He sits
out of doors, wrapped in sackcloth or in filthy rags.
Ever and anon he rolls himself, naked, in the dirt
confessing about this and that sin. He has eaten or
drunk something wrong. He has gone some way or

other which the Divine Being did not approve of.
The festivals in honor of the gods give no pleasure to
him but fill him rather with fear or a fright.
—Plutarch on melancholy, second century A.D.

The symptoms generally comprehended by the term
melancholia are taciturnity, a thoughtful pensive air,
gloomy suspicions, and a love of solitude. Those
traits, indeed, appear to distinguish the character of
some men otherwise in good health, and frequently
in prosperous circumstances. Nothing, however, can
be more hideous than the figure of a melancholic
brooding over his imaginary misfortunes. If
moreover possessed of power, and endowed with a
perverse disposition and a sanguinary heart, the
image is rendered still more repulsive.
—Pinel on melancholy, early nineteenth century

A continuum runs from pessimism through the sadness of everyday life
through mild depression to suicidal melancholia. Depression in its extreme manifestations is a mental illness that disables its victims and can
paralyze or significantly distort their behavior. In milder degree it can go
unnoticed, or the gravity of the condition and its effects can be insufficiently appreciated.

Depression is probably the most common psychiatric illness. It is appropriate to react with sadness to a loss, such as the death of a loved one or
defeat in an election. Such reactions of grief are limited in time. Some
clinical depressions are triggered by painful life events but persist. Others
are apparently triggered by biochemical changes unrelated to external
events. Depression is characterized not only by sadness but also by apathy,
fatigue, and decreased energy. The smallest task may seem difficult or
impossible. There is a pervasive sense of worthlessness, of extreme pessimism, and an excessive reaction to one's failings that may mount to the
point that the individual becomes convinced that others would be better
off if he or she were dead. There may also be serious cognitive disturbances; depressed individuals may be unable to concentrate, indecisive,
and slower thinking. Clearly the physical and psychological immobility,
disabling incapacity to do or try anything, feelings of hopelessness, help-
lessness, and apathy, and problems with concentration and attention may
profoundly affect leadership behavior.

Some psychiatric illnesses affect the mood and reality testing of the sufferer without diminishing the individual's capacity and energy. Indeed,
members of the circle surrounding a paranoid leader such as Stalin or

Hitler often wish that their chief had less stamina, was less vigorous in the pursuit of his imagined persecutors. The apathy that characterizes individuals suffering from depressive illness gives the inner circle much greater latitude to manipulate them and serve their own needs.

Abraham Lincoln was prone to episodes of depression during which he was plagued with feelings of guilt and self-recrimination. Thoughtful psychohistorians have suggested that this not only may have influenced his conduct of the Civil War but may have arisen from a feeling of responsibility for the war's initiation.[5] Major loss can precipitate depression. Such was probably the case with Lord Castlereagh, who became clinically depressed in the wake of three major losses: the death of his father, the loss of the king's favor, and a significant decline in his popular support.

Castlereagh's Suicidal Melancholia

Being under a state of mental delusion, Castlereagh
did kill and destroy himself.
—Coroner's Court, August 1822

Robert Stewart, Viscount Castlereagh, foreign secretary and leader of the House of Commons in the post-Napoleonic government of Lord Liverpool, was known to be reliable, sensible, conscientious, and mentally well balanced. Colleagues also characterized him as industrious, tenacious, and emotionally overcontrolled—features of the compulsive personality type.[6] According to his biographer Christopher Bartlett, Castlereagh was known to be "secretive, passionless, polished, . . . as imperturbable and aloof as Mont Blanc." When the poet Shelley wished to ascribe impassivity to another, he wrote that that person "had a mask like Castlereagh." To those who knew him well, however, Castlereagh had "a warm and gentle personality beneath the frigid exterior." His apparent coldness, especially in large groups, may have reflected shyness and diffidence.[7]

Castlereagh had a close marriage to Lady Emily Hobart, a marriage perhaps all the closer because they shared no children. They were nearly inseparable in spite of their quite different personalities. She dressed extravagantly and had a reputation for superficiality, whereas he presented the opposite picture. It is not uncommon for an emotionally contained compulsive man to be attracted to a woman of vivacious temperament who helps break through his shell of reserve and emotional containment. Like many of the Anglo-Irish aristocracy, Castlereagh participated enthusiastically in outdoor sports; he was also a good musician and something of a classical scholar. He showed a self-confidence that was distinctly without paranoid features. Once when a conspiracy to assassinate the Cabinet was uncovered he wanted to permit a dinner he had arranged to go forward with the Cabinet armed and prepared at the table.

For a quarter-century, from 1797 until 1822, Lord Castlereagh played a central role in some of the most important political events of his time: the union of Great Britain with Ireland, the preparation for and conduct of the wars that overthrew Napoleon, and the subsequent reconstruction of Europe. By 1821, he was at the acme of his influence and power in Europe. It was a time of immense responsibility and immense pressure. In the following year, however, when he was both leader of the Commons and foreign secretary, Castlereagh's mental state began to deteriorate. He became uncharacteristically suspicious and, even more uncharacteristically for this private man, began to air his suspicions with mere acquaintances. Just before the onset of his malady he had been working especially hard, even for him.

In spite of his eminence, Castlereagh's social position at court was threatened because of a feud between his wife and George IV's mistress. Castlereagh was excluded from several affairs of state, and he was hurt by his monarch's rejection. He became convinced that the king and Lord Liverpool had turned against him. When a close friend, Countess Lieven, intervened to mend the breach, Castlereagh, rather than expressing gratitude, angrily called her a traitor, leading the perplexed countess to remark, "Well, either I am mad, or he is."[8] He became increasingly agitated and dejected, convinced that everyone was talking about him.[9] He wept despondently in front of his brother Charles, who told Countess Lieven that Castlereagh's nerves were shattered; Charles feared a mental breakdown. "He is disgusted with everything . . . the cup has overflowed. He suspects everybody. He is broken-hearted."[10] Usually reticent, Castlereagh became voluble, speaking of his fears to relative strangers. In June 1822, his characteristically neat handwriting became almost illegible, suggesting an organic component to his illness. At that time, he raised questions about his ability to conduct his official responsibilities

Sleepless, Castlereagh appeared haggard to his friends, who maintained their loyalty despite his wary distrust. After asking Countess Lieven, "Can I trust you?" he forebodingly informed her, "In August I shall no longer be the King's Minister."[11] The countess told Prince Metternich that Castlereagh "looks ghastly; one can see he is a broken man."[12] Castlereagh became convinced that he was the object of a conspiracy, progressively suspecting everyone around him, including even his wife and his close friend Lord Wellington, whom he groundlessly believed was seeking to supplant him as foreign secretary. He told his secretary, "My mind is, as it were, gone."[13]

Castlereagh also became obsessed with the belief that accusations of homosexuality were being circulated against him. His fears in this regard were so great that he avoided being seen with the duke of Wellington out of concern that the meeting of these old friends would give rise to scandal. Convinced that he was about to be denounced as a homosexual, Castlereagh informed George IV of his fears, stating that he was receiving anonymous letters threatening to expose him. As is often the case with paranoids, there was a nub of truth to his fear. According to the Reverend J. Richardson, Castlereagh had told a nobleman of an incident that was to haunt him. Once while returning from the House of Commons, he was accosted by a prostitute who persuaded him to accompany her to a brothel. He soon found that the prostitute was a man in woman's attire. Two men then burst in and threatened to expose him for indecent behavior unless he paid them, which he did.[14] Thereafter, he was the object of blackmail.

Castlereagh did not tell the king of this incident, only of his worries. When George made light of them, Castlereagh said, "I know well that you are also my enemy. Everyone hates me and shuns me. When I walk down the street people take the opposite side to avoid meeting me." He then proceeded to accuse himself of a wide range of crimes. When the king told him he was suffering from brain fever, Castlereagh broke down, saying, "I am mad. I know I am mad. I have known it for some time." He begged the king to keep his secret from his colleagues. George pleaded with Castlereagh to seek medical attention, telling him to "have yourself bled and chase away your fit of blue devils."[15]

After this meeting, Wellington found Castlereagh to be obsessed with delusions. He believed that his horses had followed him to the castle, a sign that he should leave the country, and continued to insist that there was a conspiracy against him. Wellington confronted his friend, saying, "From what you have said I am bound to warn you that you cannot be in your right mind." Castlereagh responded, "I fear it must be so. I have an oppression of the head which distresses me perpetually and makes me fear that my ideas are indeed in great disorder." Wellington wrote to Castlereagh's physician, Dr. Bankhead, imploring him to see Castlereagh immediately: "I have no doubt he is very unwell; he appears to me to have been exceedingly harassed, much fatigued, and overworked during the late session of Parliament; and I have no doubt he labours under mental delirium."[16] Castlereagh was removed from office and placed under observation. He managed, however, to evade the vigilance of those responsible for him. On August 11, 1822, he took a small penknife and severed his carotid artery, tragically ending a distinguished public life.

The onset of Castlereagh's bizarre behavior some three months before his death was so dramatic and so obviously a consequence of mental illness that he was removed from authority, first informally and then formally. His madness thus did not affect British foreign policy. Whatever the truth may have been concerning his homosexual relations and declining political fortunes, Castlereagh's random accusations and obsessive suspicions were clearly pathological and recognized as such at the time. Probably precipitated by the perceived loss of favor of the king, the illness was almost certainly involutional melancholia, a mid-life depressive disorder characterized by extreme feelings of worthlessness, self-deprecation, and delusions of persecution. As we shall see in the next chapter, this same illness destroyed James Forrestal, the first secretary of defense of the United States, some 125 years later.

An important lesson to be drawn from the Castlereagh affair is that when the mental disease is obvious and inconsistent with the victim's previous character, it is likely to be of little political consequence. Others note the disability, and the person is removed from power. And when, as in this case, the mentally ill leader is not the principal leader, his removal is somewhat easier.

Churchill's "Black Dog"

The best documented case of depression of a political leader is that of Winston Churchill.[17] Various factors predisposed him to this illness. As a child Churchill was treated coldly and distantly by both parents, especially his mother, a pattern that psychologically predisposes its victim to depression in adulthood. On his father's side of the family, moreover, there was a history of severe melancholia. Indeed, Churchill's own description of the recurrent depressive episodes that came over him, often without reference to outside events, is consistent with an inherited major depressive disorder. He ruefully characterized his depression as "my black dog," a faithful companion, sometimes out of sight, but always returning.

Churchill was fortunate, however, in that his depression was not so severe that he was unable to combat it. Like many depressives, he was aware of the onset of the illness and could try to fight it off by intense activity. This overcompensation, psychologically painful to the man but useful to the politician, is a creative response to what would otherwise be a destructive malady. As one writer has commented: "The depressive, before his disorder becomes too severe, may recurrently force himself into activity, deny himself rest or relaxation, and accomplish more than most men are capable of, just because he cannot afford to stop. We do not know how many men of exceptional achievement have this tendency toward depression, for it may often be well-concealed. That some do, and that Churchill was one of them, admits of no possible doubt."[18]

Churchill often fought off his depression and rationalized his many real failures (such as the disastrous attack on Gallipoli during World War I) and long periods in the political wilderness by the belief that he was being saved for some great role and that he must direct his energies toward preserving himself for that role. Such fantasies are not uncommon, particularly among men in public life, and suggest a narcissistic core to Churchill's personality. The grandiose self-concept and dreams of glory characteristically sail on a sea of insecurity. Indeed, the narcissistic leader, no matter how much success and acclaim he wins, is always vulnerable to setbacks and often prone to depression. No amount of praise can fill the inner void. While it may seem strange for such dreams to persist so late in life, this is characteristic of seekers after glory. Old dreams never die. They don't even fade away. Had Churchill died in early 1939, at the age of sixty-five, he would have been considered a failure. As it was, fate and greatness did call him. He was able to say to his doctor and confidant, Lord Moran, near the beginning of World War II, "This cannot be accident, it must be design. I was kept for this job."[19] Perhaps his very exalted self-concept and long and successful personal battle against depression made Churchill an ideal figure to lead Britain in a successful denial of its desperate condition and help his country win through to victory. "It is probable that England owed her survival in 1940 to this inner world of make-believe. The kind of inspiration with which Churchill sustained the nation is not based on judgment, but on an irrational conviction independent of actual reality. Only a man convinced that he had a heroic mission, who believed that, in spite of all evidence to the contrary, he could yet triumph, and who could identify himself with a nation's destiny could have conveyed his inspiration to others."[20]

Under the depression a rage often smolders. Characteristically hostile, depressives are angry toward those who have deprived them of love or recognition but are unable to display this hostility because they continue to need these people. During periods of depression the hostility is turned inward against the self, hence the self-accusations. It is therapeutic to turn this hostility outward, but often no suitable object can be found. Further, the incidence of emotional disorder declines at times of external crisis. It is as if the need to cope with real, external dangers deflects the mentally ill from the fears of their internal world. In Great Britain during the Blitz, the incidence of psychoneuroses declined precipitously. In the aftermath of the 1989 San Francisco earthquake, patients suffering from depressive disorders reported feeling better. Rather than focusing on their internal psychological problems, they direct their attention to the crisis in the outside world. As the leader of wartime Britain, Winston Churchill found Adolf Hitler an opponent worthy of his foulest rage. Compensating depressives like Churchill find the fighting of real enemies a great relief, a legitimation of the suppressed wish to lash out. Churchill was able to find that relief in the service of saving his people.

Churchill lost his postwar bid for re-election to the prime ministership for a variety of reasons, but in one respect the British people showed a sure instinct. Churchill was magnificent as a leader in desperate battle, but not in reform or as a junior partner to the Americans in the Cold War. Because of his arteriosclerosis, increasing dependence on drugs and alcohol, and the absence of direct and violent conflict with his enemy, it was increasingly difficult for him to escape the downward pull of his depressions. He began to display mawkish emotion in public, frequently crying, for example. As we saw earlier, Churchill's various disorders, including his depression, made him a figurehead for most of his final term in office. The government simply drifted. Although the battle against depression may have improved his political abilities, in his later days, depression contributed to his downward spiral.

Oliver Cromwell: Youthful Depression, Adult Rage

Churchill was able to turn his depression-generated anger to good purpose. His countryman Oliver Cromwell was not. Six months after being elected to Parliament in 1628, the twenty-nine-year-old Cromwell visited the London physician Sir Theodore Mayerne. Mayerne noted Cromwell's stomach pains but stressed in his notes that his patient was "extremely melancholy." Cromwell's regular physician stated that Cromwell would sometimes lie in his bed "all melancholy" and would send for a doctor at various "unseasonable hours," claiming to be dying and having "fancies" about seeing a large cross in the center of town. Like Churchill, Cromwell believed that he would be "the greatest man in this kingdom."[21]

The depression must have been severe indeed for Cromwell to consult a physician, for the Puritan attitude toward this disorder was ambivalent. It was believed that those in God's favor would go through a "dark night of the soul" in which they would feel abandoned by God. Only after this experience could the sufferer become aware of a state of grace.

Cromwell, like Churchill, seems initially to have turned his depression to his advantage, by throwing himself into political activity. But the consequence of this activity for society was mixed. Although Cromwell was influential in establishing parliamentary supremacy, his manic style alienated many, and led to an extremism that eventually discredited the Roundheads and restored the monarchy. Even worse, there may have been a connection between Cromwell's depression—which seems largely to have left him in his thirties and forties—and the mania that sometimes seized him in battle.[22] The massacres at Wexford and Drogheda in 1649, when Cromwell was suppressing the Irish rebellion, were in large part due to the madness and lack of control that overcame Cromwell in battle.

But some might argue that it is only the toss of the dice of history that leads us to admire Churchill and not Cromwell. Were the firebombings of Dresden in Germany any less inhumane than the massacre at Drogheda? But Churchill's victory in World War II was complete—militarily, politically, and in the broadest sense, morally. Cromwell's place in English history is mixed. He did limit royal power, but in such a draconian manner that the monarchy was reestablished after his death. His actions in Ireland seem unforgivable today. The lesson here is that the aggressive dimension of depression—compensatory rage—is in itself neither good nor bad. Its coloration depends on the political circumstances.

Menachem Begin's Recurrent Depressions and Terminal Melancholia

Until his death on March 9, 1992, Menachem Begin fought with single-minded devotion for the Zionist dream of establishing a Jewish homeland in the biblical land of Israel. Begin was strongly influenced by the Zionist pioneer Ze'ev Jabotinsky, who advocated a policy of unremitting and ruthless struggle. Begin lost most of his family to the Holocaust, a devastating loss that led him to vow, "Never again." He came to see himself as having a special role to play in the destiny of the Jewish people, an exalted self-concept that was to sustain him through long years of political struggle as an outsider. When his idol Jabotinsky died in 1940, the mantle of the personality cult that had surrounded Jabotinsky descended upon Begin, and his belief in a divine mission was confirmed. His political party's banners read, "God Chose Us to Rule."[23] He himself acquired a reputation for such arrogance and ruthlessness that Ben Gurion and other Labor Zionist leaders compared him to a Nazi.[24] To Begin, of course, such personal condemnation showed only that his detractors were less than wholehearted Zionists. To condemn Begin, in Begin's narcissistic eyes, was to condemn the Jewish people.

Narcissists, like paranoids, make errors of reference. That is, they see events, comments, actions as being directed toward them even when they are not. This leads to a constant state of conflict. Begin once identified his credo as "I fight, therefore I am."[25] As the leader of Irgun, the underground resistance group, he played a central role in driving the British out of Palestine. Begin referred to his political party as his "fighting family," and he fought the post-independence elections with the same fierce intensity that he had employed against the British occupiers. He was a flamboyant showman, a charismatic orator, and a compulsive scrapper. There was no room for uncertainty in his doctrines or variation in his policies. Even as late as 1972, in a classically narcissistic affirmation, he stated, "We have never been mistaken. We have always judged things correctly, so we have never changed."[26]

None of his former adversaries could ever be forgiven; rather, all were to be battled, even when the lines of demarcation among friends, enemies, and neutrals were not clear and reconciliation was in the practical interests of Israel. When in the 1960s Chancellor Konrad Adenauer of Germany (who had spent part of World War II in a Nazi prison because of his opposition to Hitler) offered to make restitution for financial losses suffered by Jews during the war, Begin responded, "There is not one German who did not murder our parents. Every German is a Nazi. Adenauer is a Nazi. All his aides are murderers."[27]

After four years as prime minister, Begin suffered a series of political defeats in early 1981 and was forced to set an election for June. Polls showed that the popularity of the Likud party and Begin was at a low. But Begin appeared buoyant; he threw himself into the campaign with exuberant confidence. At rallies, his supporters praised "Begin, King of Israel," and he responded to their adulation with increased vitality. In March, Begin indicated that he felt better than at any time since he had come to power four years earlier, "because now I am in a fight." He said, "If they [Labor] win, I will lose my chance to save the Jewish people."[28] His upset victory in the 1981 election confirmed his belief in his destiny to lead Israel, the correctness of his views, and the efficacy of his highly personalistic style of leadership.

Although victory on the battlefield or in the polls confirmed Begin's exalted self-concept, political defeats and setbacks precipitated serious bouts of depression. His first recorded clinical depression was in 1939, when he was high commissioner of the Zionist organization Betar, responsible for organizing the clandestine emigration of Polish Jews to Palestine. The characteristically strong and assertive leader became paralyzed with indecision, and many have noted his failure of leadership at this crucial time, believing that more decisive action on his part could have significantly reduced the destruction of the Warsaw ghetto.

In 1951, after an election setback, Begin became depressed, decided to give up politics, and submitted a letter of resignation to his political followers (which was not accepted). In the aftermath of Camp David in 1978, Begin again began to fall into a depression. Perhaps this represented the depletion depression that sometimes occurs after sustained tense involvement. For although Camp David was a triumph, massive pressure was exerted upon Begin, from within and outside his government, and the difficult negotiations were conducted at high cost to his fragile constitution. He withdrew from active leadership at this crucial time and was uncommunicative. He seemed drained, exhausted. This led to an attempted political coup within his party, which Begin turned back with difficulty. A prominent Israeli politician commented, "When I met Begin on December 8, 1979, I could not help but be impressed that the Prime Minister is a sick and broken man. He is physically and mentally ill. Begin is a tragic figure. This poses a danger to the state."[29] In the spring and summer of 1980, Begin had several depressed periods. One was precipitated by the decision of his long-time ally and sometime rival, Ezer Weizman, to resign as defense minister. Begin himself, despite his lack of expertise in military matters, assumed Weizman's position.

When Begin entered a depressed period, he would become indecisive and inaccessible, gloomy and deeply pessimistic. As we have seen, he emerged from some of these depressive periods by taking assertive action, replacing apathy with activism. Close associates would often deliberately provoke him—by making accusations against his rivals, by telling him things that they knew would anger him—to come out fighting. It was a type of adversarial therapy.

Throughout this long and often lonely political odyssey, Begin's wife, Aliza, played an important role in blunting his depressions. She was his constant source of emotional support, his political confidante, his sounding board, his source of strength when he wavered, his reassurance when he doubted. Although she remained in the background and eschewed the limelight, many consider her Begin's most important political adviser. In her later years, Aliza struggled with cardiopulmonary illness. Begin was often torn between his official duties and his desire to be at the side of his ailing wife. In spite of suffering a setback, Aliza, in failing health, urged her husband to fly to Washington on an important diplomatic mission. While he was on this mission, on November 13, 1982, his wife of forty-three years died. Informed of her death by his daughter Lea, he cried, as he recited from Proverbs, "I shall remember you going after me on an unseen desert."[30]

Blaming himself for abandoning Aliza in the final stages of her illness, Begin became deeply depressed. The personal loss was compounded several months later by the February 1983 report of the Kahan Commission, which had investigated the massacres at Sabra and Shatila in the wake of the 1982 invasion of Lebanon. The commission assigned partial blame for this atrocity to Begin for his inattention and indifference. Standing up against the outside enemy was never stressful for Begin. He exulted in it. But to be criticized by the Israeli people—his people, to whom he had devoted his entire life—was shattering. And now he did not have his lifelong source of support, his wife, Aliza, to help him through these dark hours.

What happens to ambition unfulfilled? Does it burst into flames or wither in the grass, become the bone-dry dust of despair? Perhaps Menachem Begin's recognition that his dream of Eretz Israel—the biblical Jewish homeland—was not to be ensured in his lifetime contributed to his terminal melancholia. Rather than receive the plaudits of his nation for ending the terrorist menace through the Lebanon invasion, he was judged responsible for the massacres at Sabra and Shatila and Israel was castigated in the court of world opinion. Hoping to go down in history as Israel's savior, instead Menachem Begin became the object of criticism within the land to which he had dedicated his life.

This combination of events—the loss of his wife, his guilt over not being with her at the end, the toll of the war in Lebanon, the official condemnation by the nation to which he had devoted his life—overwhelmed Begin; he sank into a despair from which he was never to emerge. He became indifferent, apathetic, and gloomy, did not tend to his personal appearance, did not shave, sat at home in his bathrobe, lost his appetite, and suffered major weight loss. These are the classic symptoms of clinical depression, an eminently treatable psychiatric disorder. But Begin was too proud to accept psychiatric aid.

When a leader delegates effectively, his subordinates may blunt the impact of a period of incapacity. But Begin's rule had been so autocratic, his power so concentrated, that there was no one to act in his stead. Indeed, throughout his political career, if a subordinate became too popular and prominent and attempted to exert authority in his own right, Begin had cut him down. Thus not only was there no provision for succession, but potential successors were viewed as threats and eliminated.

Begin's spokesmen insisted that the government was functioning effectively and that Begin was providing his characteristic strong leadership, but this was plainly false. He was not making public appearances, was inattentive to the day-to-day running of his government, and seemed disengaged during cabinet meetings. Once a favorite of the press, with a gift for the pungent phrase, he no longer gave interviews. When an invitation to visit President Reagan in Washington was extended, he felt unable to respond, although he had been angling for just such an opportunity for more than a year and Israel desperately needed to repair its damaged relationship with Washington. The economy was ailing, but Begin was apparently uninterested. The controversial occupation of Lebanon continued, with no apparent way out, tearing at the moral fabric of his nation, producing deep divisions.

Israel is not a land that lends itself to secrecy and concealment. The general situation was public knowledge. The party faithful also recognized that Begin was no longer up to the demands of leadership, but they had no alternative. They pleaded with him to stay in office. When Begin finally announced his intention to resign in August 1983, stating, "I cannot go on," it was both sad and a relief, like the end of a terminal illness. His welfare minister acknowledged, "The government has been a ship without a captain." On September 15, 1983, almost a year to the day after the massacres at Sabra and Shatila, Begin submitted his resignation, secluded himself in his house, and withdrew from public life.[31]

Mania

Mania lies at the opposite emotional pole from profound depression. Indeed, in psychodynamic theory, it is considered a flight from and defense against depression. In striking contrast to depressives, manics experience elation, euphoria, and joy. They also experience cognitive distortions, but in the opposite direction: they are optimistic in the extreme. They have an exaggeratedly positive self-image, characteristically deny or blame others for their problems, and tend to be arbitrary in decision-making. In terms of motivation, they are driven and impulsive rather than paralyzed and apathetic. Impatient and restless, they are highly action-oriented and tend to be hyperactive—socially, sexually, and professionally. This leads to excessive involvement in activities without recognizing the risk for painful consequences—for example, buying sprees, reckless driving, sexual indiscretion. Manics have a strong desire for self-enhancement. They may suffer from delusions, but they are delusions of grandeur. Manics may regard themselves as superheroes or the reincarnation of God.

The physical manifestations of mania are striking. Like depressives, manics have sleep disturbances, but whereas depressives are characterized by insomnia and early morning waking, manics are indefatigable. Their supply of energy is seemingly inexhaustible. They demonstrate a rapid flight of ideas and a characteristic pressure of speech. They usually show an increased libido.

Clearly, many of these traits have important implications for political behavior. When mania invades the royal chamber, it can have devastating effects, especially if it goes unrecognized. Although the extremes depicted in the clinical description are unusual in high office, they have occurred. The frenzied periods of hyperactivity and excessive spending of Mad King Ludwig may well have represented manic phases of a manic-depressive illness. Cromwell's battle rage may also have been a manifestation of mania.

But if full-blown mania is inconsistent with sustained leadership performance, so-called hypomanic behavior is not. Indeed, many leaders who are seemingly endowed with extra stores of energy will drive their assistants to the point of exhaustion. This is usually not recognized as a clinical aberration. The decision-making of these leaders who are on a natural high can be very dangerous. Impulsive and impetuous, grossly overoptimistic, they make rapid decisions without judicious reflection and without thought to long-range consequences.

Paranoia: Destroyer of the Leader's People

Where lies the boundary between healthy wariness and malignant suspiciousness, between malignant suspiciousness and paranoia? Who shall be the judge, and what the criterion—that of expertise or majority rule? The seventeenth-century playwright Nathaniel Lee, calling attention to this dilemma, protested his incarceration in Bedlam: "They called me mad, and I called them mad, and damn them, they outvoted me."[32] Emily Dickinson gave poetic voice to this thought:

Much Madness is divinest Sense—
To a discerning Eye—
Much Sense—the starkest Madness—
'Tis the majority
In this, as All, prevail—
Assent—and you are sane—
Demur—you're straightaway dangerous—
And handled with a Chain.

Paranoia, the most political of all mental illnesses, best illustrates the difficulties in distinguishing between exaggerated personality traits and full-blown mental illness. The essential features of the paranoid personality are a pervasive suspiciousness and general mistrust of people. The paranoid is always expecting plots and betrayal and sees himself or herself as alone, surrounded by enemies. This attitude derives in part from an exaggerated need for autonomy: in a dangerous world, it is best to trust no one.

Individuals with this disorder are hypersensitive and easily slighted; they continually scan the environment for clues that validate their biases. Paranoids constantly try to find evidence to confirm their ideas, dismissing what is not relevant to them, and seizing upon what apparently supports them. Psychologically healthy individuals can abandon such suspicions when presented with firm contradictory evidence. Paranoids, in contrast, will become hostile, defensive, and stubborn when presented with evidence that disproves their suspicions.

Paranoids tend to be rigid and unwilling to compromise. In a new situation, they tend to lose sight of the context as they conduct a narrowly focused search for confirmation of their biases and disregard contrary evidence. Trying to breach the rigidity of the paranoid can produce unfortunate consequences. Well-meaning attempts to reassure or reason with them will usually provoke anger, and the helpful person can even become the object of suspicions and be seen as disloyal. The paranoid's hypervigilance and readiness to retaliate often generate fear and uneasiness in others. People tread lightly and carefully around a paranoid, walking on eggshells lest they provoke anger.

The paranoid leader's view of his adversary is strong and central. He sees the world as full of conflict and the adversary as evil, an immutable threat to his and the national interest. Thus, in a crisis situation, the paranoid leader will not see his adversary as eager to avoid conflict, but rather will attribute malevolent motivations, will construct a worst-case scenario. This conviction that persuasion and compromise are impossible in turn pushes the paranoid to preemptive action.

Fortunately, overt paranoids usually do not last long in a hierarchy, at least in an open society. But under the stress of crisis, the characteristic personality traits, which of course represent coping mechanisms, become exaggerated and can become dysfunctional. Thus an individual whose suspiciousness is not usually of pathological proportions can, under stress, become frankly paranoid. Several accounts of the last days of the Nixon presidency suggest that the effects of the stress of the Watergate crisis on Nixon were so severe that his close associates feared he might react in an aggressively paranoid manner. Emergency measures were instituted to limit Nixon's power as commander-in-chief to initiate conflict.

In considering the relationship between personality types and crisis-induced stress, we should not limit our attention to leaders in open societies. What of those in closed societies? As we shall see in the case of Stalin, in such a society the paranoid with power can go unchecked. To suspect conspiracy in such an environment is not only not dysfunctional but perhaps necessary for survival. And the point at which adaptive suspiciousness deteriorates into malignant paranoia may be difficult if not impossible to determine.

Individuals with strong propensities for paranoia have leadership roles in both open and closed societies. Consider Adolf Hitler in the light of paranoid dynamics, especially in his interpersonal relationships. Toward the end of the war, Hitler felt increasingly isolated, and his paranoia mounted. When his generals brought him undeniable reports of Germany's defeat, he was convinced that they were lying to him and that he could trust no one. He told his personal pilot that his tombstone should read, "He was the victim of his generals."[33] In April 1945, Field Marshal Göring informed Hitler that he was making preparations to negotiate the surrender of the defeated German forces. Hitler flew into a rage, denouncing Göring as a traitor: "Nothing is spared me!" Hitler screamed. "Nothing! Every disillusion, every betrayal, dishonor, treason has been heaped upon me."[34]

Consider the interaction between an exaggeratedly paranoid Hitler and his officers, many of whom apparently had strongly authoritarian personality dispositions. Accounts of Hitler under stress, both on the eve of the Normandy invasion and on other occasions as Germany was losing the war, suggest that the greater the stress, the more rigidly Hitler held to his construction of the world. To attempt to present him with new information or to persuade him to change his mind was to risk not only explosive wrath but even expulsion from the ranks, court martial, or worse, as the following description of a confrontation between Hitler and General Guderian exemplifies: "His fists raised, his cheeks flushed with rage, his whole body trembling, the man stood there in front of me, beside himself with fury and having lost all self-control. After each outburst of rage, Hitler would stride up and down the carpet edge, then suddenly stop immediately before me and hurl his next accusation in my face. He was almost screaming, his eyes seemed about to pop out of his head and the veins stood out on his temples."[35]

Such a reaction would inhibit even the most self-confident of advisers. But given the strong psychological need to please authority that characterized many of these individuals, not disturbing or angering the Führer took precedence over presenting one's assessment of the situation. This example, while striking, is by no means unique. It emphasizes the point that in considering the effects of serious personality disorders and mental illness on crisis reactions, one must consider the interaction between different personalities in the decision-making hierarchy.

When the paranoid ruler is not constrained by the structure of the kingdom, the consequences can be fatal for the objects of his paranoid suspicions. Such was the case with the general secretary of the Communist party of the Soviet Union Josef Stalin; the president of Equatorial Guinea Francisco Macias Nguema; and the President for Life of Uganda Idi Amin Dada.

Stalin's Paranoia

When Stalin left the seminary to follow Lenin's road to communism, he entered the world of conspiracy, where hyper-suspiciousness was required. To be open and trusting was to risk imprisonment by the czar. Yet Stalin's attraction to this conspiratorial environment probably reflected his personality bent; once he was in power, pronounced distrust continued to mark his leadership style. Nikita Khrushchev (1970) indicated that Stalin was always known as highly suspicious, even within the plot-ridden chambers of the Kremlin.[36] Khrushchev described Stalin glaring at him during party meetings, insisting that he explain why he would not meet Stalin's gaze.

At a party congress in 1923, Stalin declared, "We are surrounded by enemies—that is clear to all. The wolves of imperialism who surround us are not dozing. Not a moment passes without our enemies trying to seize some little chink through which they could crawl and do harm to us."[37] Stalin's readiness to see enemies everywhere permitted him to counter threats to his leadership. It may well be that only someone highly attuned to danger, highly suspicious of plots, could have survived. But his precautions exceeded prudence, and he became increasingly paranoid. He was obsessed with a fear of assassination. Before public appearances in Red Square he would have his security guards search more than a million people and then search them again. The harsh prophylaxis against plots to dethrone him in fact produced real enemies in a self-fulfilling prophecy. As Robert Tucker has observed: "Inside Russia, and even within its Communist party, he felt himself to be in a besieged fortress. He was driven by unconscious needs and drives to people the world around him with Stalin-hating enemies who pretended to be loyal Bolsheviks while watchfully waiting for an opportunity to strike a blow against the Communist cause and against him as its leader. Were such enemies lacking in sufficient numbers, he would have to invent them. And invent them he did."[38]

In the 1930s Stalin's suspiciousness mounted to a degree that in an open society would have warranted the diagnosis of paranoid personality disorder. But the question of pathology was masked by the extraordinarily brutal and genuinely conspiratorial environment in which he lived and to which he contributed. These tendencies grew and flourished during the 1940s. Robert Conquest has estimated that some 23 million people lost their lives in the purges as Stalin sought to eliminate all enemies of the state, real and imagined.[39] The malignancy was highly manipulable; Laventi Beria, the dread chief of the NKVD, the Soviet secret police, adroitly exploited Stalin's suspiciousness to rid himself of bureaucratic rivals. Just before his death in 1953, Stalin announced that a group of Jewish doctors, in cooperation with Western powers and their allies within the Soviet Union, were scheming to murder Soviet leaders. Another purge was clearly on the way.

By then, Stalin was in a clinical paranoid state, seeing enemies all around him.* Age and cerebral arteriosclerosis moved Stalin along the continuum from paranoid suspiciousness to full-blown paranoia. And his total con-

---

*Tucker has brilliantly exposed the relationship between Stalin's paranoid personality and his politics in *Stalin in Power* (1990), which continues his earlier delineation of the dictator in *Stalin as Revolutionary* (1973).

trol of the Soviet Union permitted his paranoia to flower unchecked. In that plot-ridden environment, moreover, the border between prudent overreaction and psychotic delusions was difficult to determine.[40] Though most people in his surroundings may have judged him mad at the end, the only vote that counted was Stalin's.

Khrushchev's memoirs offer the best evaluation of the role Stalin's paranoia played in the politics of this brutal era. It was Stalin's right to be suspicious, Khrushchev conceded, but it was not right to kill people just because he was suspicious. That, Khrushchev noted as perceptively as any political psychologist, was what made him crazy.[41]

President Macias Nguema of Equatorial Guinea: Unconstrained Paranoia, Reign of Terror

Equatorial Guinea was a colony of Spain when Macias Nguema was born in modest circumstances in 1924. He entered the colonial administration at age twenty as a clerk. Macias's education was limited, and it was remarked early that in his life he suffered from an "inferiority complex" in front of educated persons and foreigners but was arrogant toward others.

He gradually climbed the administrative and political ladder. During the constitutional conference that paved the way for Equatorial Guinea's independence from Spain, the Grupo Macias formed around Macias, violently opposed to other statesmen. Macias ran for president in September 1968, on the second ballot defeating Ondo Edu, who went into exile in Gabon. On October 12 of that year Equatorial Guinea gained its independence and Francisco Macias became chief of state of the sovereign nation of Equatorial Guinea.

Under stress, basic personality vulnerabilities are intensified; the somewhat suspicious individual can become frankly paranoid. For a man with only limited education to be chief of state, required to develop a structure of government, manage the economy, and establish foreign relations, is massively stressful. On assuming the presidency Macias crossed the border into frank paranoia.

Macias began a reign of terror that characterized his entire eleven-year rule. He acted quickly to eliminate any opponent, real or imagined. His first victim was Ondu Edo, his opponent in the presidential election. Macias lured him back from exile with false promises and had him arrested and killed, initiating a long series of political assassinations. After delivering a series of violent anti-Spanish speeches in January 1969, precipitating a military intervention by Spain, Macias declared a state of emergency and suspended the guarantees of the constitution he had helped formulate. Now Macias, who had long felt inferior toward educated people, systematically began to eliminate the source of discomfort by executing prominent intellectuals; in a short time he ordered the assassination of the ambassador to the United Nations, the president and secretary of the Parliament, and ten of his original twelve cabinet members. The word *intellectual* was prohibited, and the minister of education was fined for using it in a cabinet meeting. When portraits of Macias were slashed and anti-Macias tracts were circulated in a secondary school, the teachers, students, and parents were arrested.

Macias now began to see enemies internationally as well, and in 1970 he accused the United States government of plotting to kill him. He then proceeded to liquidate political figures he believed to be supporting the American plot. As his insecurity mounted, he constructed elaborate physical defenses to augment his psychological defenses. He evicted all people living around the palace and created a secure perimeter, surrounded by high walls topped with electrified wire. At the same time, his grandiosity was mounting. Attempting to magnify his cult of personality, Macias ordered that his portrait be placed on the altars of all Roman Catholic churches and his name included in the recitation of the Sign of the Cross. When the priests refused, he outlawed Catholicism. In 1976 he summarily announced that Guineans had six months to give up their Christian names for African ones. He changed his own name to the Africanized Masie.

Macias's atrocities were documented by several human rights organizations. On one occasion he exhibited a statistician whose fingers he had amputated because "he couldn't count."[42] He ordered two prisoners to participate in a savage reenactment of the crucifixion of Christ. Male prisoners had electric currents administered to their testicles, female prisoners had thorns forced up their vaginas. A prominent priest was frozen in a refrigerator truck; another prominent intellectual was bound and left to roast in the Saharan sand.

During this period there was an average of more than one political murder per week, including 2 vice presidents of the republic, 18 ministers, 22 provincial deputies, 7 mayors, 4 ambassadors, 15 high officials, 24 state administrators, 23 major landowners, and 123 other officials.[43] In 1974, 27 members of the Crusade for the Liberation of Equatorial Guinea were publicly executed; the remaining 87 defendants died under torture or in prison. Between 1968 and 1979, there were more than 500 political killings. Many people were arrested and simply "disappeared." In 1977, as he continued to hunt down the remaining intellectuals, Macias, projecting his insecurities onto the nation, identified the intelligentsia as Africa's most serious threat. In celebration of National Day in 1978 he ordered 32 new executions.

This reign of terror was finally ended in 1979, when Macias was toppled in a coup, captured, and executed. It was estimated that between 40,000 and 50,000 of his nation's 324,000 citizens (more than 10 percent of the population) had been killed during his despotic rule.

Macias's reign of terror well illustrates the escalating dynamics of the paranoid leader. As insecurity mounts, the leader takes ever more violent steps to eliminate imagined enemies. This in turn produces increasing dissent, leading to even crueler excesses. The imagined enemies become enemies in reality, and the circle of those he can trust becomes ever smaller, leading to a spiraling totalitarian violence.

Idi Amin Dada of Uganda: Paranoid Grandiosity and Cruel Excess

His Excellency President for Life Field Marshall
Al Hadj Dr. Idi Amin Dada, VC, DSO, MC,
Lord of All the Beasts of the Earth and Fishes
of the Sea and Conqueror of the British Empire
in Africa in General and Uganda in Particular

Born in 1925, Idi Amin grew up without a father—indeed, without knowing who his father was. He attended missionary school intermittently, leaving after the sixth grade. He had a reputation for limited intelligence but considerable shrewdness and cunning. In Uganda, then a British colony, many of those with ambition but without advanced education gravitated toward the military, and at age twenty-one Idi Amin joined the king's African Rifles, an African unit of the British army. Effective in the military suppression of the Mau Mau between 1952 and 1954, he nevertheless could not be promoted to sergeant because he could not pass the English examination.

Amin thrived on the pageantry of military life, with its military dress and colors. Throughout his military career he impressed his commanders with his conscientiousness and zeal. But he was criticized for being overzealous to the point of brutality in his attempts to disarm rural gangs and was described as a soldier constantly at war. In his pursuit of his military duties, he became fascinated with techniques of torture.

Great Britain granted independence to Uganda in October 1962, and under the new native military command Idi Amin was promoted to major. The next year he visited Israel for the first time, participating in a course for paratroopers. Idi Amin led an attack on the king of Buganda in 1966, in which hundreds were killed in a vicious assault. This led to his promotion to army chief of staff. He proceeded to build up the army by 400 percent, making it the seventh largest in Africa.

In January 1971, now age forty-five, Idi Amin took control of Uganda in a military coup. His first words were instructive, suggesting his discomfort with his role: "I am not a politician but a professional soldier. I am therefore a man of few words." This insecurity did not ease with the passage of time. Amin was later to remark defensively: "Sometimes people mistake the way I talk for what I am thinking. I never had any formal education—not even a nursery school certificate. But, sometimes I know more than Ph.D.s because as a military man I know how to act. I am a man of action."[44]

Like Francisco Macias of Equatorial Guinea, Amin found himself out of his depth as chief of state. His limited intelligence, lack of education, and inexperience left him unqualified to face the complexities of national leadership. He found cabinet meetings extremely frustrating because he could not understand the concepts his ministers were discussing or the advice they were proffering, and soon he stopped consulting them.

Amin initially courted the educated elite but found that he could not relate to them. Reminiscent of Macias in his characteristically direct fashion, Amin sought a solution to his discomfort by attempting to eliminate the educated class. Amin believed that killing the educated elite would protect him from coups.

While his cruelty had been present, if underestimated, before Idi Amin took over the reins of Ugandan power, its paranoid qualities had not been in evidence. This former sergeant with only a sixth-grade education was clearly inadequate to the task of managing a national economy, developing political and social institutions, and maintaining international relations. When an individual has a tendency to externalize, exaggerated paranoid reactions become a defense against inadequacy. This was the psychological path Amin took. The assumption of power, by increasing the stress on Amin, thus contributed to the exaggeration of his paranoid psychopathology. Criticism confronted him with his inadequacy as a leader, an intolerable situation, and he responded by eliminating his critics. If something went wrong, as it frequently did, it could not be his fault, and internal scapegoats and external enemies were quickly identified.

The term *chief of state* was singularly appropriate for Amin, for he brought to Uganda the leadership style of a tribal chief with unlimited power. Within months of assuming control, he issued decrees that gave the military unlimited powers of arrest, setting the stage for a brutal reign of terror. Yet it was some time before the world realized the magnitude of his sadism. He was considered a simple clown, a silly buffoon. To those who met him casually, Amin seemed uncomplicated, unaffected, kindly, and affable. These apparent traits led his opponents to underestimate both his cunning and his cruelty. It was difficult to take this buffoon seriously, especially considering that he was obviously an intellectual lightweight and, moreover, charming. Many who knew Amin only at a distance found it difficult to believe his sadistic personal cruelty, even when confronted with the evidence. Godfrey Lule, Uganda's former attorney general, observed, "Face to face, he is relaxed, simple and charming—he seems incapable of wrongdoing or of sanctioning any crime." His former personal secretary, Henry Kyemba, who fled, referred to Amin as "jovial and generous."[45] But those who knew him better came to fear his cruelty.

The killings began in June 1971; hundreds of soldiers whose loyalty he suspected had their throats slit. The next month, two American journalists were killed. When a chief justice declared in Masaka in August that the military had no power of arrest, Amin had him seized, and, according to a British journalist, "his ears, nose, lips, and arms were cut off and severed from his body . . . he was disemboweled and his private parts were cut off and pushed into his mouth and he was finally burnt."[46] There was no further criticism from the judiciary. The former mayor of Masaka was similarly tortured and killed. Internal opposition seemed impossible, and those who could do so fled, though the punishment for attempting to flee was torture followed by death.

Since his military training in Israel, Amin had considered that he had a special relationship with that country. When it refused his request for military assistance in his campaign against Tanzania, he was stung and humiliated and turned against Israel. He blamed the deterioration in Uganda's economy on the Jews and said, "Israelis want to destroy God, and to be a Zionist, you must specialize in murder."[47] Amin sent a message to the United Nations secretary-general defending Hitler's actions against the Jews and calling for the extinction of Israel as a state. He then expelled all Jews from Uganda. He later expelled 4,500 Asians as well, blaming them along with the Jews for Uganda's economic difficulties. When an Air France airliner whose passengers were predominantly Israelis was hijacked at Entebbe by Palestinian terrorists, Amin embraced the hijackers, calling them freedom fighters. The Israelis' dramatic raid on Entebbe to rescue the hostages was a further humiliation for Amin.

In 1977, after several plots to overthrow Amin were discovered, plainclothes elimination squads from his own Kakwa tribe began to round up "ringleaders" from a list of seven thousand Acholi and Langi tribesmen. Amin had decided on a "final solution" to what he called the "Acholi and Langi problem," which in effect meant killing virtually all the educated young men.

Hypervigilant to outside danger, Amin became increasingly paranoid, seeing himself as surrounded by enemies ready to attack him. Anyone caught listening to the BBC was labeled a traitor and killed. Amin's fear was not without basis, for in the spiraling self-fulfilling prophecy of the paranoid leader, his defensive aggression created a multitude of enemies. Anyone who was a political enemy or a friend of a political enemy was put to death. Indeed, a person could be killed for being from the wrong tribe, having a good-looking girlfriend, driving a shiny car, being too strict at the office, or offending a minor functionary.[48] "Enemies" were typically put in a special prison, identified with a sign as the "Killing Muchine [sic]," and beaten to death, though other methods of execution and torture were also commonly used. By late 1978, a press report listed those who had met this fate:

Politicians and civil servants:
Every member of President Amin's original cabinet who has not fled Uganda is now dead. Many parliamentarians and politicians have also been wiped out. Retired cabinet ministers are not immune. . . . Hundreds of civil servants have also been eliminated.

Religious leaders and followers:
[The] Archbishop of Uganda . . . was murdered on Amin's orders in February, 1977. . . . other church leaders have subsequently been picked up and killed.

Academics, teachers and students:
Uganda's chief inspector of schools was executed publicly in September, 1977, at a time when many teachers were being rounded up.

Businessmen:
Almost every Ugandan who represented a foreign company is now believed to have been killed. Businessmen are particularly vulnerable because of the near-collapse of Uganda's economy.[49]

A genocide of the country's Asian population was narrowly averted in 1978 by international pressure and the mass granting of asylum. Uganda appeared to be in the grip of a particularly sadistic paranoia. Enemies, real and imagined, were being detected—and eliminated—everywhere.

In addition to his paranoid defenses, Amin also defended himself psychologically against his insecurity and low self-esteem with compensatory grandiosity. He loved to be on center stage and appeared daily on Ugandan television. Shortly after taking power he began to send messages to foreign heads of state, criticizing their conduct of foreign affairs; for example, he criticized President Nixon for his conduct of the Vietnam War. When the Watergate scandal erupted, Amin also wrote letters of advice to Nixon concerning his difficulties. He was ostentatious in his lack of respect for the superpowers. "I do not want to be controlled by a superpower. I myself consider myself to be the most powerful figure in the world and that is why I do not let any superpower control me."[50]

In April 1979, the reign of His Excellency President for Life Field Marshall Al Hadj Dr. Idi Amin Dada, VC, DSO, MC, Lord of All the Beasts of the Earth and Fishes of the Sea and Conqueror of the British Empire in Africa in General and Uganda in Particular came to an end when joint

Tanzanian and Ugandan guerrilla forces took over the capital and most of the country. Amin fled, ultimately finding asylum in Saudi Arabia. Estimates of those killed during his brutal six-year rule range from 100,000 to 300,000.

Amin's pathology, sadistic paranoia, is highly destructive but unfortunately not necessarily politically disabling;[51] indeed, it may lead to a totalitarian state of terror in which, for a time at least, the leader's power is absolute. Actions against imaginary enemies create real enemies, which widens the area of violence until a climate develops where enemies do abound and conspiracies flourish. The enemies may eventually become so numerous that they overthrow the paranoid leader. In Amin's case (as in Hitler's), only outside forces were able to end the tyrant's rule. Sometimes, as with Stalin, the terror ends only with the natural death of the paranoid leader.

Each of the psychiatric illnesses described here clearly has important implications for leadership behavior and decision-making. The mindset and the image of allies and adversaries, the motivation and pace of activity, and the quality of relationships within the leadership circle are affected. A depressed leader, apathetic and withdrawn, paralyzed with indecision, is dramatically different from a leader in a manic state, driven to act, overoptimistic, impulsive, and impetuous. And different again from the paranoid leader, unable to trust anyone, besieged by plots, surrounded by enemies. These illnesses in blatant form will be recognized as illnesses and can usually be dealt with, although they may present problems for the system. The critical difficulties come with unrecognized mental illnesses.

For a leader to lack emotional control, to be unable to think clearly, is extremely disturbing to his followers. When a leader is affected by an illness that *primarily* affects his thought processes and emotional reactions, it therefore destabilizes the system. But even if the illness does not directly affect the ailing leader's mental state, the treatment may do so, adversely altering the ailing monarch's leadership. This is the subject of the next chapter.

3

THE ROYAL TREATMENT

EFFECTS OF PRESCRIBED MEDICATIONS AND SUBSTANCE ABUSE ON LEADERSHIP

Because they desire a leader who is all wise, all knowing, and in full control, citizens will become distressed when the leader stricken by illness seems not to be in command of his mental faculties. Even when his illness does not have a *primary* effect upon his emotions, mental processes, and decision-making, the customary medical treatment may have adverse secondary effects. Each advance in medical therapeutics poses new challenges for the court physician. Prescribed drugs can have profound cognitive and emotional consequences, and the treatment itself may impair awareness and effective functioning.

Consider, for example, the heart attack (coronary occlusion) that struck President Eisenhower (chapter 1), a common disorder among men over fifty. Heart-attack victims are routinely treated with sedatives—but sedatives diminish the patient's awareness and ability to function. Similarly, where pain is a prominent symptom of the illness, the required analgesic medication may dull mental faculties. Analgesic medication is usually required immediately after a coronary and in the recovery period following surgery. Powerful pain medication was required for President Eisenhower's attacks of and operations for regional ileitis (an inflammatory disease of the small intestine) and was required by President Reagan after emergency treatment for his shooting by John Hinckley, Jr., and after surgery for his colon cancer.

Psychological Effects of Medication

Drugs almost never act on a disease without causing their own effects. To some extent, sometimes great, each drug produces its own disease. In this era of polypharmacy, sophisticated physicians will always include in their differential diagnoses *iatrogenic* illness—illness produced by treatment. Many commonly prescribed drugs can produce adverse psychological reactions. For example, some of the most frequently prescribed anti-hypertensive drugs can produce depression. The Beta-blockers are notorious in this regard, with a depression rate as high as 12 percent in some series. The discovery of insulin promised productive lives for victims of diabetes, but many individuals find it difficult to regulate their diabetes, for stress, infections, working or exercising too hard, or simply missing a meal can lead to insulin reactions, resulting from hypoglycemia (low blood sugar) and causing confusion, nervousness, lethargy, and fatigue. The stress of political life for an individual struggling with a stress–related chronic illness such as diabetes will often require the assistance of the inner circle. Buddy Roemer of Louisiana suffered from diabetes, and his long–time personal aide and driver, Lawrence Guidry, performed the crucial function of supervising the governor's diet. We have already considered how sedatives and analgesics may dull the faculties. Some prescribed medications can profoundly alter mood and affect judgment.

The Effects of Steroids on Mood and Judgment

Adrenal steroids, which are prescribed for many illnesses, including in-flammatory diseases such as rheumatoid arthritis, allergic illnesses such as bronchial asthma, and some cancers such as lymphomas, have significant mood-altering effects.

John F. Kennedy suffered from Addison's disease, chronic adrenal insufficiency. The adrenal steroids he required as replacement therapy can produce both euphoria, with attendant overoptimism, and depression, with feelings of hopelessness and despair. Before Kennedy became president there were rumors that he had had an attack of steroid psychosis. When pressed, the endocrinologist involved was "discreetly non–committal rather than forcefully dismissive."[1]

In this connection, it is interesting to speculate whether adrenal steroids, a frequent initial treatment for the chronic leukemia from which the shah of Iran suffered, affected the shah's emotional state. The occupant of the Peacock Throne was a highly narcissistic man who thrived on pomp and circumstance. His grandiosity reached new heights during the years of his illness, as exemplified by the splendor of the celebration at Persepolis in honor of the five-hundredth anniversary of the Persian Empire. Euphoric grandiosity is a well-known side-effect of steroid treatment, and it may well be that the shah's steroid treatment magnified his psychological tendency to grandiosity.

Psychological Effects of Other Medications

Powerful psychoactive drugs were reportedly also employed to alleviate the shah's anxiety and depression. In addition to intermittently dulling his faculties and interfering with his mental functioning and decision-making, some of these drugs have major effects on mood and could have distorted his judgment. The treatment of most diseases of the blood and lymphatic systems often involves changing medications after the cancer no longer responds to the first treatment. When the shah's cancer no longer responded to adrenal steroids, he probably would have had a number of courses of powerful cancer chemotherapeutic drugs. These drugs can be extremely debilitating and would have further weakened the already enfeebled shah. Clearly the diminished stamina experienced by cancer victims, especially when undergoing chemotherapy, can adversely affect their political ability.

The days when patients with a serious medical disease were treated without psychoactive medication are probably past. From now on, individuals suffering from serious medical illnesses unaffected by mind-altering medication will be uncommon. Because often the precise amount of the drug required can be determined only by experimenting with dosage levels, even the best managed patient is likely to experience variations in mental acuity, mood, and capacity due to medication. This variation is bound to affect the leadership of the ailing monarch who insists on leading despite his illness.

The Doctor's Dilemma: Leader Competence versus Patient Comfort

A drug may relieve the royal patient's pain or stress but make him a less effective ruler. It might be better for the nation to have a leader in discomfort but cognitively sharp rather than pain-free but with dulled faculties. There are matters of judgment for the doctor and the patient in the medical management of almost every disease. If the patient expresses the desire to subordinate comfort—physical or mental—to the demands of the office, the doctor can almost always accommodate him. Nevertheless, because of the doctor's clinical imperative to relieve the patient's discomfort, the conflict between leader competence and patient comfort can lead to a problem for the physician. Often the royal physician faces not a patient eager for the relief of pain drugs can afford but an ambitious and iron-willed person who is willing to tolerate the pain and the attendant medical risks rather than fall under the influence of drugs. This is dramatically exemplified by the way John Foster Dulles faced his terminal illness. In February 1959, U.S. Secretary of State John Foster Dulles made his last trip to Europe. He knew that he was dying of cancer of the bowel. For eight days he was nearly unable to retain food, and his pain at night was so severe that he had to take sedatives. He refused to take analgesics and sedatives during the day, however, because he said the matters before him were so important as to require his full concentration, and when he was concentrating intensely, the pain was bearable.[2] But can it be that decisions made under the influence of constant pain and with awareness of the imminence of death were optimal?

It may be ambition rather than duty that prevents a leader from availing himself of medical relief. Many workaholics ignore their health and in effect suppress recognizing and reporting symptoms. Thomas Weigele, who has extensively studied the effects of stress on leadership, notes that "presidents have a tendency to be cavalier about medical advice which suggests that they moderate their activities as a result of previous illnesses or present symptomology."[3] Lady Bird Johnson has revealed that one of the reasons she pressed Lyndon Johnson in 1968 not to run for a second term was concern for his health. He had already suffered a nearly fatal heart attack and was under immense stress because of the unpopular Vietnam War. The First Lady was concerned about her husband's tendency to suppress symptoms and was worried that should he suffer another coronary his drive to lead the country would cause him to deny his symptoms and refuse medication lest it compromise his mental acuity.[4]

Leaders may also refuse medication for fear that it will damage their political reputation. Many politicians, energetic and ambitious as they often are, are rightly afraid that illness will weaken their attractiveness to their followers. They are especially concerned to avoid even the hint that they might be suffering from a psychiatric disorder. In chapter 2 we observed the rapidity with which Senator Eagleton was dropped from the Democratic ticket as vice presidential candidate when his history of electroshock treatment for depression was revealed. This drove home a powerful lesson for political hopefuls. That former senator Lawton Chiles took Prozac, an anti-depressant, because of feeling "burned out" was used by his opponent in the Florida gubernatorial contest of 1990 to challenge Chiles's stability, although Chiles did eventually win the election.

The physician today has the means to alleviate the pain, mental or physical, that his royal patient feels. Thus the doctor must bear part of the responsibility for the sometimes debilitating and mood-altering effects a course of treatment has on the leader. The ethical responsibilities of a leader's doctors as they attempt to navigate a course consistent with the responsibilities of multiple roles are not always clear. The fatigue, tension, and stress of dealing with a continuing crisis may lead the patient to request stimulants, tranquilizers, and sleeping pills, an alternation of uppers and downers that can impair awareness, clarity of thinking, and effective functioning. Decisions made under the influence of stimulants, which can produce a heady overoptimism, are quite different from those made under the influence of tranquilizers, which may cloud the sensorium. Yet the leader may insist that he needs these medications in order to function in the crisis.

It is not always possible to distinguish with total confidence between drugs that are ethically prescribed by a physician and drugs that are prescribed to pursue some unethical end. Some physicians may put personal and political considerations before ethical ones and prescribe medications at the request or demand of their royal patient. In fact, many of the problems with VIP health management concern self-indulgent behavior by the patient that the physician, because of the status of the VIP patient, does not counter. The patient may demand psychoactive medication that will interfere with the discharge of his responsibilities. Doctors may yield to pressure from their royal patients for medication that they would not prescribe for commoners. This may lead to physician-assisted substance abuse.

Thus physicians may in effect become legally sheltered procurers of such drugs as minor tranquilizers, sleeping pills, narcotics, and stimulants for their VIP patients. Failure to set limits for their famous patients may contribute to addiction. Republican Senator John P. East of North Carolina committed suicide in June 1986 by taking an overdose of prescribed sleeping pills and tranquilizers. In his suicide note, he blamed a physician at the U.S. Capitol, Dr. Freeman H. Cary, who, East asserted, "had failed to diagnose my hypothyroidism" and instead, at East's request, had prescribed addictive medication for the senator's anxiety, depression, and insomnia—frequent symptoms of thyroid disorder. The same physician had prescribed Placidyl, a powerful hypnotic, to future Supreme Court Justice William Rehnquist "over a nine-year period in doses that exceeded the recommended limits."[5] This drug is ordinarily not prescribed for longer than two weeks because of the hazard of addiction. Rehnquist had to undergo a drug-withdrawal regimen in 1981. Not only was this a physically and psychologically harrowing process, but Rehnquist's previous dependence on Placidyl was raised in Senate hearings for his confirmation to the Supreme Court. This concern was well placed, for when royal patients become dependent on drugs, psychologically or physically, their leadership and decision-making can be greatly compromised.

The specter of senior world leaders wrestling with complex politico-military crises while under the influence of narcotics, stimulants, sedatives, or alcohol is dreadful to contemplate. Contributing to the rejection of President George Bush's first nominee for secretary of defense, Senator John Tower of Texas, were concerns about his reliability in the nuclear chain of command because of suspected alcohol abuse. In fact, the history of the twentieth century is marked by leaders whose decision-making was affected by substance abuse. And in a number of these instances the leader's physician facilitated that very dependence.

Amphetamine and Alcohol: The VIP's Drugs of Choice

Amphetamines and alcohol are the two most commonly abused drugs, especially among leaders. Characteristically provided by physicians, amphetamines are especially attractive to leaders in crisis because the initial effects on the user are increased alertness, a feeling of well-being, lessened fatigue, and a diminished need for sleep. With continued use, the feelings of well-being can mount to euphoria, elation, and grandiosity. In a crisis, an individual high on stimulants may be insufficiently cautious, unduly optimistic, and impulsive. Under sustained stress, some individuals will use stimulant and depressive drugs serially in a high-low sequence: feeling wired from the excitement of a crisis and from such stimulants as amphetamines, they may require hypnotics such as barbiturates for sleep and then stimulants for alertness. During a crisis, many doctors find it difficult to resist the pleadings of a president or a prime minister for amphetamines.

Individuals taking amphetamines demonstrate other maladaptive behavior effects in addition to impaired judgment. They may become highly irritable, as was Anthony Eden, and embroiled in arguments. There is a tendency to loquacity, loss of emotional control, and hyperactivity. Hypervigilance and suspiciousness emerge and mount, as do aggressiveness and hostility. Continued amphetamine abuse can lead to confusion about time and place, distractability, vagueness, rambling speech, delusions of persecution, hallucinations, and psychotic behavior resembling paranoid schizophrenia. The paranoid delusions may induce violent behavior against perceived enemies. Amphetamine abuse is the most dangerous form of drug abuse for people in positions of power.

Getting High in High Places
Ups and Downs on Downing Street

Winston Churchill drank heavily throughout his career. A man of patrician taste, he favored cognac and champagne. During World War II, his heavy drinking continued, augmented by "reds" (barbiturate capsules), which he required for sleep. Churchill of course had no problem getting alcohol and drugs. His personal physician, Lord Moran, supplied him with all the chemical stimulants and depressants he wanted, with little or no warning as to their effects. Yet few would fault Churchill's performance as wartime commander.

As prime minister during the 1950s, Churchill became increasingly dependent on drugs, especially after his stroke in 1953. He even named his tablets: majors, minors, reds, greens, and "Lord Morans." He sometimes took these medications during the day and with alcohol, itself a central nervous system depressant that can magnify the effects of some drugs, especially sedatives and tranquilizers, producing clouded reasoning and confusion. Increasingly enfeebled, he took stimulants to project an image of vitality. As we observed earlier, cerebral arteriosclerosis was probably the principal cause of Churchill's progressive incapacity, but excessive use of alcohol and drugs hastened his decline and magnified that incapacity.

Anthony Eden's Amphetamine Addiction

While the public image of Churchill's successor was that of a suave, urbane, self-contained man, Anthony Eden was extremely high-strung, with a noticeably nervous temperament. His twenty-one months in office from 1955 to 1957 were marked by a number of severe national and international crises, including the Suez debacle. Especially under the stress of crisis decision-making, his leadership behavior was apparently degraded by prescribed medication and self-medication.

While in office Eden intermittently suffered debilitating fever probably associated with his chronic gall bladder difficulties. There is reason to believe that he became dependent on narcotics during a painful, sustained bout of blockage of the biliary tract in the early 1950s. At this time he carried with him a box containing a variety of medicines, including morphine.

But it was addiction to the powerful stimulant amphetamine that rendered this previously thoughtful and moderate statesman erratic and injudicious and undoubtedly contributed to his disastrous leadership during the Suez affair. Sustaining himself on less than five hours of sleep a night, Eden has acknowledged that he "was practically living on Benzedrine" during the crisis.[6] According to one witness he was "almost in a state of exaltation" during this time.[7] Another witness said he talked ceaselessly and was given to hysterical outbursts whenever Gamel Abdul Nasser's name was mentioned.[8] A concerned physician confided that "Anthony could not live on stimulants any more."[9] The deleterious effects of amphetamine were not fully known at the time, but the historian William Manchester observed that "years later medical scientists discovered that amphetamines could rob a sensible man of his good judgment, and this is what happened to Eden in 1956."[10]

John F. Kennedy's Vigor: Chemically Assisted?

Amphetamine abuse, which had spread to the general population in the 1960s, began among elite groups in the 1940s and 1950s.[11] "Celebrity doctors" may have played an important role in establishing this pattern.

Doctor Max Jacobson had fled Hitler's Germany in 1936 and soon took up medical practice in New York City. Although he had no staff privileges at any hospital after 1946, during the 1950s he acquired a reputation as a doctor for celebrities, among whom he was known as "Doctor Feel-Good." Anthony Quinn, Cecil B. DeMille, Emilio Pucci, Alan J. Lerner, Otto Preminger, and Tennessee Williams were among his patients. Jacobson provided vials to Tennessee Williams for daily injections. After being on this regime for an extended period, Williams developed a paranoid psychosis requiring psychiatric hospitalization. Jacobson also treated John F. Kennedy and is depicted in an intimate family photograph in a published album of Kennedy family pictures.[12]

Jacobson's popularity with celebrities appeared to be derived in part from the energizing injections of amphetamine he gave them. Amphetamines are usually given by mouth; administered by injection, their effects are especially powerful. Several patients suffered from amphetamine poisoning while under Jacobson's "care," and at least one, the Kennedy family photographer Mark Shaw, died. The official autopsy showed no major evidence of heart disease but did report heavy residues of methamphetamine in Shaw's organs. Under questioning, members of Jacobson's staff admitted to buying amphetamines in quantities sufficient to give many large doses daily. In 1969 the Bureau of Narcotics and Dangerous Drugs seized all controlled substances in Jacobson's possession. Six years later Jacobson's license was revoked by the New York State Board of Regents.

What was Kennedy's relationship to Jacobson? Although their association is authenticated, medical records are not available. Harvey Mann, a Hollywood casting director who claimed to have been an assistant to Jacobson in the 1960s, wrote that on at least one occasion he mixed a solution containing 85 percent amphetamine for hypodermic injection, accompanied Jacobson to the presidential suite in New York with this material, and saw Jacobson and the president retire to another room. Mann then found the empty vials and a used syringe. The president, according to Mann, had the flushed appearance characteristic of people who have recently been injected with amphetamine. A member of the White House staff has confirmed that Kennedy received injections of an energizing tonic from Dr. Jacobson. Still, without Jacobson's medical records there is no way to verify that Kennedy received amphetamine injections from Jacobson or that he was aware of their content if he did.

The physicians who participated in the University of Virginia's Public Policy Commission on Presidential Disability and the Twenty-fifth Amendment noted the widespread rumor in medical circles that Kennedy had selected Jacobson as his physician precisely because of the amphetamine injections and that Kennedy was under the influence of amphetamines during his famous "Ich bin ein Berliner" speech at the Berlin Wall.[13] Though the evidence is highly suggestive, it is nevertheless circumstantial, and the allegation must be considered unproven.

Adolf Hitler's Polypharmacy

Perhaps the most remarkable case of drug abuse by a twentieth century leader, and one that shaped history, was that of Adolf Hitler. Over seventy "medicines" were given to Hitler by his doctor, Theodore Morell, widely known as a quack. Nicknamed "the Meister-Jabber" by Hermann Göring, Dr. Morell recorded in his medical diaries seventy-three medications he administered to his famous patient, including a wide array of sedatives, hypnotics, stimulants, tonics, vitamins, and hormones. Included in the pharmacopoeia were Cardiazol, a cardiac stimulant; several variants of belladonna; barbituates; cortisone; Orchikrin, a combination of male hormones; an extract of bull testes; hormones from the female placenta; an array of powerful narcotics; and laxatives and enemas.[14] Moreover, Morell daily gave his own golden Vitamultin tablets to Hitler. On chemical analysis, these were found to contain both caffeine and Pervitin (methamphetamine), a form of amphetamine. He also injected Hitler with Eukodal (Percodan), a narcotic of equivalent strength to morphine, for his abdominal pains.

Late in the war, ranting about his inability to trust his generals, Hitler spoke of his dependence on Morell and, by implication, on the stimulating effects of the drugs Morell administered. "If I had not got my faithful Morell I should be absolutely knocked out—and those idiot doctors wanted to get rid of him. What would happen to me without Morell?"[15] But powerful as they were, amphetamines were not the most powerful drugs administered to Hitler.

Hitler's Intranasal Cocaine

Thou hast the keys of Paradise,
Oh just, subtle, and mighty Opium.
—Thomas De Quincey, "Confessions of an English
Opium Eater"

After the attempt on his life in July 1944, Hitler began receiving daily cocaine treatment for chronic sinusitis.* The drug in 10-percent concentration was frequently swabbed on Hitler's nasal linings,** and Hitler himself used an inhalator containing cocaine twice a day. Hitler's ear, nose, and throat physician, Dr. Erwin Giesing, later testified that Hitler was "not your common drug addict. . . but his neuropathic constitution led to his finding certain drugs . . . like the cocaine in the sinus treatments I gave him, particularly pleasurable; and there was a clear indication toward becoming an habitual user of such medications as he himself admitted to me."[16]

Like amphetamine, cocaine produces a sense of well-being and confidence that can mount to feelings of elation and grandiosity. Other symptoms are restlessness, excitement, excessive loquacity, loss of appetite, and diminished need for sleep. Paranoid ideas are frequent, and judgment is characteristically impaired.

The precise effects of this pharmaceutical cocktail of cocaine, amphetamines, and other stimulants on Hitler's mental state are difficult to gauge. Suffice it to say, in the jargon of the street, that Hitler was simultaneously taking coke and speed. Methamphetamine alone would have had major deleterious effects on Hitler's decision-making. Many of the effects of amphetamines would have been augmented by cocaine. The following description of Hitler under stress was quoted earlier in the discussion of Hitler's paranoid reactions. It is so striking that we repeat it here, because it suggests that his paranoid reactions may well have been compounded by effects of the stimulant and narcotic medications he was taking. "His fists raised, his cheeks flushed with rage, his whole body trembling, the man stood there in front of me, beside himself with fury and having lost all self-control. After each outburst of rage, Hitler would stride up and down the carpet edge, then suddenly stop immediately before me and hurl his next accusation in my face. He was almost screaming, his eyes seemed about to pop out of his head and the veins stood out on his temples."[17]

Biographies of Hitler and memoirs of German generals provide descriptions of Hitler's distractibility, irritability, and sudden, apparently arbitrary decision-making. To confront Hitler with bad news was to precipi-

---

*In defense of the medical profession of the day, when cocaine was first introduced into the pharmacopoeia it was viewed as a wonder drug. In fact, before turning to psychoanalysis, Sigmund Freud, then practicing as a neurologist, prescribed cocaine for his patients, wrote a major medical article extolling its benefits, and relied upon cocaine himself from time to time, until the tragic death of a colleague from cocaine use. Thus the hazards of cocaine and its potential for abuse were not yet known at the time.

**Before the era of crack-cocaine, the preferred route of ingestion by cocaine habitués was intranasal because of the drug's rapid absorption through the mucous membrane.

tate an attack of rage and risk losing one's job. Many of these behaviors were in evidence earlier in his career before he was operating under the influence of drugs. Almost certainly the use of multiple drugs would have magnified the observed characteristics.

The Drugging of President Hácha of Slovakia

Another use of "prescribed" medication should be noted, though it largely falls outside our topic: the coercive or secret use of medication to affect behavior. It was the German policy in 1939 to induce Czechoslovakia to surrender rather than be conquered. To this end, President Emil Hácha of Slovakia was forced to travel to Prague to meet senior officers in the chancellery at 1 A.M. There is controversy as to what occurred then.[18] One description states that under mental coercion and sleep deprivation, and after collapsing several times, Hácha was injected with some substance and capitulated. Some historians argue that the injection was dextrose (sugar) and vitamins. Others have observed that since the notorious Theodore Morell, who was not noted for his devotion to medical ethics, was the administering doctor, the injection more than likely contained a powerful compliance-inducing blend of barbiturates and amphetamines.

Alcohol: The Lubricant of Politics

The substance most frequently abused by political leaders is, without question, alcohol. It is certainly the most common agent of self-medication, regularly employed to relieve both anxiety and depression. It often produces both mental and physical pathologies affecting behavior, which may then require medical treatment. It is not possible here to give a full exposition of the effect of this central nervous system depressant and the different types of alcoholism. Suffice it to note that each of the variants of alcoholism can have major effects on political functioning and leadership.

Alcohol is not commonly thought of as a depressant because one of its characteristics—a feature that accounts for much of its popularity—is that it decreases inhibition. Users and abusers of alcohol become relaxed and behave in ways that their sober selves would never permit. The world of politics is a particularly salutary environment for the concealment and facilitation of alcoholism. Politicians are expected to socialize, and in most Western countries socializing involves drinking. What begins as a pleasant duty may become a painful addiction. But the association of alcohol and politics is so pervasive that reporters and political opponents characteristically do not report or exploit incidents, even after frequent repetition. Witness, for example, the numerous stories about the heavy alcohol consumption, especially during crises, of former president Richard Nixon. One story that was widely circulated but not reported was that Nixon was drunk upstairs during the most critical hours of the 1973 Middle East War and that Henry Kissinger made the critical decisions.

Only when alcohol consumption leads to flagrant public misbehavior does it make the news, as it did in the incident that ended the career of the powerful Democratic congressman from Arkansas, Wilbur Mills. Mills, who served in Congress from the late 1950s to the early 1970s, known as a heavy drinker for many years, was found wading in the reflecting pool on the Washington Mall early one morning, obviously intoxicated, in the company of a prominent Washington stripper, Fanny Fox.

Public knowledge of alcohol dependence sometimes comes to light only years after the victim's death. Senator Estes Kefauver of Tennessee was to be his parents' replacement for the brilliant older brother who had died before having a chance to succeed. Among a breed of driven men, politicians seeking the presidency, Kefauver was particularly obsessed. It seemed to many close to him that alcohol was the volatile fuel that kept him going. At a hotel on the campaign trail for the 1960 nomination, a reporter recounts how Kefauver would awaken:

> Though the room was darkened, Earl [Mazo, a campaign reporter] recognized Kefauver lying on his back, flat out on top of the bedspread, completely naked, sleeping the sleep of the dead. Dick Wallace [a campaign aide] filled a glass almost to the top with straight Scotch whiskey, carried it to the bed, and touched Kefauver's shoulder, saying, "Senator, it's time to get up."
>
> Kefauver began to rise stiffly. As he came toward the full sitting position, one arm rose as though grasping for something to pull himself up with. Wallace put the glass of whiskey in the outstretched hand, and Kefauver brought it to his lips and drained it.[19]

Kefauver lost the nomination to John Kennedy.

Severe alcoholism may not appear, or at least not become a problem, until middle age. Characteristically denied by the individual and his or her family and friends, alcoholism is frequently insidious in its development over many years until its grip becomes too blatant to deny. A leader by that time has often achieved significant influence and political security. When a leader is afflicted with alcoholism, it affects not only his personal life and career but also the well-being of the state. How dangerous for the state alcoholism among leaders can be is dramatically illustrated by the failed Soviet coup of the summer of 1991.

The Role of Alcohol in the Soviet Coup

History will record that the planning and execution of the failed coup—surely a critical event in the history of the Soviet Union and one that hastened the collapse of communism—were strongly influenced by heavy drinking among the plotters. The short-lived coup of August 19–21 by right-wing forces failed because of "the sheer incompetence of the coup leaders," according to both official Soviet and press accounts.[20] Many observers were puzzled by the leaders' failure to act decisively and, in particular, by their permitting Boris Yeltsin to remain as a rallying point and allowing continuing communication with the West.

Apparently, heavy alcohol consumption contributed strongly to the ineptitude of the plotters. Former Soviet vice president Gennady Yanayev, front man for the coup, drank heavily throughout the affair. He was found "in an alcoholic haze" in his office after the coup collapsed. Former prime minister Valentin Pavlov began drinking the first night of the coup, according to his own report. Pavlov ineptly tried to trick the government into approving a resolution calling for a state of emergency. According to Deputy Prime Minister Shcherbakov, Pavlov appeared sick "or more likely drunk." According to Shcherbakov, Yanayev and Pavlov had been drinking heavily when they were summoned by then KGB chief Victor Kryuchkov and the other conspirators on August 18. Pavlov had confided to his deputy on that day, "I am sitting here with my son, and we're drinking." Shcherbakov observed derisively, "I know these people, and they'll sign anything while they're drinking." When Yanayev was arrested, he was "asleep, incoherent and appeared to have been drinking heavily."[21]

Stress and the Precarious Balance of the Alcoholic Leader: Senator Key Pittman's Alcoholic Decline

The alcohol abuser's personal life situation, political capacity, and work circumstances may coexist in a precarious balance until a change in any one of these precipitates a major episode or a permanent condition of alcohol incapacity. An alcohol abuser might manage reasonably well as long as his or her spouse is alive but become incapacitated by the death of that spouse. Or he or she might function successfully as a minor cabinet official but not in a more demanding role.

The best known instance of alcohol abuse in high office is that of President Andrew Johnson, whose alcoholism figured in the debate concerning his impeachment. The best documented case of a decompensating alcoholic under the stress of excessive responsibilities, however, is that of Key Pittman, chairman of the Senate Foreign Relations Committee during Franklin Delano Roosevelt's presidency.[22]

Pittman was elected to the Senate from Nevada in 1913, and in 1916 he gained a place on the Senate Foreign Relations Committee. When the Democrats regained control of the Senate in 1932, Pittman's lengthy tenure led to his ascension to the chairmanship, and early auguries were that he would be effective. A skillful politician, he had a great deal of common sense and a reputation as a loyal Democrat. He was a moderate internationalist, supporting Wilson on the League of Nations and apparently getting along well with the new president. A *U.S. News and World Report* profile of the new chairman was laudatory: "One of the three best strategists among Democratic congressmen; a level headed individual who manages to be politically astute without sacrificing his integrity; the kind of man you would want for secretary of anything rather than for President of it; one who never did a bad job of anything; not a creative genius or a hard worker but a good legislator and a skilled artisan in the political technique of legislation and statesman."[23]

With Roosevelt's election, Pittman fully expected to be a major architect of foreign policy. He sought, and made it clear to Roosevelt's inner circle that he expected to have, great influence almost to the point of absolute control over Roosevelt's foreign policy. But in fact, Pittman was barely controlling a severe drinking problem. Much of the control rested in a masochistic relationship with his cold and sexually promiscuous wife. As their relationship deteriorated, Pittman's responsibilities as chairman of the committee greatly increased. International issues concerning repayment of World War I debts, international currency and silver agreements, and America's movement away from neutrality and entry into the newly approaching world war made the Foreign Relations Committee a focus of intense pressure.

Pittman responded to that pressure with increasing alcohol consumption. Roosevelt and his inner circle did not give Pittman the role in policy formulation he desired and increasingly distanced themselves from him. As his disappointment mounted over the failure of his expectation of playing a prominent role, so did his alcohol consumption. This led to inappropriate social and political behavior, including extremely careless public speech and the tendency to enunciate policies at variance with those of his party and administration.

A dramatic example occurred in the late 1930s, at a time when feverish diplomatic efforts were underway. Without clearing his statement with the White House, Pittman made a disastrous public pronouncement:

1. The people of the U.S. do not like the Government of Japan. 2. The people of the U.S. do not like the government of Germany. 3. The people of the U.S., in my opinion, are against any form of dictatorial government,

Communistic or Fascistic. 4. The people of the U.S. have the right and the power to enforce morality and justice in accordance with peace treaties with us. And they will. Our Government does not have to use military force and will not unless necessary.[24]

Such careless behavior further degraded his influence, which led to increased alcohol consumption—a tragic downhill spiral.

Like many alcoholics, Pittman did not recognize the degree of his disability and continued to harbor the ambition to be selected as vice-presidential nominee, despite the manifest contempt in which he was held by the Roosevelt administration. By 1940, his health was severely compromised, yet he undertook a campaign for a sixth term. Six days before the election he became ill, apparently the consequence of a secret binge. Although he managed to win the election, he died five days later, the pitiful victim of alcohol abuse in a man whose alcohol consumption and ambition knew no bounds.

The treatment of powerful political leaders for drug and alcohol dependence is extremely difficult. Denial is a prominent symptom in nearly everyone who has a substance abuse problem, delaying diagnosis and making treatment difficult. Special difficulties attend this denial with the famous and powerful because of their characteristic feelings of invincibility and their preoccupation with image. Public acknowledgment not only would bring humiliation but might spell the end of a political career.

The circle around the prominent individual may facilitate the addiction. As the director of the Silver Hill Foundation, a nationally known facility for the treatment of substance abuse, notes, "The careers of subordinates are often dependent on preserving the public image. They may be in awe of the person or need a figurehead, even if he isn't performing up to snuff. What often happens is that the person gets propped up—even though there's carping behind the scenes."[25] The director of the Alcohol and Drug Clinic at Georgetown University Hospital observes that the longer the duration of the problem, and the more prominent the addict, the harder it is to break through the denial. "When someone has been very successful for a long time and the people around them have been protecting them, that just reinforces it."[26]

A personality type common to prominent political leaders—the narcissistic personality—augments the denial. And the effects of drugs magnify some of the characteristics of the narcissistic personality. Thus the narcissist will often feel above the rules that govern others. Mayor Marion Barry of Washington, D.C., in an interview with the Los Angeles Times boasted about his invulnerability weeks before being apprehended for cocaine possession. He bragged that he was "invincible . . . what I have done nobody knows about because I don't get caught."[27] Commenting on this pattern, the medical director at Silver Hill has observed: "The higher the stakes, the more exciting it is for some people to get away with it. Some people are incredibly turned on by the excitement. They crave it. It's not at all unusual for a public official to feel immune to the laws that govern the rest of us. And success generates a sense of immunity."[28] This interaction of illness with personality affects the course and treatment of every illness that affects prominent leaders, particularly when it is substance abuse.

Indeed, in the early stages of drug use, the politician's success may depend upon a drug. It would be simplistic to say that drugs always damage a politician's efforts for election. Washington psychiatrist Frederick K. Goodwin tells the story of a politician who experienced extreme mood fluctuations. When he was up, it was during an election and he would do well, though he was difficult to live with and was himself very unhappy. The politician's physician prescribed lithium carbonate, a mood regulator, to moderate his emotional swings, eliminating the extremes of both mania and depression and producing a much calmer disposition. This not only made the patient happier but made those around him happier as well. However, he lost the following election.[29]

Substance abuse by major political leaders is not a private illness. For the leader under the influence of drugs or alcohol, whether senator or congressman, president or prime minister, every aspect of functioning is affected—perceptions, judgment, decision-making, relationships with subordinates, and the balance between personal needs and those of the followers. Especially during crises, when the mighty are high, the lowly should tremble.

4

The Royal Physician

The Medical Environment of the Ailing Leader

In the previous chapter, we observed the multiple pressures that bear upon the king's physician in dispensing medications to the leader. The royal physician must always bear in mind the effects of the treatment on the decision-making of the patient, which may be in conflict with his medical welfare. The physician's role in the medical management of the ailing leader is inherently conflictual as he or she attempts to navigate a course consistent with the responsibilities owed the patient, the larger society, and the ethics of the medical profession.

Deception in the Service of Patient Privacy

A major ethical issue concerns patient privacy. Do citizens give up the right to privacy when they enter public office? Many would argue that to some extent they do, just as airplane pilots or officers commanding troops in the field must subordinate their right to privacy to the rights of passengers or troops to have their lives and welfare protected. These issues are complicated by the peculiar environment within which the king's physician must operate. Physicians in private practice are able to function autonomously and in familiar circumstances. They are in charge of the case and are usually accorded special deference because of their expertise. Moreover, they have unrestricted access to other medical specialists should the need for consultation arise. They rarely need to consider their responsibility to anyone except their patient.

This is assuredly not the case with the royal physician, who is *not* in full control of the medical management of the patient. It is impossible for an attending physician to do more than is permitted by those who have chosen and can replace him or her. Royal physicians operate simultaneously in several systems. As physicians they are bound to principles of medical ethics. But like it or not, they are also members of a political system whose requirements at times will conflict with their responsibilities as physicians.

The problem royal physicians face is not that the ethical problems are new (see appendix A) but that they must weigh them on unfamiliar scales. That is, the circumstances surrounding their decisions are unlike any that ordinary physicians are likely to have encountered. Dealing with a royal patient is like treating a combination of god and master.

The Leader Held in Awe
George III and the Mad-Doctors

The general conduct of the physicians has not been
so decided or firm as the occasion of their attendance
has required. They appear to shrink from
responsibility and to this time they have not
established their authority, although pressed by
every attendant. . . . The task becomes more
difficult from the intricacies of various controls and
various interferences [from members of the court].
We ought not to be embarrassed by fluctuating
decisions nor puzzled with a multitude of
directions from the other Quarters.
—Lord Greville, December 1788

So far, we have emphasized the nature of the illness and its consequences. We shall do so in the case of George III of Great Britain as well, but here we shall stress a factor that has until now in our discussion figured only marginally: the distorting effect that a leader's high status has on the relationship with his doctors.

In contrast to Mad King Ludwig and King Talal, George III was not chief of government, though he had great political influence. Controversy continues to surround the nature of his mental illness. Because of the recurrent delusions to which George III was subject, earlier medical historians have suggested that he suffered from a form of schizophrenia. Prime Minister

William Pitt the Younger found "the King in an agitation of spirits bordering on delirium."[1] The contemporary diarist Fanny Burney indicated that he conversed "with that extreme quickness of speech and manner that belongs to fever; and he hardly sleeps, he tells me, one minute all night."[2] Greville observed that the king talked incessantly and very fast. After only two hours of sleep, "he talked for nineteen hours without scarce any intermission."[3] These symptoms suggest a rapid cycling manic disorder.

But the abruptness with which the symptoms appeared and the nature of the symptoms, which resembled a toxic delirium, suggested to the medical historians Macalpine and Hunter that the periodic psychotic episodes were a result of a rare metabolic disorder, porphyria. This in turn has been disputed by later medical psychohistorians. McKinley Runyan has suggested that George's mental symptoms may have been produced by plumbism (lead poisoning).[4] While this diagnostic arcana is interesting to medical historians, for the purposes of this study, it is not necessary to diagnose the specific malady from which George suffered. What is important is that the king of England was subject to recurrent psychotic episodes during which he had bizarre delusions, experienced hallucinations, and displayed prolonged mania.

George III's psychotic episodes were too frequent and too extravagant to be kept secret.[5] The monarch suffered open displays of insanity in 1765, 1788, 1789, 1801, 1804, and from 1810 to 1820, the year of his death. They were noted at court and talked about throughout the country. Lady Harcourt, a member of the court, wrote in her diary: "Every alarming symptom seemed increased; the bodily agitation was extreme, and the talking incessant, indeed it was too evident that his Majesty had no longer the least command over himself . . . the veins in his face were swelled, the sound of his voice was dreadful; he often spoke till he was exhausted . . . while the foam ran out of his mouth."[6]

George III's episodic psychotic illness was characterized not only by delusions (he sometimes congratulated individuals on their mutual wedding, which never took place and had never been planned) and hallucinations (he claimed to have seen London flooding) but also by periodic states of extreme agitation and anxiety. There was no question when George was mad. In November 1788, Richard Warren, one of the royal physicians, noted in his diary, "rex noster insanit" (our king is insane).[7]

In fact, there was no question when an attack was imminent because George displayed clear prodromal symptoms that resembled the full-blown symptoms. King George himself knew when these agitated episodes were beginning that he was not himself but protested, "I am nervous—I am not ill."[8] The king usually was able to acknowledge his distorted ideas and behaviors. At one point he apologized for his "wrong ideas" and for having revealed them. Another time, when making architectural suggestions, he wryly noted, "Not bad for a man who is mad."[9] There was also no doubt when he had recovered. In between psychotic episodes, King George was ordinarily calm and sensible. King Ludwig and King Talal, in contrast, were both subject to intense episodic fluctuations, but their leadership was impaired in a continuing fashion by the ravages of mental illness. When George III was sane, he was the model of sanity: honest, calm, sensible, and humane. Political problems arose not because of uncertainty as to whether the king was sane but because of the unpredictability of the disorder's occurrence. When he was sane, George was an effective player within Britain's political system. When George had one of his fits of madness, no one gave him any responsibilities or followed his directions.

This type of illness, coming on unexpectedly and lasting for extended periods, could not be covered up. There would have been strong motivation to do so. If George had been judged insane the Prince of Wales would be appointed regent, with full royal powers. This eventually occurred, but only after a long rear-guard political battle by the king's supporters. It would have been greatly in the interest of the king's party to cover up their leader's mania, but it was not possible. At the end, George was lost in a psychotic world. "He appears to be living . . . in another world and has lost almost all interests in the concerns of this."[10] Not only preoccupied with apocalyptic hallucinations, he was regularly talking with the dead.

Of course, there were efforts to cure the king's illness, but these were frustrated as much by the patient's high status as by the low level of eighteenth-century psychiatric medicine. Lord Greville's description of the medical treatment of George III, quoted at the beginning of this section, makes it clear that his physicians, Sir George Baker and Dr. Richard Warren, were unable to cope with their patient's royal status and that his treatment suffered as a consequence. The demands of royal etiquette conflicted with the requirements of the doctor-patient relationship. No one, including his physicians, spoke to the king unless spoken to. Moreover, despite the medical tradition of "doctor's orders," it was the king who gave the orders, and the courtiers, including the royal physicians, who executed them. On one occasion, the delirious King George refused to admit Dr. Warren to his chambers. Despite his patient's manifest incapacity, Warren dutifully attempted to make a diagnosis by observing the king through the keyhole. This led Greville to comment: "The King certainly did not feel Himself got the better of in the late struggle, and therefore He still aimed at Authority, which He seemed conscious He had not lost, tho' it had been impeded."[11]

In this struggle for authority, the senior physician, Sir George Baker, was regularly overcome with awe for his royal patient and behaved inconsistently and indecisively, in effect yielding control over medical treatment to his patient. One does not lightly manhandle one's king, but the stormy illness of George III, who was often physically aggressive, required just that, a requirement Baker was not up to. On one occasion, King George pinned him against the wall and taunted him for being an old woman too nervous to speak to him.

The court noted both the deterioration in the king's condition and the absence of medical authority. In desperation they turned to the Reverend Doctor Francis Willis, a renowned "mad-doctor" with a strong reputation as a disciplinarian. Not armed with tranquilizers or electroshock therapy, the "mad-doctors" had a fairly simple theory of mental illness and its treatment: the mentally ill person was overexcited and out of control. It was the task of the doctor to induce a state of calm by exerting control over the patient. A remarkably self-confident man convinced of the soundness of his therapeutic approach, Dr. Willis applied his techniques to his patients without regard for rank. As he explained, "As death makes no distinction in his visits between the poor man's hut and the prince's palace, so insanity is equally impartial in her dealings with her subjects. For that reason, I made no distinction in my treatment of persons submitted to my charge. When therefore my gracious sovereign became violent, I felt it my duty to subject him to the same system of restraint as I should have adopted with one of his own gardeners at Kew. In plain words, I put a strait waistcoat on him."[12]

As is often the case with famous patients, there was a profusion of physicians, rivalrous and competitive. Greville dryly noted "jealousies among the medical corps." That Dr. Willis had entered the case did not mean that Baker and Warren had withdrawn or that they had overcome their deference to royal authority. Thus when the king ordered Warren to remove the straitjacket that Willis had put on his overexcited patient, Warren obeyed, whereupon the king tore off his bandages and worked himself into a frenzy.[13]

Physicians are members of the court, subject to its pressures and intrigues, sharing its values and animosities. Except where powerful persons, traditions, or well-established institutional arrangements provide otherwise, it is not to be expected that in donning their professional white coats the physicians will discard political and personal considerations. In all our research we have not found a case of a physician working to persuade members of the inner circle to remove a disabled leader, and we have only found two cases of court physicians trying to persuade their patients (Prime Minister Winston Churchill and Prime Minister Sir Henry Campbell-Bannerman, prime minister from 1905 to 1908) to retire.*

In fact, the political context of the conflict-ridden court may cast doubt on the doctor's motives. Warren's close relationship with the prince of Wales, who would be regent if the king were deposed, was well known, so when Warren insisted that the king's case was hopeless and that he could not recover, his motives were considered suspect. Despite his madness, the king had not lost his political acuity, and he came to call Warren, whose motives he, too, suspected, "Richard Rascal."[14] In fact, after two months of firm medical control by Willis and his team, the king had improved remarkably, to the point that he was able to resume the throne just before the Regency Bill would have been enacted.

In Greville's judgment, the stance of authority that Dr. Willis adopted was critical to his success in bringing King George and his illness under temporary control. He saw as a turning point in the treatment an incident when the king was out of control and shouting at his doctors.

Dr Willis remained firm, and reproved him in determined language, telling him he must control himself or otherwise he would put him in a strait waistcoat. On this hint Dr Willis went out and returned with one in his hand. . . . The King eyed it attentively and alarmed at the doctor's firmness, began to submit. . . . On Dr Willis wishing him good night and recommending composure and moderation, he retired.

I was much struck with the proper manner and the imposing style of the authoritative language which Dr Willis held on this occasion. It was necessary to have this struggle. He seized the opportunity with judgment and conducted himself with wonderful management and force. As the King's voice rose attempting mastery, Willis raised his and its tone was strong and decided. As the King softened his, that of Dr Willis dropped too. . . . The King found stronger powers in Doctor Willis . . . gave way and returned to somewhat of composure. . . . This seems to have been the first solid step leading to permanent recovery.[15]

*Woodrow Wilson's physician, Dr. Cary Grayson, apparently *initially* attempted to persuade the president to resign on grounds of health. In late January 1920, Wilson, whose leadership was significantly impaired as a result of the major stroke he had suffered the previous year, discussed resigning with Dr. Grayson, who "advised it strongly, especially on health grounds. But Mrs. W. objected" (Link et al., eds., *Papers of Woodrow Wilson,* 64:362–63). However, as Wilson's resolve to resign faltered (detailed later in this chapter), so did that of the loyal doctor, who no longer pressed Wilson to resign. Rather, in league with Edith Wilson and Chief of Staff Tumulty, Dr. Grayson actively supported the president's desire to stay in office, shielding the degree of Wilson's impairment from public view—and from his patient.

In fact, the posture of self-confident authority that Dr. Willis brought to his daunting task was exceptional. The stance of awe that Drs. Baker and Warren brought to their royal patient, which seriously degraded the efficacy of their treatment, is much more frequently encountered when physicians undertake the treatment of the famous and the powerful.

No long-term disadvantage to Britain seems traceable to George's madness. It was disruptive and distracting, but not consequential. Even the loss of the North American colonies, which took place during George's reign, occurred in a period when the king was free of symptoms. Indeed, George III had been told over and over when he was a child, "George be King—George be King," and set himself as an adult to restore the royal prerogative at the expense of Parliament. His madness made him less effective in this retrograde activity, and his replacement by his notoriously ineffectual and dissolute son, George IV, further damaged the royalist cause. Had George III been saner, the development of British parliamentary democracy would have been made more difficult.

Atatürk of Turkey: Collective Denial of Mortality

At least George III's physicians acknowledged their monarch's disease. Sometimes the leader's physicians are unable to see the obvious because they hold their ruler in such awe. One of the most extraordinary examples of such denial concerns the founder of the modern state of Turkey, Atatürk.

Born Mustafa Kemal in 1881, Atatürk embodied his nation's struggle for independence and its pride. A true charismatic, he was treated as a godlike figure by his followers. At the end of his years, Atatürk began to suffer from a continual itchiness. His officials searched the presidential palace from top to bottom to locate the insect and destroy the infestation that surely must be causing their leader's discomfort. Only when Atatürk left Turkey for a neighboring nation did a local physician recognize the obvious stigmata of terminal liver disease—ascites (swelling of the abdomen), sallow, jaundiced skin, and spider nevi (characteristic venous malformations). These, along with itchiness, were clear signs of cirrhosis, terminal liver failure, a frequent late consequence of chronic alcoholism.[16]

This pattern of symptoms is one any second-year medical student can recognize, yet the otherwise competent physicians in Atatürk's retinue did not. They, like the other people of Turkey, saw Atatürk as immortal and could not admit that their president was dying, especially from a disease that many, especially in this Moslem country, would see as deriving from self-indulgent behavior.

The medical environment around a political leader cannot be assumed to be an island of objectivity in a sea of intrigue. In some cases, it might be.

For the most part, however, the medical delivery system should be seen as an integral part of the political one, and there lies the heart of the doctor's dilemma. To whom does the doctor owe primary allegiance? Is it the suffering human being, the individual in a special role, the institution surrounding that role, or the public at large?

We have seen that impairment of the chief executive can be highly consequential. We have also noted that the relation between a president and his doctor is problematic. Franklin Delano Roosevelt's and Woodrow Wilson's attending physicians treated their charges as they would wealthy old patients who had no responsibility for others, ignoring the fact that they were treating political bodies, disregarding their responsibilities to the body politic. This narrow approach served their country, as well as their patients, badly.

Woodrow Wilson's Physician: Loyal to a Fault

Woodrow Wilson wished the United States to enter the League of Nations as a full member. He had been the prime mover in the creation of the world peace organization, and he saw America's entry as the capstone in his long career of successful reform, at home and abroad. There were those who opposed America's entry, however. For the United States to enter the League of Nations two-thirds of the Senate would have to ratify the treaty. In the late summer and fall of 1919, though fatigued from his European efforts and in failing health, Wilson undertook a grueling campaign to convince the American people to elect League of Nations supporters to Congress.

Wilson should never have attempted that campaign. On returning from the Paris Peace Conference, he complained of severe headaches. He was physically and psychologically depleted by his ordeal, and the headaches magnified the concern of his personal physician, Dr. Cary Grayson. With the support of Joseph Tumulty—Wilson's close personal political aide— Grayson strongly counseled Wilson to cancel the scheduled speaking tour of the western states, but Wilson stubbornly insisted on making the trip to rally support for his cherished League of Nations. In his memoirs, Tumulty recalled: "Admiral Grayson . . . who knew his condition and the various physical crises through which he had passed here and on the other side, from some of which he had not yet recovered, stood firm in his resolve that the President should not go West, even intimating to me that the President's life might pay the forfeit if his advice were disregarded. Indeed, it needed not the trained eye of a physician to see that the man . . . was on the verge of a nervous breakdown." Wilson heard these warnings but ignored them. Continued Tumulty: "I took leave to say to the President that, in his condition, disastrous consequences might result if he should continue the trip. But he dismissed my solicitude, saying in a weary way: 'I know that I am at the end of my tether, but my friends on the Hill say that the trip is necessary to save the Treaty, and I am willing to make whatever personal sacrifice is required.'"[17]

During the trip, Wilson continued to complain of headaches and double vision. On September 25 in Pueblo, Colorado, the president began to show loss of motor control as the consequence of a transient ischemic attack (a vascular spasm that often presages a stroke). He stumbled often and generally showed signs of weakness. Previously an outstanding speaker, he now slurred his words and lost the thread of his argument. On the twenty-sixth, the facial muscles on the left side of his face were paralyzed, so that his formerly beaming smile was now grotesque, only the right facial muscles responding. On the morning of the twenty-ninth, he suffered a particularly painful headache. A further loss of control of the facial muscles followed, leading to drooling and severe difficulty in speaking. The paralysis soon spread to his left arm and leg.

Any competent physician would have known that Wilson would be disabled for an indeterminate time. He had apparently suffered a thrombosis of the right internal carotid artery. But at this moment the medical cover-up began. As so often is the case with diseases of the mighty, truth became the second casualty. The balance of the speaking tour of course had to be canceled, but in making the announcement to the press, Dr. Grayson significantly understated—indeed, lied about—the gravity of the president's condition. Grayson publicly stated that the president needed only a short rest—that he was not seriously ill and had suffered no organic damage.[18] Perhaps Dr. Grayson had fallen victim to self-deception. In his *Woodrow Wilson: An Intimate Memoir* (1960), based on his diaries, Grayson repeated his insistence that Wilson's "intellect was unimpaired."[19] But even in a closed society, it is almost impossible to conceal an incapacitating illness. On the train trip back to Washington, Wilson waved to nearly empty streets as if to a massive crowd. The rumor spread that the president's mind was failing.

On October 2, back in Washington, the progressively developing stroke extended further and was quite severe, affecting Wilson's entire left side. His physicians diagnosed a massive cerebral thrombosis. He developed acute urinary retention and had to be catheterized. Grayson was frequently summoned to the president's bedside. The respiratory distress Wilson experienced on lying prone suggests that he was in mild congestive heart failure with fluid in the lungs.

According to his wife, Edith, who survived him, Wilson's first words when he regained the ability to speak directed her and close friends (including Grayson) not to describe the nature of his illness if it proved to be serious. Grayson did announce that "the President has suffered a complete nervous breakdown,"[20] but in the parlance of the time this signified not a psychotic episode but so-called nervous exhaustion. Grayson persisted in vague circumlocutions that minimized the seriousness of the president's condition, denied its organic origin, and implied that Wilson would soon return after a much-needed rest.

The lid on medical information was very tight; only Edith Wilson, Tumulty, and Grayson were allowed at Wilson's bedside. Rumors flew in official circles that Wilson had suffered a stroke, which Grayson consistently denied. On October 6, the Cabinet received a medical report from Grayson that Wilson was suffering from a "nervous breakdown, indigestion, and a depleted system."[21]

In fact, Wilson was unable to function. He could not read or dictate, was confused, and stared vacantly into space. Wilson denied the extent of his impairment, as stroke victims frequently do. Official Washington was at a standstill, paralyzed by the president's paralysis. Official papers were generated from the White House, attributed to Wilson but prepared by Tumulty and Edith Wilson. Senior officials, especially Secretary of State Robert Lansing, doubted the authenticity of the documents but could not penetrate the barriers the inner circle had so carefully constructed around the disabled president. Grayson described the First Lady as standing "like a stone wall between the sickroom and the officials."[22] When told that it was essential for the nation's welfare that the president be directly consulted, she replied: "I am not thinking of the country now, I am thinking of my husband."[23] As Grayson noted admiringly, "During the four and a half years of his illness she thought of practically nothing else."[24] The rationalizations she gave for walling off her husband were ascribed to Dr. Grayson: "It is always an excitement for one who is ill to see people. The physicians said that if I could convey the messages of Cabinet members and others to the President, he would escape the nervous drain audiences with these officials would entail."[25]

Finally, Secretary Lansing insisted on calling a special meeting of the Cabinet to discuss what he believed to be the medical incapacity of the president and its constitutional implications. Tumulty recounted his and Grayson's confrontation with Lansing in anticipation of the special Cabinet meeting.

A few days after the President returned from the West and lay seriously ill at the White House, with physicians and nurses gathered about his bed, Mr. Lansing sought a private audience with me in the Cabinet Room. He informed me that he had called diplomatically to suggest that in view of the incapacity of the President we should arrange to call in the Vice-President to act in his stead as soon as possible, reading to me the [disability clause in the U.S. Constitution]. . . .

Upon reading this, I coldly turned to Mr. Lansing and said: "Mr. Lansing, the Constitution is not a dead letter with the White House. I have read the Constitution and do not find myself in need of tutoring at your hands. . . ." When I asked Mr. Lansing the question as to who should certify the disability of the President, he intimated that that would be a job for either Doctor Grayson or myself. I immediately . . . said: "You may rest assured that while Woodrow Wilson is lying in the White House on the broad of his back I will not be a party to ousting him. He has been too kind, too loyal, and too wonderful to me to receive such treatment at my hands." Just as I uttered this statement, Dr. Grayson appeared in the Cabinet Room and I turned to him and said: "And I am sure that Dr. Grayson will never certify to his disability. Will you, Grayson?" Dr. Grayson left no doubt in Mr. Lansing's mind that he would not do as Mr. Lansing suggested. I then notified Mr. Lansing that if anybody outside of the White House circle attempted to certify to the President's disability, Grayson and I would stand together and repudiate it.[26]

Tumulty and Grayson were supported in their refusal by Vice President Thomas R. Marshall, who refused to act as president.[27] Naturally, Lansing made no further attempt to institute ouster proceedings against his chief. But no good deed goes unpunished. Just as Grayson and Tumulty defined their responsibilities entirely in terms of personal loyalty, so Secretary Lansing's concern for the nation was subsequently seen by President Wilson as an act of personal disloyalty; Wilson requested his resignation in February 1920.

The president was not well enough to hold a Cabinet meeting until 13 April 1920, nearly seven months after his stroke, and on that occasion he was obviously still debilitated, his left arm paralyzed, his face sagging, his voice weak. He was not oblivious to his depleted strength, ruefully acknowledging to Grayson: "I don't know whether it is warm or cold. I feel so weak and useless. I feel I would like to go back to bed and stay there until I either get well or die."[28]

As is often the case with depressed and denying patients, Wilson was mindful of his responsibilities while not admitting that he was violating them. Grayson describes how "one night he summoned me to his room, and asking the nurse to leave us, he said: 'I have been thinking over this matter of resigning and letting the Vice President take my place. It is clear that I should do this if I have not the strength to fill the office.'"[29] He declared to Garyson, "I am seriously thinking what is my duty to the country on account of my physical condition. My personal pride must not be allowed to stand in the way of my duty to the country. When I am well, I feel eager for work. I judge my condition because now I do not have much desire for work."[30] Wilson then described in great detail how he would summon Congress in special session, be wheeled in to the House chamber, read his resignation himself or have the Speaker read it "if my voice is not strong enough," and then "be wheeled out of the room." Yet he never, despite his evident incapacity, made the smallest move toward relinquishing the presidency. Reflecting his consistently narrow and personal perspective on the nature of his role, Dr. Grayson did not construe it as his responsibility to confront his patient with the magnitude of his executive incapacity.

Grayson was a determined stonewaller. A later bulletin referred to exhaustion and nervous breakdown. Grayson stated on September 29 that he believed the president to be free of any organic trouble. It was not until *February* 1920 that he suggested any degree of paralysis, and this was described as trivial. Brain damage was specifically ruled out.[31] Grayson stated that Wilson suffered only from breakdown, exhaustion, and indigestion. Rather contradictorily, he then warned that the Cabinet should do nothing to upset the president as that might kill him.

And so for seven months, from September 1919 to February 1920, Edith Wilson, Grayson, and Tumulty ran the U.S. government. They decided what the president could read, what he would say, when he would appear. Sometimes messages were answered from the sick room, sometimes not. Twenty-eight bills became law without his signature. There were no proclamations and no pardons. Various branches of the government were told to present reports, and these reports were cut and pasted together to form the State of the Union address. The public was told that the president was in control, though resting a good deal. At one point a delegation of congressmen came to visit President Wilson. He was propped up, with his useless left arm hidden. The name of each congressman was whispered to him so that he could offer the appropriate greeting. It was a successful deception by the president's inner circle and a successful self-deception by Congress.

Inevitably, Wilson's illness became involved in partisan politics. Democrats felt they had to stand by their leader and turn a blind eye to what they knew was happening. Yet at the same time, they accused the Republicans of driving their "martyred" president to serious illness. Republicans recognized that they were likely to hurt themselves as much as Wilson if they attacked a clearly sick man in his final days as president. So Wilson went on "ruling" the country until the end of his term. He even hinted that he would be available for a draft for a third term and was surprised and disappointed when his fellow Democrats ignored his hints. The lies and half-truths continued even after his leaving office. Only gradually, long after his death, did the true story come out.

Deception in the Service of Patient Privacy

Doctor Ross McIntire's *White House Physician* (1946) was published to dispel the rumors that President Franklin D. Roosevelt was more seriously ill than McIntire had said and also to counter the suggestion that Roosevelt's senior physician had withheld this information from the American public. As A. Merriam Smith asserted: "To his credit, McIntire never lied about Roosevelt's condition. He told the truth, but in language that could easily be misleading."[32] For the most part, McIntire's deception was conducted through a highly selective use of statements that were essentially true but incomplete. This modus operandi is readily apparent in the doctor's memoirs, but it did not end with him. Since then, on occasions when the White House has not chosen to be candid, deception rather than outright lying has been the favored means of news management.

In matters of health, there is a practical reason for this preference for deception. The media watches the president's health with great interest. If they become aware of an illness (through public announcement or rumor) it will be reported on. It is not a great exaggeration to say that when the president is under the weather, the Dow Jones average drops forty points. This is especially the case if the hard currency of fact or at least of official information is not provided, for then rumor will be reported and discussed. Giving information, candidly or deceptively, is the best way for the White House to control the discussion.

Should there be no medical secrets at all? The president may want—and need—to discuss his symptoms and his treatment in confidence. If he cannot confide in his doctor, he might well choose not to report the symptoms, and a potentially treatable problem could go untreated. Moreover, a worrisome medical report at certain junctions could lead to overreaction or to the weakening of the government in a crisis. This was the rationalization for the shah of Iran's not making his illness public, and with good reason, though the shah should have informed his inner circle and allies. Secrecy and the ability to deliberate in private play a legitimate role in effective government. But as we have seen, when the secrecy conceals the illness of an ailing leader, the gamble is great indeed.

Special Conditions of the Physician-Leader Relationship

The cases of George III and Atatürk, as well as those of Wilson, Roosevelt, and Churchill, permit us now to describe some of the peculiarities of the physician-leader relationship.

1. *The influence of those around the patient (the inner circle) is apt to be great and so to influence medical management.* Typically, physicians are part of the political-social entourage surrounding the leader. While they are sometimes only minor players, peripheral to the inner circle (like King George's Dr. Willis), in other circumstances (as exemplified by Dr. Grayson's relationship to the Wilson White House), royal physicians will be central members of the intimate inner circle. Indeed, they are likely to have received their positions on the recommendation or through the introduction of someone in the entourage. Members of the entourage will evaluate the physician's performance in treating their leader, second-guessing diagnoses and treatments. At the same time, physicians will inevitably have frequent personal contact with the entourage, and likes and dislikes, alliances and rivalries, will doubtless develop. Often they provide, on a formal or informal basis, medical treatment to others around the president—his family, administrative assistants, and close political associates.

The breadth of the doctor's responsibilities as White House physician is illustrated by quotations from two former White House physicians, Roosevelt's doctor Ross McIntire and Nixon's physician William Lukash:

> I had not been in the White House for any length of time before I discovered that I did not have just one patient but a *family*. Not a small one either, for aside from the secretariat and the workers in the executive offices, there were the Secret Service men, the White House police, the ushers, the domestic help, and so on.[33]

> I treat the entire White House complex, but my primary responsibility is the care of the President and the First Family. The White House staff accounts for about 1,500 people. My own staff functions in the category of physician extenders or assistants: nurses and corpsmen with training in clinical and ambulatory care. The majority of our treatment is focused on ambulatory care and preventative medicine, i.e., keeping people comfortable, healthy, and happy so they can do their jobs.[34]

Royal physicians thus find themselves in close contact with the entire court and will become aware not just of the medical histories and diagnoses of the court but of sensitive personal and political matters affecting every aspect of the system.

Questions of factional politics and policy can become entangled with questions of health: Is the prime minister well enough to attend a summit? Should the president be permitted to campaign for his supporters? If so, how much and when, and perhaps even under what climatic conditions, in which states at what time of year? If there is a question concerning the disability of the president, can the physician evaluate this question objectively without considering his or her own evaluation of the vice president?

The chief's physician is not just treating a patient, important as that patient is; he or she is also treating—and affecting—an institution and an entire political process.

The royal physician is buffeted by multiple, often conflicting pressures in the immediate environment. In addition to caring for the leader, the doctor must always be mindful of the ruler's public relations image. A bizarre example of this is afforded by the revelation, decades after the fact, that Lord Dawson of Penn, physician to King George V, hastened the death of his patient with an overdose of morphia so that the death would occur in time to be reported in the morning edition—the optimal time for public attention.[35]

These role conflicts and special conditions regularly affect the physician's role and the treatment of special patients. Ethical principles developed in the consulting room or the hospital ward are in a radically different environment here. Politics, of course, is not absent from the hospital or clinic, but it is much more in evidence and more consequential at the court.

2. *The status of the patient is far higher than that of the attending physician.* When a patient asks that something unethical be done—for example, the prescription of inappropriate drugs or a request to keep secret a situation that might threaten the lives of others—the physician is typically in a position to invoke his or her special status as a medical expert as well as code of medical ethics to resist the patient's demand. Dealing with any high-status person reverses the typical status roles, however, and it will be an unusually clear-headed and self-confident physician who will resist the royal patient's imperious demands. For Doctors Baker and Warren, their subordinate status as royal subjects took precedence over their medical status. When the nation is in a major crisis, as Great Britain was during the Suez crisis, how can the physician resist the prime minister's urgent requests for Benzedrine, which he insists he needs to keep going? Recall that when a usually strong-minded and outspoken physician was brought in to examine the failing Churchill, he was unable to inform the aging prime minister that he was suffering from dementia. How does one tell one of the nation's greatest heroes that he is losing his mind? The awe with which physicians approach the throne of the powerful regularly compromises their judgment.

Even when a physician has directly observed a fellow physician giving inadequate treatment to a VIP, that doctor may do little better when confronted with the problem. Recall how clear it was to Lord Moran, when he accompanied Churchill to Yalta, that Dr. McIntire's professional care and treatment of President Roosevelt was woefully lacking and that McIntire was blinded by his patient's status. Ironically, Lord Moran was later in a position much like McIntire's and did not do a great deal better. His special patient was just short of his seventy-seventh birthday when he became prime minister for the second time in 1951 and stayed in office until he was over eighty. As has been noted, during this second term as prime minister of Great Britain, Churchill was afflicted by a progressive dementia, having suffered a series of major and minor strokes. He became but a shadow of the extraordinary leader he had been during World War II, suffering a major decline in stamina and concentration. His waning skills and his performance at what were increasingly infrequent public appearances were bolstered by Moran's administration of central nervous system stimulants.[36]

3. *The physician is likely to lose professional status and other types of rewards if dismissed by the royal patient. In some societies physicians may lose their freedom or even their life.* It is commonly assumed that the chief of state is the beneficiary of the best medical care in the land. Accordingly, in many societies, having the imprimatur of being the leader's physician suggests that the occupant of that esteemed role is the best physician in the land. Doctors are highly competitive people and many are drawn to practice medicine because of the prestige of that profession. Examples abound of physicians to the rich and famous who were chosen not because of their medical competence but because of their social prominence. Often social climbers whose primary dedication was to self-promotion, they had probably left medicine behind many years earlier. To the public, of course, taking care of important people is a mark of elevated status. To be dismissed from the position of royal physician would be a public humiliation proportionate to the former honor.

Being or having been the leader's attending physician has material as well as symbolic rewards. Even after the chief's doctor leaves that post, the fact of having been the physician to the president or the prime minister or the generalissimo will make the doctor attractive to other high-status and high-paying patients. Many doors—both professional and private—will open. Physicians to the famous and powerful have profited by writing articles and books on their experiences. The royal physician, moreover, may be tempted—and able—to benefit from information and opportunities gleaned by virtue of this exalted position. Walter Graham, Harry Truman's personal physician, for example, was accused of using privileged information to speculate on the grain market.[37]

So it is that the royal patient can greatly change the doctor's status, income, and future well-being—even to grant or deny the physician a place in history. Doctors often temper their ethics under far less demanding circumstances. When a doctor is under the control of the patient, especially a strong-willed leader accustomed to getting his own way, and there are many other doctors standing in the wings ready to take over, it takes great strength of character and courage to resist the monarch's demands.

4. *The physician's medical management may have major societal and historical consequences.* Third-person ethical problems are not unusual in medicine. They regularly arise in the treatment of contagious patients or in treating individuals, such as airplane pilots, who are responsible for the safety of others. What should a physician do if a commercial airline pilot has an intermittent cardiac arrhythmia that may not be detected during the pilot's routine company examinations? Or if in the course of therapy the doctor learns that the pilot has been abusing alcohol? Should the physician serve the public's interest and inform on the patient, violating the confidence of the consulting room? In so doing, does the doctor inhibit other impaired airline pilots from seeking therapy? Similarly, what is a physician's responsibility when he or she comes upon an infectious physician who carries out medically invasive procedures?

If this is a concern for physicians treating individuals with public responsibilities, it is assuredly a concern for physicians treating chiefs of state. And, to reassert a point made throughout this book, our concern is not for the obviously disabled leader (or airline pilot) but with the subtle partial disability, not readily discernible.

When a leader's judgment is growing "softer," when there are edges of paranoia, when a mortal illness is being concealed, when alcohol is being abused, especially during times of crisis, and decision-making is being affected—these are especially difficult circumstances for the physician to manage. They are all the more difficult if powerful factions within the court are manipulating an ailing leader into making decisions that reflect their wishes.

Of all the illnesses of the mighty, Roosevelt's at Yalta has evoked the most intense controversy. As described in chapter 1, Roosevelt, weakened by chronic pulmonary disease, severe hypertension, and arteriosclerosis, lacked the physical stamina and intellectual edge to engage in demanding negotiations. He should never have gone to Yalta.

But did it matter? The assumption of this book is that individuals, their intellectual capabilities, physical stamina, and style of leadership can matter, can change history. But to say that individuals *can* matter is not to say that they always do matter; to say that individuals can change history is not to say that historical changes are always caused by individuals.

Historians continue to debate the controversial summit at Yalta. The frequent accusation that "The Sick Man of Yalta" was responsible for surrendering control of Eastern Europe to the Soviet Union ignores the military and political strengths Stalin had at his disposal. Roosevelt had to make concessions in order to gain two important goals: that the Soviet Union would enter the war against Japan and that it would participate in the United Nations.

On the other hand, as one of the foremost historians of the period points out in regard to Yalta: "International relations reflect and are shaped by a combination of diverse factors and trends, but the actual conduct of diplomacy is still affected by individuals. Their skills, ideas and moods cannot be overlooked. Never an outstanding diplomat and seriously handicapped at Yalta by bad health, President Roosevelt continued to rely on his political instincts. Harry Hopkins (Roosevelt's close associate and adviser) was also ill at Yalta and not very active."[38] Yet there were powerful factors that even a fully healthy Roosevelt would have had to face. Poland was probably the principal issue to be dealt with at Yalta, and Poland was the most important state in Eastern Europe for Stalin. It was the geographical key to controlling Germany, an essential part of any structure of postwar Soviet domination of Eastern Europe, as well as a source of additional territory for an expanding Soviet Union. Stalin was not likely to give way on this issue. And he already had troops on the ground in Poland to enforce his will. These important geopolitical factors aside, the Polish question had largely been settled well before Yalta, at Tehran in November and December 1943 and at several preconference meetings in Malta.[39]

Still, the policy Roosevelt adopted was weak: he went out of his way to reassure Stalin that there was no "Anglo-Saxon" conspiracy against him, going so far as to denigrate Great Britain behind Churchill's back. At best, he made a "half-hearted" effort to protest Stalin's brutal plans for Eastern Europe.[40] At worst, he acquiesced to them. Would a stronger stance have saved Poland? No. Would it have better served America's long-term interests and national honor had Roosevelt protested (even if he had not resisted) this violation of international law, human rights, and his country's obligation to a loyal ally?

As the memoirs of many of the participants at Yalta clearly demonstrate, this acquiescence was by no means Roosevelt's personal policy. For the most part, Roosevelt followed the advice of the principal American diplomats. To assert, as Dr. McIntire has, that ill health did not interfere with Roosevelt's negotiations at this crucial summit would be to ignore the historical record, but whether FDR's evident enfeeblement affected the outcome is quite another matter. Given the magnitude of the geopolitical forces arrayed against him, it seems unlikely that even the vigorous Roosevelt of 1936 could have exerted the will and intellect to make a difference at Yalta. The fading man of 1945 was clearly incapable of doing so.

It is easy to criticize the physicians of Presidents Wilson and Roosevelt for deception; the political consequences were adverse. The medical officers serving President Cleveland were also guilty of deception, but we have found no condemnation of their actions. In this respect, the medical decisions the leader's physician makes will always have political implications and are necessarily political decisions. Like it or not, the decisions the royal physician makes in regard to the medical treatment of the royal patient will be judged by history like other political decisions: not by whether they conform to an abstract doctrine of right and wrong but by whether their consequences were in the nation's interest.

5. *The relation between the leader and his personal physician is likely to be one of extraordinary intimacy.* Good medicine is preventive medicine. A principal obligation of the royal physician is to maintain the health of the royal patient in optimal condition so that he will be able to withstand the stress of high office and address the tasks of leadership with full effectiveness and vitality.

Effective preventive medicine and health maintenance require careful monitoring. The leader, ill or well, is apt to see his physician often. Roosevelt's physician, for example, saw his patient at least three times a day. Nothing will be more important to the physician than the well-being of his special patient, and there will be no limit placed on his access by the court. The degree of intimacy differs from president to president, of course. Doctor Daniel Ruge, President Reagan's physician, said he purposely tried to keep out of Reagan's view because he considered it "unnatural and disconcerting" for a healthy person to see his doctor every day. "We had a little game going. When I wanted to watch him in the hall, I would keep the door of my office ajar. But when I stood outside on the carpet as he passed by in the morning, he knew he should stop by when returning to the residence for an allergy shot or something else."[41] The contact between President Reagan and Dr. Ruge was not as close as that between several other presidents and their physicians. Where the contact, physical and emotional, is very close, an unusual degree of intimacy results that has important consequences for the physician's judgment and for the health management of the physician's special charge.

Earlier in this chapter we described the deception practiced by Woodrow Wilson's physician, Dr. Cary Grayson. Given the intimate contact between Grayson and Wilson, it would have been very difficult for Grayson to have acted other than as an exclusively personal physician. Grayson was extremely well connected socially, and his social status and charming manner are assuredly what recommended him to Wilson.* Certainly Grayson's training and prior experience were not the bases of his selection as White House physician, for previously he had served only an internship in obstetrics and gynecology at the Columbia Hospital for Women in Washington, D.C., and a brief stint at the U.S. Naval Hospital—not a background that would equip a physician to cope with complex neurological and cardiovascular problems.

Wilson was captivated by the young physician's pleasant personality. The two shared leisure moments, enjoyed trading stories, and, despite the age disparity, became close friends. Feelings of warm caring and love are incompatible with objective medical care, which is why most physicians will not treat family members or close friends. An overly close relationship with his patient is always harmful to a physician's capacity to maintain an appropriate professional stance with the patient. Embarrassing or painful questions and procedures are avoided under such circumstances and slowly developing but important mental and physical changes may not be noted. Wilson treated his closest subordinates as members of the family. As a member of this inner circle, Dr. Grayson would have found it even harder to retain clinical objectivity. There is reason to believe that Grayson's close relationship to Woodrow Wilson and his family contributed to the severity of the depression Wilson experienced at the death of his first wife, Ellen, in 1914. Grayson was himself extremely upset and apparently lacked the courage to tell Wilson or the family that Ellen Wilson's death was imminent. It fell, belatedly, to Dr. Edward O. Davis to do so.[42] By not helping Wilson to prepare emotionally for his wife's death, instead fostering and reinforcing his denial of the gravity of her illness, Grayson not only failed to diagnose and treat a reactive depression that exceeded normal grief but helped to create it. During his depression Wilson felt emotionally paralyzed and publicly stated his feelings of inadequacy to provide presidential leadership. His emotional impairment and consequent indecisiveness may have contributed to bringing the United States and Mexico close to war.

*Park (1986) has detailed the social circumstances that led to Grayson's appointment as presidential physician. Grayson first came to Wilson's attention during a White House reception in which he administered prompt but minor first aid to the president's sister, who had suffered a minor injury in a fall. Grayson was related by marriage to Presley Marion Rixey, surgeon general of the navy and the White House physician to both Theodore Roosevelt and William Taft. The personable young physician served in the Taft administration and was well known to the White House medical circle. Wilson appointed Grayson to be his White House physician on the basis of his social connections and Taft's recommendation.

In 1919, Grayson's role as family intimate and close personal friend again took precedence over his role as physician. Again he lost perspective, was unable to maintain an objective stance, and could not deal frankly with either Wilson or his family. Moreover, he was not frank with the officials who needed to be apprised of the gravity of Wilson's illness, again fostering denial.

This pattern was repeated twenty-five years later as Roosevelt's illnesses were hidden from the public. Again social connections, not medical expertise, played a large role in the selection of the president's doctor. And again the unusual intimacy of the president and his physician impaired objectivity. Yet again the necessary stance of objectivity was lost, so that McIntire fostered denial by the president and his family of the gravity of Roosevelt's illness. As we observed earlier, McIntire was selected on the basis of Grayson's recommendation, in large part because of their shared conviction that illness in the White House should not be revealed, that priority should be given to maintaining the privacy of the president.

An additional note on the medically marginal leader: often it is not the health-care professionals who are the key monitors of the leader's health. Often it is some intimate, a spouse or an aide. We have mentioned, for example, that former governor Buddy Roemer of Louisiana suffered from diabetes and that the duties of his personal aide, Laurence Guidry, included not only his being Roemer's driver but also his food checker. As reported by the political journalist Mary Durusau, "Although it is not technically part of his job, Guidry also tries to see that Roemer isn't served things he doesn't like, or, as a diabetic, can't have."[43]

Being a VIP Can Be Dangerous to Your Health: Subordinating Medical Risk to Political Risk

So far, we have discussed the effect on the government of hiding an illness. Obviously, a cover-up poses major risks to the leader as well. Consider the candidate who on the eve of an election, an election that polls suggest will be very close, becomes ill, suffering, let us say, the pain of angina pectoris—not a frank coronary occlusion, but a premonitory sign. With proper treatment, including rest, sedation, and coronary vasodilators, a full-blown heart attack might be averted. However, even to suggest that the candidate is not healthy and vigorous might well tilt the balance in favor of his or her opponent, so that there would be a premium on concealing the illness and acting as if nothing untoward had occurred. Even a medical compromise can be dangerous.

This was in fact what happened to former governor Earl Long of Louisiana. Long was in a hard fought race for a congressional seat in 1960. On the morning of election day, he suffered a heart attack. Fearing that news of the illness would cost him the election, he chose to stay at home, claiming indigestion. He did not enter a hospital until the polls closed that evening. The tactic worked, and Long won the seat by a narrow margin. But he never occupied the seat; nine days later the sixty-five-year-old newly elected congressman was dead.

This added dimension of the negative impact of public knowledge of the leader's illness creates what is in effect a medical-political paradox: to submit to optimal medical treatment can be *politically* fatal; to subordinate medical considerations to political considerations can be *medically* fatal.

The Long case and that of Tancredo Neves of Brazil, discussed below, raise an interesting question concerning the physician's role and the limitations upon his or her responsibility. Assuredly Long's physician would have recommended immediate hospitalization and warned Long of the extreme hazard should he refuse to follow this medical advice. But suppose Earl Long had followed the doctor's advice and as a consequence had lost the election. Long ate, breathed, and dreamed politics. A life out of the political maelstrom was unthinkable for him. For Long, to be physically alive but out of office would have been a living death.

The fear that there *might* be a medical problem, which *might* result in unfavorable publicity, apparently led at least one leader to avoid a medical evaluation. We know that physicians discovered benign polyps in Ronald Reagan's colon about two years before he underwent his operation in July 1985. Sound medical practice would have called for either colonoscopy or a barium enema at that time. Did he receive bad medical advice? Or, more likely, did he wish to avoid a definitive diagnostic procedure before he ran for president a second time? If the latter, he was taking a great risk: if a polyp had penetrated the colon wall and entered his liver, Reagan would have had a life expectancy of just one to eighteen months.

Just because a leader *can* get the best medical care does not mean that he will, for two reasons. The first is more obvious to physicians than to laymen. Doctors who hold high academic rank, have won prestigious research prizes, or are high medical administrative officials may not be particularly good clinicians. If called to Pharaoh's bedside, however, they may not acknowledge this limitation. We have noted that the principal specialization of Woodrow Wilson's physician was gynecology; Franklin Delano Roosevelt's was otolaryngology. Furthermore, the process of selecting the court physician can be intensely political, with back-biting and controversy, and various medical "experts" attempting to intervene.

The medical care of political elites differs from that of ordinary mortals in a number of respects, each with potentially negative consequences for the patient and the nation:[44]

- The referral channel is indirect, and often even unusual;
- Too many or too few are often involved in the care;
- The assignment of medical responsibility is often diffused and confused;
- Clinical attention is often misdirected, often centering on seemingly trivial details;
- There is exceptional disagreement about diagnosis and treatment.

In some cases, these factors alone or combined can become so strong as to result in the leader's death.

Too many cooks can spoil the broth, and too many doctors can hurt a patient. Before the eighty-six-year-old Ayatollah Khomeini died on June 3, 1989, he was attended by forty Iranian physicians, who debated every aspect of his care and recorded every moment of his final days on a hidden video camera.[45] His great enemy, the shah, had a similarly unhelpful complement of doctors. He was receiving medical care from eight medical teams from five countries—France, the United States, Mexico, Panama, and Egypt—at the time of his death in Cairo in 1980.[46] During Generalissimo Francisco Franco's prolonged terminal illness, one of the attending physicians remarked wryly that so many doctors filled the hospital room that there was scarcely room for the patient.

Tancredo Neves, President Elect of Brazil:
Dying of High Status

The most bizarre case we have found of medical mobbing and rivalry at the expense of the patient is that of Brazil's Tancredo Neves. Neves was elected president of Brazil on January 15, 1985, ending twenty-one years of military rule. The immensely popular seventy-five-year-old Neves was the first civilian to be elected since the military took over Brazil's leadership in 1964. But he never assumed the presidency. On March 14, the eve of the scheduled inauguration, he underwent emergency abdominal surgery. Six more operations followed in the next month, and Neves died on April 21. A review of the events between the election and the scheduled inauguration makes it clear that political considerations took precedence over medical concerns and thus contributed to Neves's death. His death was announced as being caused by respiratory failure following a generalized bacterial infection that had caused a progressive collapse of vital organs and necessitated the use of artificial lung and kidney machines for almost two weeks. In fact, Tancredo Neves died of high status.

Neves had been suffering from diverticulitis for months, according to a physician in his home town. A common problem of adults over forty, diverticulitis is an infection of intestinal pouches. Treated effectively, it rarely poses more than a minor difficulty. It generally responds to intensive antibiotic treatment, although a relatively low-risk surgical procedure is occasionally required. Neves had a health crisis shortly before traveling to the United States to meet with President Reagan in January. But he kept his ill health secret, dosing himself with antibiotics. His self-medication and later resistance to routine surgery reflected a situation in which political concerns outweighed medical considerations.

The election of 1985 was a landmark in Brazilian history. Paulo Salim Maluf, the fifty-three-year-old former governor of São Paulo, was the candidate of the pro-military Liberal Front party and was backed by the junta. Tancredo Neves, the governor of Minas Gerais, had been nominated by the opposition Democratic Movement party.

The outgoing president, General João Baptista Figueiredo, had opted against handpicking his successor, but there was widespread apprehension that the military would control the election to ensure the selection of their candidate. While Figueiredo and his junta colleagues favored Maluf's candidacy, they did not actively intervene during the campaign to oppose Neves and were stunned by the upset landslide victory of the self-described "left-of-center reformist."[47]

Neves's medical condition worsened in the months preceding the inauguration, but he resisted entering a hospital for definitive treatment because of his fear that the outgoing military leaders would not hand over power to vice president-elect José Sarney. While the fears may have been exaggerated, they were not without basis. In contrast to Neves, who could rally and unify diverse political factions, Sarney was mistrusted by all sides. He had been president of the pro-military Democratic Social party until 1984, when he joined the Liberal Front party to support Neves. He was considered a defector and traitor by the pro-military Democratic Social party because of his previous connections to the military government, and he was mistrusted by the Liberal Front party.

The smooth transition to civilian rule during the interregnum was a testimony to the confidence all sectors placed in Neves. Widely divergent political forces were held together solely by their loyalty to him. Fearing that even a temporary absence for medical or surgical treatment could provide the impetus for a reversal of the military's decision to support a civilian government, Neves continued to treat himself through the early months of 1985, concealing his illness from public view. He planned to make it to the inauguration on March 15 and be sworn in as president, then step aside temporarily to receive proper treatment.

Neves almost won his calculated gamble. Doctors first learned that

Neves had a serious abdominal infection on March 12. Two days later he underwent a two-hour emergency surgical procedure for diverticulitis less than twelve hours before the scheduled inauguration. The surgery was conducted in Brasília, the political capital, although São Paulo, the thriving commercial metropolis, has superior medical facilities. Neves, for political reasons, was reluctant to leave the capital.[48]

The medical emergency precipitated a political crisis. It was widely believed that only Neves could hold the fragile political coalition together, and the country faced serious economic and political difficulties requiring strong leadership and difficult decisions that could not be delayed. Thus the implications of a prolonged convalescence were grave.

On March 15, José Sarney was sworn in as interim president despite opposition from the political leadership, the Democratic Movement party, which would have preferred the president of the Chamber of Deputies, Ulysses Guimarães, Neves's natural ideological and political successor. On March 19 a hospital physician reported that Neves was suffering from respiratory difficulties. The following day Neves underwent a second surgical procedure to relieve intestinal obstruction. Surgeons from São Paulo were brought to Brasilia for the three-hour operation.[49] This represented, in effect, a medical coup, precipitated by the family's dissatisfaction with the original treatment. To smooth over the displacement of the original medical team, the high-powered team from São Paulo devoted nearly as much time to producing a report evaluating the initial treatment as "correct" as it did to the care of Neves.

Neves's VIP status again contributed to poor medical treatment. It is reported that he was continually negotiating with the physicians to alter his treatment. A drainage tube that had been inserted through the nose and threaded through the esophagus into the stomach was removed prematurely to permit him to discuss the political crisis freely with his deputy and to sip tea. This deviation from standard procedure led to intestinal paralysis, gaseous distention, and vomiting.

During this interval, the medical reports were that Neves was recovering satisfactorily, when in fact he was not. The intestinal paralysis required an abdominal X-ray, a simple medical procedure, but because of the national attention focused on the ailing president-elect, it was politically complex, for the X-ray suite was two floors below the surgical floor. That an X-ray was required would cast doubt on the report that he was recovering satisfactorily and might produce public panic. To conceal the X-ray procedure, a sheet was put over Neves's body on the gurney, and he was smuggled down to the X-ray suite disguised as a corpse.

By now no fewer than twelve physicians were attending Neves, three from the original Brasília team and nine specialists from São Paulo. The unity in the team was fragile at best, and as Neves's condition deteriorated, it broke down, precipitating what was described as "the war of the stars" between the São Paulo group and the Brasília team. A political minister caustically observed that "the best equipment in Brasília is the air shuttle." Doctor Pinotti, head of the São Paulo group, replied, "Brasília has excellent equipment. What's missing is cerebrum."[50]

Complicating the situation, the hospital staff in Brasília lost control of the hospital to the politicians and journalists. To the despair of Neves's wife, Risoleta, there were often a dozen or more politicians and reporters in her husband's room. This assuredly did not aid the weakened Neves in his recovery. Moreover, Mrs. Neves, a former nurse, sensing her husband's embarrassment over being tended by female nurses, ordered that male nurses be brought in from a military base, indicating that she would give her husband his required injections until they arrived.

The São Paulo team finally gained control, and the second operation was carried out by a team accustomed to working together. As soon as the incision was made, the problem was apparent. In fact, the second surgery was required because the internal wall of the abdomen was coming apart, a result of inadequate surgical suturing technique in the first procedure, compounded by poor post-operative care.

On March 26, Neves was medically evacuated to São Paulo hospital, where he underwent abdominal surgery for a third time, this one a four-hour procedure to halt internal bleeding, requiring removal of a small segment of intestine. On April 2, he sustained his fourth abdominal surgery, and two days later a fifth abdominal surgery was performed for two new abscesses. Now Neves was listed in critical condition because of pulmonary complications, with fluid in the lungs and irregular cardiac rhythm.[51]

The nation was transfixed by Neves's health crisis. Prayer meetings and special masses were held. White-clad members of the Afro-Brazilian animistic spiritual sects appeared on the streets, releasing doves, sprinkling holy water, chanting, and burning candles. Despite his deteriorating condition, Neves asked to be released from the hospital, stating "I need to take command."[52] He requested a telephone, a radio, and newspapers.

On April 9, Neves underwent his sixth operation, a tracheotomy to assist with respiration, and was placed on a respirator. On April 11 he had abdominal surgery to remove three abscesses near the kidneys. The next day Neves's kidneys shut down, and he was put on kidney dialysis. By the fifteenth he was febrile, with rapid heart rate and dangerously low blood oxygen. Doctors opined that his medical condition was nearly irreversible. Thirty thousand striking steel workers interrupted an angry rally to clasp hands and pray for Neves. National "chains of energy" were called for, and the nation's many Pentecostal sects and spiritualist groups organized simultaneous prayer meetings. Some clergymen preached that God wanted Brazilians to be united and so chose Neves's suffering to send his message at Easter time.

The highly respected and admired politician Tancredo Neves died on April 21. He was never sworn in as president. After Neves's death, wide-ranging accusations were uttered against the medical teams that had treated him. On April 22, the head of the São Paulo surgical team received death threats—and police protection—amid rumors that Neves's medical care had been inadequate. Neves's brother claimed that doctors had inoculated Neves with bacteria, causing the fatal infections. His family maintained that Neves was the victim of medical incompetence. During the first operation, according to Neves's son, nearly fifty people crowded into the operating room and were "breathing above the wound, climbing on stools to see better. . . . If I had been familiar with the Brasília hospital, I never would have allowed my father to be taken there." He remarked that before the operation the chief physician had to return home to get his glasses and that his father had initially been taken to the wrong operating room. He said that Neves later complained that "they almost ripped off my finger" when removing his wedding ring.[53]

The São Paulo specialists who treated Neves also accused the Brasília medical team of negligence and incompetence. The operation, they claimed, was performed too quickly, without adequate preparation. (Surgery for abdominal infection is usually preceded by several days of intensive intravenous antibiotic treatment to avoid later abscess formation.) There was a strong implication in press accounts that had a routine procedure been performed in a timely fashion, the fatal complications might well have been averted.[54] Probably the infected diverticulum burst, leading to peritonitis and generalized bacterial infection. If so, timely surgery of the infected diverticulum could have cured the problem with full recovery. It seems clear that Neves's VIP status adversely affected the judgment and performance of his physicians in Brasília.

But some of the blame attached to the doctors probably belonged with Neves himself. He was ill during his election campaign and was in great pain immediately before the inauguration but refused hospitalization until his very life was at risk. Days before the inauguration, an archbishop presciently compared him to Moses, leading the country to the promised land but never to enter it. Even on the eve of what was to have been his inauguration, after he had suffered convulsions, Neves at first refused to enter the hospital. "Go to [the] hospital? Today I could not even go to the dentist," he reportedly told his doctor.[55] Neves transformed a treatable problem into a critical and ultimately fatal illness.

No less tragic than the death of Neves was that of James Forrestal after an equally distinguished career, a career terminally blighted by a depressive illness. The context of Forrestal's VIP status was quite different from that of Neves, though no less fatal.

Secretary of State James F. Forrestal: Dying of an Excess of Respect

> Thy son is in a foreign clime
> . . . Worn by the waste of time—
> Comfortless, nameless, hopeless save
> In the dark prospect of the yawning grave
> . . . Oh when the pride of Graecia's noblest race
> Wanders, as now, in darkness and disgrace,
> When Reason's day
> Sets rayless—joyless—quenched in cold decay,
> Better to die and sleep
> The never waking sleep than linger on,
> And dare to live when the soul's life is gone . . .
> —Sophocles, chorus from *Ajax*

James Forrestal was copying this melancholic poem immediately before he leapt to his death from the tower of the Bethesda Naval Hospital.*

On July 27, 1947, having served as secretary of the U.S. Navy for more than three years, James Forrestal was confirmed by the Senate as the nation's first secretary of defense. He had played a major role in shaping the National Security Act of 1947, which established the National Security Council and firmly placed the military services under civilian control. There was widespread admiration for his perceptive understanding of the international arena. He was considered "tough"; his was a clear voice concerning the dangers posed to the free world by the Soviet Union.

Forrestal had achieved notable success in the private sector before his appointment as naval secretary in 1944. He had a distinguished career as an investment banker, having risen to the presidency of the investment banking firm of Dillon, Read and Company at age forty-six. Both on Wall Street and in Washington, he was noted for his intense involvement with his work (he often worked sixteen hours a day) and for his mastery of

---

*This poignant observation is made by Rogow in *James Forrestal*, from which much of the following chronology is drawn. Had Forrestal been hospitalized in a conventional psychiatric ward, an alert staff member might well have inferred the suicidal nature of his preoccupation from the morbid content of the poem he was copying.

details. He was, moreover, a good person to work for: considerate, generous, and conscientious, though demanding.

When Harry S Truman succeeded Roosevelt on April 13, 1945, Forrestal indicated that his time of public service was drawing to a close, and on numerous occasions over the next years he publicly stated his need to leave government service because of the strain he had long been under. In January 1946, for example, he declared his intention to resign that year: "The President knows I want to get out. I'm no believer in the indispensability of one man."[56] Yet despite these frequent public protestations, it was clear that he had caught the Washington virus. When Truman expressed his desire for Forrestal to continue as secretary of defense after the election of 1948, Forrestal was gratified. No longer did he profess his desire to leave the center of power. In January 1949, asked whether he expected to continue as secretary of defense, he responded, "Yes. I am the victim of the Washington scene."[57]

And indeed he was. To be at the center of power is to be at the center of controversy, a lightning rod for criticism and attack. Sharing the widespread conviction that the Republicans under Governor Thomas Dewey of New York would win the election, Forrestal had signaled his willingness to remain in the Cabinet, as either secretary of defense or secretary of state, in a Republican administration. Politically ambitious, Forrestal had approached Dewey during the campaign of 1948, deploring the condition of the nation's defenses. Though Forrestal was a Democrat, the defeat of his party would have been to his private political advantage. Forrestal came from a different wing of the Democratic party from Truman, more conservative and more tied to East coast international and banking interests. Had Truman lost, power in the defeated party would have flowed to the faction less associated with the electoral loss—Forrestal's faction. Indeed, Forrestal had been mentioned as a future presidential candidate, and it is possible that he entertained such ambitions in the event of Truman's defeat.

Soon after the Democrats' upset victory over Dewey, a swirl of controversy developed regarding not only Forrestal's loyalty to the Truman-Barkley ticket but also his lack of financial support to the Democrats. Particularly damaging was a story that ran in January alleging that he had contributed to the Democratic party only after its upset victory.

By now there was a virtual drumfire of stories attacking Forrestal's integrity, loyalty, and courage. Journalists Drew Pearson and Walter Winchell, who had targeted Forrestal from the time of his appointment as secretary of defense, led the pack. Other stories Pearson and Winchell propagated in January alleged Forrestal's cowardice during a robbery of his home in 1937 and claimed that he had profited from investments in

Germany in the period between the two world wars and that he had spared Krupp industries from bombing attacks because of those investments. Forrestal was stung by the stories. He attempted to defend his reputation and counter these criticisms, but to no avail. After Forrestal's death, Representative Hale Boggs of Louisiana cited as a major cause of Forrestal's emotional breakdown the fact that he, "probably more than any man of our time, was subjected to a campaign of abuse and vilification the like of which I have never heard. . . . In this Capitol of the United States the most devastating weapons used—more devastating than machine guns or mortars or the other weapons of battle—are the cruel weapons of distorted words, and they were used against this great man in a most unfair, uncharitable, and unthinkable manner."[58]

The barrage of criticism hit a Forrestal already exhausted from the mammoth challenges of unifying the staunchly independent military services under the civilian control of the secretary of defense. Contemplating the formidable tasks of his new office, Forrestal had wryly commented in 1947 that by the end of the year he would "probably [need] the combined attention of Fulton Sheen and the entire psychiatric profession," an ironic presentiment of the emotional price he was to pay.[59]

The onset of Forrestal's psychiatric disturbance can be dated to the spring of 1948. Subject to periods of depression, he was suffering from insomnia, loss of appetite, weight loss, and fatigue, classic symptoms of a major depressive disorder. It was affecting his leadership of the Department of Defense in important ways, for he had been noted for his decisiveness as an executive, and was now inattentive, indecisive, his mind often wandering. By autumn 1948, Forrestal was emotionally and physically depleted, experiencing extended periods of depression and having lapses of memory.

Forrestal was also exhibiting paranoid symptoms. He became obsessed with the belief that he was under surveillance and that his telephone was being tapped. According to V. E. Baughman, chief of the Secret Service, he became preoccupied with unnamed dangers, and when anyone rang the doorbell or opened the front door, he would look out secretly to ensure that the visitor was a friend. His paranoia was pervasive. One day, while walking along the beach with a colleague, he pointed to metal receptacles for beach umbrellas and said quietly, "We had better not discuss anything here. Those things are wired and everything we say is being recorded."[60] The paranoia extended to concerns about the nation's security. He was convinced that the Communists were planning to invade the United States and at times spoke as if the invasion had already occurred. In his view the Communists had penetrated the highest levels of government, including the Defense Department and the White House. Forrestal believed that because of his knowledge of their plot to take over the government and his attempts to alert the American public to the dangers they posed, he had been chosen their prime target for elimination.

By late 1948, Forrestal had acquired a large number of sleeping pills and had made out his last will and testament. By late 1948 or early 1949, Baughman was convinced that Forrestal was experiencing "a total psychotic breakdown . . . characterized by suicidal features" and informed President Truman.[61] Neither Truman nor Forrestal's colleagues thought he was suffering from anything more serious than exhaustion. Not fully sharing this denial, Forrestal acknowledged he needed a rest. Several friends realized that he was ill, recognized that it was an emotional illness, and urged him to resign.

In spite of his own recognition of the toll the office was taking and the barrage of media attacks impugning his character, Forrestal's ambitions were not stilled, and he could not bring himself to resign. Truman had not sought Forrestal's resignation after the November election victory, but neither had he asked Forrestal to stay on. In January, Forrestal indicated his wish to remain secretary of defense. His moves toward Dewey and the controversy surrounding him, however, had fatally compromised his chances to continue in office. Later that month Forrestal was informed that Louis "Iron Pants" Johnson would succeed him on May 1. Nevertheless, when Truman requested his immediate resignation on March 1, Forrestal was shocked, as if it was a total surprise. Despite his foreknowledge, he could not emotionally accept the loss of power and position. He was unable to sleep that night and on arrival at work on March 2 seemed depressed and exhausted. Writing the simple letter of resignation was immensely difficult for Forrestal, and he obsessed over it.

Forrestal had little in life except politics. His home life was largely barren. His old friend Robert Lovett had moved from Washington, furthering Forrestal's isolation, for he lacked the capacity to establish a circle of close friends. He had been raised a Catholic, and he feared that his falling away from the church had led God to abandon him. To the lonely Forrestal, for whom work, achievement, power, and prestige were everything, the loss of position was the loss of meaningful life, precipitating his final decline and the full-blown syndrome of involutional melancholia.

The Navy psychiatrist who supervised his treatment, Dr. George Raines, has described the classic pre-existing personality pattern and attitude toward work seen in individuals who suffer involutional melancholia in mid-life, and this pattern fits Forrestal almost exactly. The victim typically displays a hard, cold, conscientious "office personality" to all but his or her intimates. The individual's basic personality is that of the driven compulsive (a personality type frequently found in successful executives).[62]

Characteristically such individuals show a focus on detail and organization, and keep their feelings under tight control. Such individuals demonstrate a devotion to hard work and pride in work. Many of those who develop the illness are sensitive, meticulous, over-conscientious, busy active people. They have been described as showing a narrow range of interests, poor facility for readjustment, asocial trends, inability to maintain friendships, intolerance, . . . a pronounced and rigid ethical code and a proclivity to reticence.[63]

Colleagues and friends knew how important work was to Forrestal. They observed that the only time he was truly happy was when he was at work—as if work were his hobby. Work seemed to be his way of compensating for underlying insecurities. Aware of the central importance of his work to Forrestal, the political columnist Walter Lippman wrote after Forrestal's death that one reason for Forrestal's breakdown was that he was being cast aside in mid-career, that if he had known he was needed and wanted in another job he would not have suffered an emotional breakdown.[64]

Forrestal's tragedy was not simply that he was removed from high status but that his high status followed him into the military hospital, where it compromised the objectivity of those treating him, distorting his treatment and resulting in his death. Rogow's account of Forrestal's death by suicide suggests that because of Forrestal's special status he was not placed under the close supervision and suicide constraints customary in a case such as his.[65] Indeed, the "special" treatment of this "special" patient is a textbook example of how VIP status can interfere with optimal medical treatment and prove dangerous to one's health. In Forrestal's case, it was to prove fatal.

As we have noted earlier, the polity's collective wish to have leaders who are all strong, all wise, and all powerful contributes to a public reluctance to accept illness in leaders. This is especially the case with psychiatric illness, with its potential for loss of control and erratic decision-making, which often contributes to delaying diagnosis or excusing clear signs of major emotional disorder as the consequences of "exhaustion."

This was the case with Forrestal's involutional melancholia. For nearly a year preceding the dramatic final illness, as we have earlier described, Forrestal had been exhibiting signs of psychological distress. His friends and colleagues did not suggest a psychiatric consultation but attributed his reactions to "exhaustion" from the extreme stress of work.

After the ceremony installing Louis Johnson as Forrestal's successor as secretary of defense, Forrestal's aide found him in his office, dazed and uncommunicative. Alarmed, he escorted him home and called his close friend, the New York investment banker Ferdinand Eberstadt, suggesting to Eberstadt that Forrestal could benefit from a rest at Hobe Sound in Florida, where his friends were vacationing. Eberstadt found Forrestal extremely depressed and agitated. He condemned himself as a total failure and told Eberstadt he was actively thinking about suicide. He also shared his delusions that he was being pursued by Communist and Zionist agents. It was clear to Eberstadt that his friend was seriously mentally ill, yet he went forward with the plan for Forrestal to travel to Hobe Sound. Eberstadt arranged for transport on an Air Force Constellation through Secretary Louis Johnson, whom he informed of Forrestal's condition. That Forrestal was not immediately hospitalized was a major departure from what was clearly medically required.

At Hobe Sound, Forrestal told friends and family of his paranoid fears. His first words on deplaning, to his good friend Robert Lovett, were, "Bob, they're after me."[66] During the next days, he made several suicide attempts, so that sharp objects were kept away from him. On the day of his arrival, he agreed to a psychiatric consultation with the world-famous psychiatrist Dr. William Menninger, with whom Forrestal had consulted on personnel matters during the war. Menninger flew to Hobe Sound and had several psychiatric interviews with Forrestal. Doctor George Raines, the chief psychiatrist at Bethesda Naval Hospital, had also been called in, but he declined to become involved in the case so long as Dr. Menninger was present: "I felt it improper to see Mr. Forrestal since he had designated a physician of his own choice."[67] Raines did consult with Menninger, who believed that Forrestal was "suffering with a severe depression of the type seen in operational fatigue during the war."[68]

Referring later to this diagnosis, and reconfirming the public myth that great men do not suffer from mental illness, only exhaustion, the *New York Times* likened Forrestal's condition to the physical and emotional reactions of soldiers "that came from fighting too long without respite . . . . Every man has his breaking point, and when this point comes, he must rest."[69] The *Washington Post* observed that the former secretary of defense was "worn out."[70]

It was then—finally—decided that the gravity of Forrestal's psychiatric illness required hospitalization and that the Bethesda Naval Hospital was the preferred venue. It would not, for one thing, have the stigma of being a psychiatric hospital that would attend confinement at the Menninger Clinic in Topeka, and friends and colleagues would be readily available to offer support. Menninger and several aides escorted Forrestal to Bethesda on April 2 in a private plane. Though heavily sedated, Forrestal was extremely disturbed, talking incessantly about the plot to get him. During the automobile ride to the hospital, he tried several times to leave the car and had to be physically restrained.

There was confusion early in the hospitalization concerning who was in charge. Doctor Menninger stayed on for several days and had extensive interviews with Forrestal. Only after he left was Dr. Raines placed unambiguously in charge of the case. But, in fact, even then he was not fully in charge, for this was no ordinary case and no ordinary psychiatric hospitalization. Forrestal was not confined to the psychiatric ward, where the physicians, nurses, and attendants were highly experienced in dealing with patients with psychiatric illness and in observing the subtle changes in mood that may presage suicide. One of the major challenges in dealing with severe mental illness is overcoming the patient's denial. Psychiatric milieu therapy in a group setting was developed during World War II. It is designed to help in confronting denial, combating delusions, and helping the patient to accept that he or she is indeed emotionally ill, the first step to recovery. Forrestal's VIP status and the classified information he may have incorporated into his delusions would have presented problems in group therapy, but such a setting could have been extremely supportive. It would have been best had his doctors not continued the isolation that had started in the Pentagon and now was continued at the hospital.

In response to the intercession of Pentagon and White House officials, the hospital commandant overrode Dr. Raines's strenuous objections and arranged for Forrestal to be hospitalized in "the tower," a VIP suite on the sixteenth floor, which was not designed for psychiatric patients.* Because of concern that he might attempt suicide, a navy medical corpsman or a medical resident was assigned to spend the night in a room adjoining Forrestal's suite.

Raines prescribed the treatment regimen of the day for the "operational fatigue" diagnosis made by Dr. Menninger—a week of barbiturate-induced narcosis followed by insulin coma treatment. In fact, as mentioned above, Forrestal was displaying the classic picture of involutional melancholia. Electro-convulsive therapy (ECT), a treatment modality first introduced in 1938 and in wide use at the time Forrestal was hospitalized, can be a life-saving therapy for a suicidal patient suffering from involutional melancholia. Why ECT was not employed is puzzling. In fact, Dr. Raines was overruled on at least one occasion concerning the administra-

---

*This is a classic example of the reduced authority of the physician in charge of the VIP patient. Sometimes well-meaning members of the inner circle, sometimes superiors in the hierarchy who lack the necessary expertise, intervene with damaging consequences. At a medical military hospital, Dr. Raines was placed in the position of defying a superior officer.

tion of a treatment he felt was in order. If Raines was also blocked from using ECT, this almost certainly contributed to Forrestal's death.

Moreover, Dr. Raines was unable to control the environment, a crucial factor for the hospitalized psychiatric patient. He was unable to limit the access of important visitors to Forrestal, two of whom—President Truman and Secretary of Defense Louis Johnson—were causally linked to Forrestal's depression. Thus Dr. Raines had responsibility without authority. Non-psychiatrically trained administrative physicians were intervening in decisions without understanding the destructive medical ramifications of their special arrangements.

Because of the significant suicide attempts early in his illness and his suicidal rumination, Forrestal was subject to restrictions early in his hospitalization. He resented these restrictions, assuring Dr. Raines that if he were bent on killing himself, he would do it by hanging and not by jumping out a window. Although the insulin treatment helped Forrestal's condition less than had been hoped, he showed some signs of improvement and restrictions were gradually eased. Raines's hope was that Forrestal would take this as a sign that he was seen as improving. Forrestal was accorded privileges denied other patients. Of particular significance, he was granted unaccompanied access to a small kitchen across from his suite. Unlike the windows on the hospital rooms, which had locked heavy metal screens, the kitchen window screen was fastened by hooks.

By mid-May, Forrestal's condition had improved considerably. His spirits seemed lighter, to the point where Dr. Raines, who had already cut back on the daily psychotherapy sessions, felt able to leave Bethesda to attend a professional meeting in Toronto. He also told Forrestal's family of the improvement in his patient's condition and advised his wife that she could depart the country for a European vacation. Raines saw Forrestal on the morning of May 18, before leaving for Toronto, and found his spirits much improved over the preceding week, when there had been some depression. On Friday, May 20, a visiting admiral noted that Forrestal had "a sparkle in his eye."[71]

A hazard during recovery from suicidal depression is the appearance of significant improvement and mental ease; often this apparent improvement is associated with the patient's having come to a calm resolution to take his or her life and thus being at peace at last. In retrospect, the apparent improvement in Forrestal's mental state probably represented just such a period. Doctor Raines later commented on the difficult period for the recovering depressive as it related to Forrestal.

[I] felt . . . that he was nearing the end of his illness and that the next thirty days should see him ready to leave the hospital. I further recognized the well-known psychiatric fact that the next thirty days would constitute the most dangerous period of the illness as far as suicide was concerned, inasmuch as suicidal preoccupations had to be present and at the same time privileges had to be extended to the patient to allow his full recovery.[72]

On the evening of May 21, Forrestal declined his customary sleeping pill and told his medical corpsman that he intended to stay up and read. The corpsman looked in on him briefly at 1:45 A.M. and found him writing. Shortly after this check, Forrestal walked into the kitchen, took the sash from his bathrobe, tied one end to the radiator and the other around his neck, and went through the window, falling to his death on a third-floor passageway thirteen stories below.

Severe suicidal depression is an extremely dangerous condition; some patients bent on committing suicide will succeed despite the best professional care. But involutional melancholia is an illness of limited duration; treated optimally, most afflicted patients will recover.

Forrestal's case illustrates two important principles. The first is that high status poses a danger to the proper medical treatment of any leader. Because of his special status, James Forrestal received less than optimal treatment. Had he been treated as an ordinary patient, confined to the psychiatric ward under the supervision of a highly skilled psychiatrist able to employ the full range of possible treatments and to control the environment, Forrestal might have recovered from his severe depression, and this extraordinary public servant might again have been able to contribute to the nation.

The second principle is more reassuring: when, as in this case, a change in behavior is fairly rapid and fairly obvious, the system adjusts and little harm is done. As in the case of Castlereagh, it would seem that the bizarre suspicion and hostility that heralded the onset of paranoid illness were obvious to all and defined as illness because the symptoms were so at variance with his previous psychological pattern. The political system had no trouble dealing with either man. Both were recognized as mentally ill and incompetent to lead, and hence they were removed from office.

To be sure, the gravity of Forrestal's condition was recognized belatedly. He was initially considered to be suffering from exhaustion, and his removal from a position of decision-making was delayed for months. But during his last months in office, he was excluded from meetings of the Joint Chiefs of Staff and insulated from active participation in important decisions. In any case, Forrestal's paranoia was characterized more by fear than anger. He was more likely to warn about or flee his enemies than to confront them.

The tragic case of James Forrestal demonstrates how the high status of the patient can compromise the authority of the treating physician and lead to impaired clinical judgment and insufficient and life-endangering treatment. On some occasions, the high status of the patient produces such a state of awe in the treating medical personnel that they are unable to function with customary skill. Their reaction to the fame of the individual under their care impairs their ability to minister to him as a desperately ill patient.

Stage Fright in the Operating Theater

"Please! Just Treat Me Like Anybody Else"
—Cardboard sign taped to his chest by a prominent
physician about to undergo an operation at his
own hospital

Beyond the politicized nature of the medical process, VIPs face another largely unexpected medical difficulty. Health-care personnel often suffer something very much like stage fright when treating a leader, a celebrity, or a fellow physician. The most carefully selected nurses may make inaccurate blood pressure readings; orderlies known for their skill may probe time and time again for a vein;, and conscientious, highly experienced, ordinarily careful doctors may record the wrong data or administer the wrong medication. Indeed, it is a commonplace that doctors frequently receive especially bad treatment because they are treated specially.

The physicians who successfully treated President Reagan for the gunshot wound he suffered in 1982 in the assassination attempt boasted that he was treated "just like anyone else who got shot up in downtown Washington."[73] Indeed, a major reason that things went so well at George Washington Emergency is that the president's arrival was unexpected and several of the key people caring for him were so busy administering life-saving treatment that they initially had no idea who their patient was.

Choosing Doctors on the Basis of Political Affiliation

When Ronald Reagan was brought into the emergency ward after the attempt on his life, he jokingly expressed the hope that the doctors were Republicans. He need not have feared; as one of the attending doctors replied, "We are all Republicans now."[74] But in some situations the political loyalty of the doctors involved can matter a great deal.

If court physicians are deeply involved in the political system, and that political system deals with its opponents by inflicting injury and murder, will not the court physicians be involved? The answer, of course, is yes.

Indeed, in a murderous political system, the medical system associated with the inner circle will become as much a source of danger as the military, the secret police, or any other branch of government with the ability to do harm. In fact, despite their vow to Hippocrates, *primum non nocere* (the primary duty is not to do harm), physicians have not infrequently played a murderous role in history,[75] notably in the Renaissance and in the circles surrounding Hitler and Stalin.[76] Poison has always been the instrument of preference in such matters. Cesare Borgia, the consummate Renaissance prince, was a frequent user of this instrument, aided by such doctors as Girolamo Cardano:

Poisoning was an art much practiced all over Italy. The mathematician and doctor Girolamo Cardano related that four members of his family had died by poison. Cesare's old enemy, Caterina Sforza, had written of poisons in her *Experiments* and claimed to concoct a *veleno attermine* that gave "perfect sleep." In Rome, it was not thought strange that cardinals should attend a banquet each with his own steward and his own wine, and this practice was done "without insult to the host". . . . When Cesare Borgia came to this part of the murderer's trade he looked into it with his usual skeptical thoroughness. During the first steps of his conquest he had addressed to Lorenz Behaim, the scientist of the papal court, ninety questions on scientific matters, thirteen of which were about poisons; he wished to know the ways of poisoning cups, perfumes, flowers, saddles, and even stirrups, and the formula for *veleno attermine,* the notorious white powder that killed with a delayed but sure effect. Lorenz Behaim, who found these enquiries quite normal, forwarded them to Willbald Pirkheimer of Nuremberg, a foremost European authority.[77]

Even in minor illnesses, members of Hitler's entourage feared to see any doctor not associated with their faction. Stalin guarded his medicines jealously, fearing poison (though it has been alleged that medicine might have been switched without his knowledge).

Physicians have also been involved in the medical use of coercion against their country's enemies or those they wish to influence. In the previous chapter, we described the role of Hitler's physician Theodore Morell, who injected President Hácha of Slovakia with something, probably a powerful compliance-inducing drug, immediately before he capitulated. The willingness of German physicians to conduct sadistic medical experiments on concentration camp inmates is one of the most horrifying—and puzzling—aspects of the Holocaust. Loyal citizens and devoted family men, these physicians walled off this aspect of their professional lives through a process that Robert Lifton has called "doubling."[78] The fear of medical murder or induced disability probably contributes to the tendency of chiefs of state to choose their physicians from political or international allies.

Putting demonstrated loyalty over medical competence is not without risk. When the leftist president of Guyana Forbes Burnham fell ill in 1985, he asked for a team of Cuban doctors to attend him. Perhaps he wanted the ideologically compatible Cuban physicians because he feared harm at the hands of Western doctors, or perhaps he simply wanted to affirm his dedication to the socialist ideal. The three-man medical team soon arrived in Georgetown, the capital.[79] The reportedly minor throat operation would typically have been completed in no more than thirty minutes, but this procedure took an hour and forty minutes. The practice of medicine at Georgetown Hospital, where Burnham died, was apparently rather primitive. The hospital did have a cardiac monitor with which Burnham's heart could have been monitored, but it remained in storage. The Cubans brought sophisticated medical equipment with them, but it was not installed. Had Burnham simply chosen the best medical care—which would have had to have been merely competent, given the minor nature of his illness—he would have lived.

On the other hand, if a politician's health, mental or physical, becomes a political issue, he or she would be wise to choose physicians whose loyalty was without question. And the physicians, if they intend to stay in the government's good graces—and in some cases, out of prison—will conclude that they have no choice but to support their patron. It is likely that such pressures were bearing on the Nazi doctors. In democratic societies, too, physicians can facilitate the goals of their political masters. The career of Governor Earl Long of Louisiana demonstrates how physicians and other health-care personnel can participate in highly partisan activities.

Governor Long's Medical Accomplices

Governor Earl Long had frequently displayed signs of severe psychiatric disorder—manic-depressive psychosis, pre-senile dementia, or vigorous eccentricity, depending upon the medical acumen and partisan position of the speaker. There were also rumors that Long had cheated on his income taxes, and others who might be implicated, such as his estranged wife, Blanche, would be legally more secure if it could be shown that Long was mentally unbalanced when he committed those acts.

In May 1959 Long had acted in a manner that many considered manic during two appearances before the Louisiana legislature, appearing to be under the influence of liquor and using strong language. Soon afterward Blanche invited six physicians to the governor's mansion: the Longs' family doctor; a cousin who was a physician but not a psychiatrist; another cousin who was a psychiatrist; and three other physicians known to Mrs. Long. Some of the doctors diagnosed Long as suffering from acute manic-depressive psychosis and believed that he should be hospitalized; some did not.*

Long's nephew, Senator Russell Long, received assurances from federal authorities that if a plausible case were presented that hospitalization outside the state was in the "patient's" interest, a kidnaping charge would not be leveled. The group realized that there would be political problems if Long were hospitalized in Louisiana. When Long was told that he would be placed under psychiatric restraint he said, "But why? If I'm crazy, I've been crazy all my life." Nevertheless, Long was sedated and flown out of Baton Rouge to the Harris Psychiatric Clinic in Galveston, Texas. It is an interesting constitutional point that the legislature did not act to remove Long from office. Rather, he was removed by his family and selected physicians in ordinary civil proceedings.

At the clinic Long was given tranquilizers. An announcement was made that he had probably had a series of light strokes. Long was not content with this state of affairs. He was, after all, still governor. Shouting out his hospital window to reporters, "I'm no crazier than you are!" he appealed for a writ of habeas corpus. He appeared before a sanity hearing and, over the objections of his Texas doctors, managed to work out an agreement with his wife and nephew permitting him to return home.

Long checked into Ochsner Clinic in New Orleans on his return, as he had promised in Galveston, but almost immediately checked out again. He was then arrested by state police for violating the terms of the court decision. On the recommendation of a coroner (the principal medical officer of a parish in Louisiana) and a local psychiatrist, he was committed to the state mental hospital in Mandeville, Louisiana. Although Long was still governor, now it was evident that he could not serve as such, at least for the indefinite future. Nevertheless, who would be acting governor was a legal tangle.

Although Mandeville was a state hospital, it was affiliated with the schools of medicine of Louisiana State University and Tulane University, Tulane's school of social work, the Louisiana State University Psychology department, and the Southwestern Louisiana Institute of Nursing. Many fingers were stuck in the pie, some public, some not. Doctors at Mandeville said it would take thirty days to make a diagnostic determination, a typical requirement for a diagnostic commitment, but Long managed to

---

*The medical-political chronology that follows draws on Johnson, "Governor Earl K. Long."

117

engineer his release within a week. "[The] press was swarming around the piney-wood facility; some reporters donned white lab coats in an effort to visit Long. Dave Bell, a driver for Long, crawled up to the governor's window at night, rolled up one-hundred-dollar bills and slipped them through the steel screens. Long wanted to bribe the [staff] in Mandeville." Everyone at the hospital knew that Long might well return to full power, and he had wide appointive powers.

Long and his supporters were convinced that he was simply the victim of a political maneuver. Long smuggled a message out of Mandeville, which was widely published and carried on radio and television. Released for his sanity hearing, Long convened a meeting of the state's hospital board. At Long's urging, they dismissed the state director of hospitals and the superintendent of Mandeville Hospital and replaced them with Long supporters. The new superintendent of Mandeville announced his intention to release the governor from any restriction, the state attorney general withheld objections, and on June 26, 1959, Long was a free man. He promptly fired the superintendent of state police and forty others. He appointed three psychiatrists from outside the state system to supervise him but noted, "My intention now is to do what the doctors say. But if I think they might be erroneous, I'd reserve my rights to do otherwise."

Basically, Long fired the doctors and politicians who said he was crazy and then appointed others who said he was not. It is not possible to determine at this remove which group acted more properly. Unquestionably, becoming involved with a major political figure affected the careers and quite likely the decisions of everyone involved. And whereas in this circumstance the psychiatrists and other officials on the losing side only lost their jobs, in another country the losing side could have been dealt with considerably more severely.

Keeping a Dead Leader Alive in the National Interest

The general topic of this book concerns how illness harms the political system. Yet we have already noted in the case of George III of England that the leader's illness can be a positive influence on history, if not on the leader himself. Recall that George's mania and delusions lessened the ability of those who wished to prevent the rise of parliamentary sovereignty. Modern medicine may keep terminally ill persons alive for an extended time. There are many disadvantages to such situations, but a curious positive effect is that such circumstances can facilitate a difficult political transition.

Franco of Spain

Generalissimo Francisco Franco of Spain ruled his country for well over a quarter century, at first with great severity but toward the end of his rule with increasing moderation. We know that he showed clear signs of diabetes and Parkinson's disease as early as 1963.[80] His decline was gradual, and it coincided with the acceptance of Spain back into the councils of a democratic Europe. As his death approached in the mid-1970s, Europe was at peace, Spain was increasingly prosperous, and a transition to democratic rule was possible. Yet many in Spain wanted a continuation of authoritarianism. Even more threatening, strong antagonisms and vendettas still hung over from the bloody Spanish Civil War. Many feared that the death of Franco would bring the return of civil strife and the eventual continuation of authoritarianism. Yet, so long as Franco was alive, no one was willing to make the necessary practical arrangements for a democratic succession.

If Franco were alive, there was no problem. If Franco suddenly died, there was a great problem. But if Franco were somewhere between life and death, breathing but terminally unconscious, arrangements might be made for the succession. This is what happened. At the very end, Franco was maintained on life-support systems for much longer than a commoner would have been. Some said Franco lingered so long because he had such a powerful physical constitution; others said he was being treated like anyone able to receive advanced medical care; others said that he was continued because no one was brave enough to pull the plug.

In any event, Franco's twilight state went on for so long that jokes began to circulate about it. One, which revealed the political anxiety produced by the coming end of fascist rule, described a cabinet minister approaching Prince Juan Carlos (who did become king on Franco's death) and telling him:

"I have good news and bad news, Your Excellency."
"Tell me the good news."
"Franco is dead."
"Good! What is the bad news?"
"You will have to tell him."

During this prolonged period, Spain's power brokers "came to pay their respects to the Generalissimo" but in fact ignored the wired and tubed chief of state as they successfully worked out the final details of the transition from a fascist dictatorship to a democratic and constitutional monarchy. Had the transition not been so gradual, the authoritarian rule of the dying Franco may well not have died with him.

Tito of Yugoslavia

A similar gradual transition from strong autocratic leadership was to occur during Marshal Tito's prolonged decline in 1980. Like Franco, during his final days the eighty-eight-year-old Tito was maintained for an unusually long time on life-support systems, during which period a transition was made from one-man rule to collective leadership. The violence and disorder that overtook Yugoslavia in the early 1990s was thus postponed.

It is appropriate that this chapter ends with a description of a political system that did not permit its leader to die. In chapter 5 we deal with the more dangerous situation in which dying leaders refuse to let their countries live without them.

5

SITTING CROWNED
UPON THE GRAVE

EFFECTS OF TERMINAL LEADERSHIP
ON POLITICAL BEHAVIOR

Sitting crowned upon the grave thereof
—Thomas Hobbes, *Leviathan*

The passions are the winds that drive us along.
—Voltaire

Though he watched a decent age go by,
A man will sometimes still desire the world.
—Sophocles, *Oedipus at Colonus*

For life moves out of a red flare of dreams
Into a common light of common hours
Until age brings the red flare again.
—William Butler Yeats, *The Land of Heart's Desire*

How the king reacts to his mortal illness will determine its political consequences. And this in turn will depend upon his personality, his motivation for leadership, his attitude toward illness, and his view of his own mortality. Men are impelled to seek high office for diverse reasons. Some wish to sit upon the throne in order to savor the perquisites of high office. Others desire to wield the scepter of power. Still others pursue a quest for glory, seeking to be inscribed in the pages of history. When one's entire sense of self is bound up in being a revered leader, when the exercise of power is compensation for inner insecurity, giving up the heroic life is inconceivable. In contrast, the leader imbued with healthy self-confidence, with a sense of himself apart from his leadership and a sense of the finitude of life, recognizes that the exercise of his abilities must inevitably yield to the passage of time.

Facing Death: Political Consequences of the Leader's Acceptance or Denial of the End of Life

It's still the same old story,
A fight for love and glory,
A case of do or die . . .
—Herman Hupfeld, "As Time Goes By"

Some persons facing death accept that inevitability. The leader or ordinary citizen completes what can be completed of life's affairs. He or she provides for valued matters in the future—money may be left to family members and charities—but the future is to be affected, not controlled, and the individual recognizes the limits of influence, as of time.

Others refuse to accept death. They try to avoid it, even to trick it. Nonacceptance most often takes the form of the person identifying life itself with some important aspect of their life, most often their occupation or sexual performance, and refusing to give that up. It is as if they were saying: *To give up my job is to give up my life. If I can keep my job, I will keep my life.* For political leaders, the "job" is their political position. Lord Moran cites this as an important motivation for Churchill's insisting on staying in office, even though manifestly impaired, observing, "He could not bear to give up power; there would be no purpose left in life."[1]

Some leaders simply refuse to admit that they are dying. Sir Henry Campbell-Bannerman of Great Britain "never resigned of his own free will, fighting on his deathbed to hang on to the Premiership." Finally his doctor took matters into his own hands and essentially forced the premier to resign.[2] But such medical advice and such acquiescence by the leader are very much the exception.

Non-acceptance of mortality can take another form, especially among political leaders. The leader may identify his life with the achievement of some ambition or ideal, believing that if this ideal or ambition is fulfilled, he will not really die but will live on symbolically. It is instructive to contrast the last years of the two giants who shaped the course of Chinese communism—Mao Zedong and Chou Enlai.

The Last Acts of Mao Zedong and Chou Enlai

The Cultural Revolution, which gripped China in the late 1960s, was an explosion of factional struggles, regional antipathies, personal conflicts, ideological differences, and bureaucratic competition. Yet no serious observer denies the impact, the determinative role of the strong personal leadership of China's leader, Mao Zedong. Mao initiated the widespread disorder and near civil war, encouraged it while it was underway, legitimated it throughout, and went to his grave in 1976, after the movement had run its disastrous course, still praising it.

The economic and political goals of both the Great Leap Forward during the late 1950s and the Cultural Revolution were not necessarily misguided in the view of many China scholars. The problem was the pace Mao set to actualize them. Given the state of societal inertia in China, the programs being enacted might well require decades to accomplish rather than mere months. But Mao did not have decades. It was as if by an act of revolutionary will he could pull the People's Republic of China into the twentieth century and consolidate the revolution. Seriously ill, aware that little time was left, Mao reacted to impending death by imposing his personal timetable on the nation. His intimations of mortality contributed to his sense of urgency and to the wrenching and destabilizing chain of events of the Great Leap Forward and of the Cultural Revolution.

In his psychobiography of Mao, Robert Jay Lifton argues that the Cultural Revolution was Mao's attempt to achieve immortality by identifying himself with a set of symbols that would live on after his death. Mao believed, justifiably, that his successors would reject his highly personalized revolution.[3] He feared that they would move closer to the "imperialist" powers and work to dilute his strict communism. For Mao, the meaning of his life could be ensured—and his immortality achieved—only by becoming part of an ongoing revolutionary process. Continuing revolution became the essence of Mao's struggle against death. Though he rejected the divine, in striving to ensure the perpetual pursuit of an egalitarian utopia, Mao sought quasi-holy status.

Not every revolutionary leader is so consumed. Every political system has leaders who face their death bravely and seek to serve the people until their final moments. By Mao's side until his own death was Mao's loyal premier Chou Enlai. Reflective and judicious, Chou retained his emotional and political balance as he sought to moderate Mao's excesses, aiming to sustain the gains of the revolution without permitting its architect to destroy them. Only after Chou died was it revealed that he had been suffering from carcinoma of the stomach, a painful and debilitating disease, since at least 1972. Chou was first hospitalized in the spring of 1974, but the world did not hear of his ailment until that summer. He was stoic and self-contained until his death in 1976. Only then was Deng Xiaopeng brought back into the power structure.

Chou and Mao were contrasting personalities whose reactions to their terminal illnesses could not have been more different. Chou was psychologically mature, content within himself, structured, well organized. Mao epitomized the narcissistic charismatic leader, consumed by a messianic vision; his reverential followers ascribed godlike status to him. For the leader who seeks glory, there is never enough glory, never enough time, and facing the end of life is intolerable. And thus it was that Mao Zedong, at the end of a remarkable revolutionary life, clearly to be enshrined in the pantheon of history's great leaders, was not fulfilled. Whatever the evaluation of the outside world, Mao's inner drive was undiminished, his ambition for revolutionary glory unfulfilled. His appetite for glory and a role in history was insatiable. The specter of reaching the end of life before he had consolidated his revolution was intolerable, precipitating his terminal rush to glory.

Ferdinand Marcos of the Philippines: Terminal Control

When a leader places great emphasis on strength and control, the onset of serious illness can be extremely threatening. Illness episodically affected the controlling Ferdinand Marcos from his twenties on and played a major role in his authoritarian rule. In August 1942, while fighting a guerrilla campaign in the jungles of the Philippines against the Japanese invaders, Marcos, then twenty-four, was afflicted with an illness characterized by fever and abdominal pain that left him bedridden for five months in a guerrilla camp. This illness recurred in June 1943, when it led to hospitalization. His brother, a physician, diagnosed Marcos as suffering from an ulcer and from blackwater fever, a serious form of malaria that affects the kidneys. A third episode in 1944 was again diagnosed as blackwater fever. In retrospect, this may have been the onset of the disease of the connective tissue—systemic lupus erythematosus—that later led to kidney failure and ultimately claimed his life.

After the war, Marcos entered political life.* Intellectually acute, early in his career he demonstrated a subtle leadership style and a mastery of the political process both domestic and international. He served in the House of Representatives from 1949 to 1959, was a senator from 1959 to 1965, and was president of the Senate from 1963 to 1965. At the age of thirty-seven, Senator Marcos married Imelda, who would play an important role as a political wife and became a political power in her own right. In 1965, at age forty-seven, Marcos was elected president of the Philippines.

The communist insurgency of the New People's Army, which continues today, began in 1969. Its continuing goal has been to destabilize the democratic regime through the use of violence. As Marcos struggled to contain the mounting violence, he was also struggling with ill health. By age fifty-

---

*The depiction of Marcos's political career draws heavily on Seagraves, *Marcos Dynasty*.

four, the difficulties that had episodically plagued Marcos were definitively diagnosed, and he secretly began to consult with a kidney specialist. Marcos, who had always been extremely concerned with his health, questioned his doctors closely. When he learned of the grave prognosis, he insisted that the illness be kept a closely guarded secret. For the most part, he and his inner circle were successful in concealing from public view at first the existence, and later the gravity, of his illness.

In 1971, the year the diagnosis was established, Marcos initiated emergency steps to contain the increasingly violent activity of the rebels, suspending the writ of habeas corpus. In 1972, he imposed martial law. Although there had been significant insurgent violence, the imposition of martial law was controversial, viewed by many as an unnecessarily harsh and disproportionate reaction. Marcos further consolidated his political control in 1973, naming himself prime minister under the new constitution while remaining president under the old. Although the instability of the environment required strong leadership, Marcos's political opponents argued that he was exploiting the political instability to justify his dictatorial bent. We believe there was also a more personal reason for the extremity of his actions. Facing the ebbing of his physical strength and the progressive loss of control over his own body, Marcos needed to demonstrate his political will and control.

By 1978, at age sixty-one, his progressive illness could no longer be concealed. He was having difficulty rising from his chair without assistance. The next year, the characteristic rash of lupus was explained away as a simple skin rash, but his face was puffy, and he was suffering from arthritis of the hands, other symptoms of lupus. By 1980, his kidneys were failing, prompting U.S. specialists to recommend an immediate kidney transplant. The palace staff now knew of his illness, and word leaked to the press.

As his health declined, his leadership became more controlling. In September 1980, Marcos secretly signed the Public Safety Act, giving him extraordinary powers; the next month, the government prepared to revive an old murder case against Benigno Aquino, his principal political adversary. Marcos's zeal to eliminate any threat to his political health was given added force by the threat to his physical health. Adding to the arrows in his authoritarian quiver, in January 1981 he secretly signed the National Security Act. In anticipation of the visit of Pope Paul II, he lifted martial law, which had been in place for nine years, but the broad discretionary powers granted him under the Public Safety and National Security acts still enabled him to exercise unconstrained power. Within the year, he had purged the government and military of anyone who threatened his rule.

As his control over his body continued to decline, Marcos took increasingly extreme measures to retain control of the government. During the summer of 1982, Marcos, now sixty-four, was hospitalized twice. He appeared on television to deny rumors of his failing health, but on a visit to Washington, D.C., he had two dialysis machines available at the Philippine embassy. It was no longer possible to conceal that he was suffering from kidney failure and required regular dialysis to sustain him. Friends speculated that he was near death. Given that an immediate kidney transplant was recommended in 1980, he had probably been undergoing dialysis, a daily reminder of his mortality, at least since the late 1970s.

As is almost always the case, the illness exaggerated its victim's preexisting personality. Marcos throughout his political career had left nothing to chance. Trusting no one, he had developed competing sources of information and frequently traveled throughout the Philippines to take the people's pulse. But these methods of keeping informed were now denied him, for Marcos's illness severely curtailed his mobility. He rarely left Malacañang Palace.

Moreover, because of Marcos's vulnerability to infection, access to the ailing leader was sharply reduced. By now, the circle around the stricken king had contracted. Marcos had indicated that in the event of his death, Army Chief of Staff General Fabian Ver would have "certain powers." His wife, Imelda, and General Ver controlled almost all the information that reached the largely bedridden leader. With Marcos rarely in public view, it was unclear who was making decisions. For the last four years of his rule, the ailing Marcos and his constricted leadership circle represented a striking case of a captive king and his captive court.

August 1983 was a month of medical and political crisis. In early August, decrees were issued affirming Marcos's right to imprison suspects in cases of subversion and deny them access to the courts. As his political control was reaffirmed, Marcos's condition was declining precipitously. By now the disease was affecting his brain, and his mental processes were clouded. In late August, he underwent an emergency kidney transplant.

The period immediately following a transplant is critical. In order to guard against rejection of the transplant, immuno-suppressant drugs are administered which make the patient extremely susceptible to infection and the patient is usually kept in isolation. Marcos was rumored to be semi-comatose. Even if he were reasonably alert, he would not have been able to participate in thoughtful political decision-making. It was during this crucial recovery period, on August 21, that Benigno Aquino, Marcos's chief political opponent, returned to the Philippines. As he was disembarking from the plane, but before he actually set foot on Philippine soil, he was assassinated. Many believed that Imelda had engineered the public assassination, because a soothsayer had warned her of grave consequences should Aquino set foot on Philippine soil. Indeed, in May 1983 Imelda had flown to New York to warn Aquino never to return. Aquino's murder was a catalytic event, provoking vocal protests against the Marcos regime, which was widely held to be responsible.

Marcos's immune system ultimately rejected the transplant, requiring continuing dialysis, but in September, his health status partially improved. He threatened once again to impose martial law. Tensions between the Marcos government and the United States over Marcos's authoritarian rule increased. In October, a civilian investigative panel named Marcos's crony General Ver and others as indictable for the premeditated murder of Aquino. Marcos was pressured to relax his authoritarian control by the United States, but in late October, the regional secretary of the opposition party was assassinated.

As public discontent with his rule mounted and his health became seriously compromised, Marcos might well have stepped down or at least announced that at the completion of his term in 1987 he would end his years of public service for health reasons. But no longer in control of his own body, Marcos psychologically could not yield political control. To do so would be to give up the fight for his life. On November 6, 1984, despite terminal kidney disease, he announced that he would run for re-election in 1987. The elimination of leading opposition figures continued with the assassination of Mayor César Climaco.

Shortly after the announcement, Marcos disappeared from public view, giving rise to rumors, soon confirmed, that he was seriously ill. He underwent a second kidney transplant and during the recovery developed serious respiratory difficulties, requiring an emergency tracheotomy. On November 21, the opposition filed a motion for a caretaker government, and on December 3, 1984, the government confirmed that Marcos was seriously ill, the first official acknowledgment of the gravity of his health.

Marcos's last year in office, 1985, was marked by increasingly blatant manipulation of the political system, as Marcos and his entourage frantically tried to hold onto power. Each violation of democratic norms further delegitimized Marcos's leadership. Evidence of the complicity of General Ver and his cohorts in the Aquino assassination was so overwhelming that an indictment could not be avoided; it came in February amid widespread skepticism that Marcos would permit a fair trial. That August, Marcos proposed an early election to forestall the development of an organized opposition (his personal timetable was foreshortened, however, and this probably also pushed him to secure his hold on power). Under intense U.S. and international pressure, Marcos decided to call a snap election for early 1986.

The much heralded and internationally watched trial of Ver for the assassination of Benigno Aquino ended predictably with Ver's acquittal and the implication of the Communist party leader Galman, even though Galman himself had been assassinated by then. This mockery of justice was the last straw for the Filipino people. The day after the verdict was announced, Aquino's widow, Corazon, announced her candidacy for the presidency. When the election was held in February 1986, under close domestic and international monitoring, it was clear that Corazon Aquino had won. But despite the close observation of the election, the magnitude of fraud was staggering, and Marcos was declared victor. This was the final delegitimation of Marcos; under the leadership of Defense Minister Juan Ponce Enrile and General Fidel Ramos, army deputy chief of staff, a successful bloodless coup against the Marcos regime was staged.

Ferdinand and Imelda Marcos and their entourage fled the Philippines, eventually settling in Honolulu. Despite the widespread support for Corazon Aquino and despite or perhaps because of his failing health, in January 1987 Marcos and his followers attempted a coup but were foiled by U.S. intervention.

In 1988 Marcos was diagnosed as chronically ill and unlikely to recover, thus avoiding trial for fraud and embezzlement in the United States. It is fitting that 1989, a year so many autocratic leaders fell, was the year the Marcos era ended. After a final ten months of hospitalization, during which he was often semi-comatose and had numerous emergency surgical interventions, Marcos finally succumbed to cardiac, pulmonary, and kidney failure. So large was his reputation, so strong the support he still had in his homeland, that Corazon Aquino for four years refused permission for him to be buried in the Philippines.

Ferdinand Marcos had played a giant role in the history of his nation, but his great achievements will be overshadowed by the desperate lengths to which he went at the end of his life to retain and even to regain control. While complex political forces were assuredly at play, the shadow of serious illness influenced his entire twenty-three-year presidency and significantly distorted his leadership during the final eight years. The degree of his authoritarian control, the sustained period of martial law, the assassination of Benigno Aquino, his inability to relinquish the reins of power, the decision to run for another term, and the final, flagrant electoral fraud that precipitated the bloodless coup—these benchmarks in the decline of his leadership occurred as his health was failing.

Marcos held desperately onto political power as a way of holding onto life. Had he accepted the verdict of the democracy he had helped to establish, Marcos could have retired with honor, his reputation in history intact. But in the end, his judgment increasingly failed, and he behaved more impulsively, less judiciously, perhaps influenced or controlled by the frightened and greedy courtiers around him. The more desperate his efforts to hold onto control, the more he damaged his reputation in history and the harder it became to yield power.

Andreas Papandreou of Greece: Terminal Machismo

For some narcissistic political leaders, the confrontation with mortality produces instability in the leader's personal life that has secondary destabilizing political effects. Such was the case with Andreas Papandreou, prime minister of Greece in the 1980s.

Controversy had always surrounded Papandreou. The son of Georgios Papandreou, a highly popular prime minister of Greece in the early 1960s, Andreas seemed throughout his life to be bent on establishing his identity by opposing authority. He attended graduate school at Harvard University and taught economics at the University of Minnesota and at Berkeley. Papandreou became a major influence in U.S. Democratic party politics, serving as a member of Adlai Stevenson's inner circle during his unsuccessful run for the presidency.

During his academic career the thirty-three-year-old Andreas met and married an American woman, Margaret Chant. Despite, or because of, these strong American connections, Andreas made anti-Americanism a rallying cry of his intensely nationalistic politics when he returned to Greece in 1974, after the military junta was overthrown, and succeeded to the prime ministership. Through his stormy thirty-seven-year marriage, Andreas developed a reputation as a womanizer, which probably enhanced his popular appeal. As one Greek commentator observed, "We love love affairs. It's in our blood. But at the same time, we take the family very seriously. You don't fool around with that."[4]

But in his seventieth year Papandreou crossed the line from macho but stable family man to foolish old goat in his headlong pursuit of a woman thirty-five years his junior, the former Olympic Airlines stewardess Dimitra (Mimi) Liani. What pushed Papandreou, a lifelong hypochondriac, over that line was the diagnosis of coronary artery insufficiency requiring a triple bypass operation. It was his voluptuous mistress, not his wife, who accompanied Papandreou to London in autumn 1988 for the required cardiac surgery. Without leaving anyone in Athens to mind the store, Papandreou spent two months in London, attempting to run the government by telephone from his hospital bed.

The prime minister became an object of ridicule. One joke circulating in Greece was that Papandreou had added a position to the *Kama Sutra,* the Indian erotic manual: one foot in the bed, the other in the grave. Photographs of his well-endowed mistress topless at a beach appeared in the Greek press. Political plays mocked the Papandreou government, focusing

on the seventy-year-old prime minister's neglect of official duties to concentrate on his thirty-four-year old mistress. Helen Vlachos, a senior
Greek newspaper correspondent, commented, "Suddenly he has lost control. The Greek people who sort of admired the macho side of having an
affair have begun to think this is too much."[5] A Greek diplomat observed,
"The question became not that he was having an affair with a woman
young enough to be his daughter, but that he was a doddering old man
being manipulated by her."[6] Papandreou even brought his mistress to
Parliament for the annual presentation of the budget.

Putting the final scandalous nail in the coffin, Papandreou announced his
intention to divorce his wife of thirty-seven years. In concert with financial
improprieties in his government and charges of corruption, his personal
indiscretion led to a marked decline in his popularity (45 percent in the
1985 election) and assuredly contributed to his loss of the election in June
1989, when he garnered just 20.5 percent of the vote.

P. W. Botha of South Africa: Terminal Stubbornness

> What must the king do now? Must he submit?
> The king shall do it: must he be depos'd?
> The king shall be contented: must he lose
> The name of king? i' God's name, let it go.
> —Shakespeare, *King Richard II*

Loss of control is especially threatening to authoritarian personalities.
Highly sensitive to position in the hierarchy, they are notably unreceptive
to advice from subordinates. They have extremely strong needs for autonomy and tend to become oppositional in the face of strong pressure,
conveying stubbornness and rigidity. Having a strong need to be right,
authoritarian persons do not easily admit error or change positions.

On January 18, 1989, a week after his seventy-third birthday, South
Africa's President Pieter (Pik) W. Botha suffered a "slight cerebral vascular
incident"[7] (a mild stroke) that left him partially paralyzed on his left side.
His obstinate clinging to his office for the next seven months also left his
government paralyzed at a time when strong and flexible leadership was
needed.

The illness could not have struck at a worse time. The government faced
massive problems: mounting international and domestic pressure to dis-
mantle the system of apartheid; the decision when or whether to release
jailed African National Congress leader Nelson Mandela, counter to the
wishes of the conservative Afrikaaner population who feared for their
survival; slowed economic growth and soaring inflation because of puni-

tive international sanctions; and the transfer of control of Namibia from South Africa to an independent government.

Botha's illness immediately kindled speculation that he would retire. Medical experts opined that even if he recovered quickly, it would be extremely dangerous for him to return to office: "If he wants to live to see his next birthday, he should immediately cut all the stress out of his life."[8] Rumors during the preceding year that Botha was in poor health gained force when he chose not to deliver the traditional New Year's message to the nation. In an interview in 1988, reflecting on the pressures of the office, Botha had indicated, "If I am to be honest, I have to say that you can only do this job while you are healthy. If my health is of such a nature that I cannot continue doing it, I myself will decide to go."[9]

But the first thing Botha did on returning to his official residence in Cape Town to convalesce two weeks after the stroke was to order that a desk be moved into his bedroom, making clear his intention to remain on the job. Ironically, Botha had come to office in 1978 after leading the effort to force the resignation of Prime Minister B. J. Vorster when financial improprieties in his government were revealed. Vorster had been suffering from a chronic blood disease for years and had clung to office despite his poor health.

Known as "The Great Crocodile" for his imperious manner and total control of his government, Botha was not one to relinquish that power easily. In early February 1989, taking even his senior cabinet members by surprise, he abruptly quit as head of the National party but resisted calls for his resignation as president and indicated his intention to serve out his term, elevating the presidency above partisan politics and making it "a unifying force in South Africa."[10] This, according to National party sources, would fulfill his long-held dream of finishing his political career as a senior statesman pursuing his vision of granting some power to the country's black majority of 23 million without taking power from the 4.5 million whites. In fact, the move created a peculiar political anomaly, essentially making it impossible for his successor as party leader Frederik W. de Klerk to lead effectively.

There was growing sentiment within the party that Botha should resign the presidency, too. But on March 2, Botha defiantly announced that he would resume his official duties later that month, asserting, "I am not looking for power for the sake of power . . . I do not cling to posts. But now I am healthy."[11] Afrikaans newspapers, which traditionally reflected National party views, suggested that Botha should resign to allow de Klerk to guide the reform process. On March 13, in a stunning rebuke to Botha's defiant stand, the 133 members of the parliamentary caucus of the ruling National party, which Botha had led for eleven years, voted unanimously in support of a resolution recommending that Botha step aside so that de Klerk could replace him as state president. But on March 15, as promised, Botha returned to office, leading one senior party official to remark: "The Great Crocodile is going to fight this one out to the end, and I wouldn't be surprised if he manages to bite a couple of people where they sit before this thing is all over."[12]

Liberal newspapers had a field day with Botha's bulldog insistence on retaining his position. A South African business newspaper editorialized that "the spectacle of President Botha clinging to high office like a two-year-old to a toy has been so unedifying that it is hard to see how he can rescue much dignity."[13] A South African daily ran an article under the headline "Botha Stands Alone" and editorialized that Botha's defiance was "quite irrational. The real interests of this country . . . are certainly more crucial than *the quirks of a fading strongman reluctant to let go of power.*"[14] Over the next several months, there was a standoff between Botha and de Klerk, and ill feelings between the two grew. A South African professor of political studies observed, "In the past five months, P. W. Botha has done everything he could to hamstring his successor. This shows how even astute leaders like P. W. Botha lose touch with reality. He clearly ought to have retired with honor after he had his stroke."[15] The government-supported newspaper *Citizen* referred to Botha as "totally unpredictable . . . yesterday's man" and urged de Klerk to "be strong in the showdown with the president."[16] Finally, on August 15, 1989, the embittered seventy-three-year-old president resigned. Appearing gaunt and nervous, he complained petulantly in his resignation speech, "It is evident to me that after all these years of my best efforts for the National Party and for the government of this country . . . I am being ignored by ministers serving in my cabinet. I consequently have no choice other than to announce my resignation."[17]

How sad, as the South African academic quoted above observed, that he could not retire with honor after his stroke, for he had during his eleven-year rule made quiet but significant progress in granting increased power and political participation to the nation's black majority while preserving the rights of the white minority. But his dream had not been achieved. Indeed, Botha was in fact "a fading strongman reluctant to let go of power."[18]

The exercise of power and control gave meaning to Pieter Botha's life. To yield the reins of power was akin psychologically to forfeiting life itself. To acknowledge his incapacity as a leader was akin to yielding to death's embrace. In denying his incapacity and fighting for his personal survival, Botha gravely damaged his nation.

The Narcissistic Personality and the End of Life

I have no spur
To prick the sides of my intent but only
Vaulting ambition, which o'erleaps itself
—Shakespeare, *Macbeth*

The love of power is the love of ourselves.
—William Hazlitt, *Political Essays*

Death always comes too soon, but when a leader has established a timetable to achieve his mark in history and the shadow of mortal illness abbreviates that schedule, it is especially threatening. Confronted with the approaching end of his life, he will experience a feeling of urgency to accomplish his goals for the nation before his time runs out. Thus his personal timetable takes precedence over his nation's timetable.

The specter of the end of life may ignite a frantic last-ditch attempt to ensure immortality, rather than despair. So Mao at the end of his days instigated the Cultural Revolution. But Mao's excesses affected the People's Republic almost exclusively. His terminal spasm pales by comparison with the international consequences precipitated when the shah of Iran learned he was afflicted with a form of cancer of the white blood cells.

The Shah's Quest for Glory: Terminal Urgency

In chapter 1, we described how the shah concealed from public view and from his principal ally in the West, the United States, that he was attempting to lead his embattled nation while fighting cancer and the debilitating effects of chemotherapy. Unaware that the shah was seriously ill, the United States government, which received almost all of its information from the shah's inner circle, once again banked on his ability to exercise effective leadership and resist the rising tide of discontent that threatened his regime.* His inability to do so paved the way for the Islamic revolution.

In fact, we believe that the psychological effects of his illness had an even more important impact on the shah's leadership than the debilitating physical effects of the disease and its treatment. Learning first that he was seriously ill and then that he had cancer and that his lifespan would be foreshortened meant realizing he would not have time to achieve his place in history.

The shah had spelled out his dreams for his nation, what he called the "White Revolution," in 1960 in his book *Mission for My Country*. He

*The U.S. government had acquiesced to the shah's demand that it utilize SAVAK as its source of intelligence and not independently mount intelligence operations.

believed that his firm leadership was necessary to achieve his ambitious plan to modernize Iran. He wished to turn over the reins of leadership to his son only when his mission for the country had been accomplished, which would require patience and persistence over many years. Then in his early forties, the shah assumed that he would live into his seventies or eighties, with two, three, or even four decades to shepherd Iran's advance into the twentieth century.

The shah became seriously ill in 1973.[19] He declined alcoholic beverages, citing "dyspepsia." He was observed to be gaunt and drawn, but that was attributed to the stresses of office. Early in 1974, the shah noticed a swelling in his abdomen. When his Iranian physicians found a massively enlarged liver and spleen, they called in French specialists, who informed him in April 1974 that he was afflicted with Waldenstrom's macroglobulinemia, a rare disease that could ultimately prove fatal.

Though his physicians had soft-pedaled the diagnosis and assisted in maintaining a veil of denial concerning the gravity of the illness, the shah knew. He had been confronted with his mortality. It was unlikely that he would live as long as ten years. Clearly, his plan for his country's development could not be accomplished in his lifetime.

The year the shah became seriously ill, 1973, was the year he broke with OPEC (the Organization of Petroleum Exporting Countries), leading to a quadrupling of oil prices. The sudden infusion of vast oil revenues into an economy with a poorly prepared infrastructure led to massive societal dislocations and a revolution of rising expectations.

The shah was playing a desperate game, gambling that he could speed up the White Revolution and yet control it, hoping to accomplish his goals in his few remaining years.* But the forces he unleashed were powerful, and rather than harvest the gratitude of the Iranian people for his dedicated leadership, he was to reap the whirlwind. Employing skillful vitriolic demagoguery, the Ayatollah Khomeini developed an unlikely coalition of peasants and the members of the bazaari, or merchant class. These disparate sectors of the polity were united only in their common hatred of the shah and their common desire to end his rule.

---

*Demonstrating the sense of urgency that consumed the shah, Seyyed Nasr, former president of Aryamehr University, recalls meeting with the shah in late 1973 to make a major budgetary request for a new campus. Expecting the shah to counter with a lower figure, Nasr was startled when the shah replied, "You may have it all, and even more. But spend it as quickly as you can" (personal communication with Seyyed Nasr, May 14, 1992).

As protests mounted, many urged the shah to deal with his opponents with an iron fist, as his father would have done. The ravages of illness, powerful medication, and American exhortations to observe the civil rights of his opponents weakened his resolve, and his obsession with the continuity of the throne constrained him from employing ruthless methods to suppress the Islamic revolt. He told friends and allies in the final months of his rule that he was determined not to unleash the full force of the army and secret police against the Iranian people, because he hoped that some day Iran would turn again to his dynasty. After the victory of the Islamic Revolution, he wrote from exile,

> I am told today that I should have applied martial law more forcefully. This would have cost my country less dear than the bloody anarchy now established there. But a sovereign cannot save his throne by spilling blood of his fellow-countrymen. A dictator can do it because he acts in the name of an ideology which he believes he must make triumphant, no matter what the price. A sovereign is not a dictator. There is between him and his people an alliance which he cannot break. A dictator has nothing to pass on: power belongs to him and him alone. A sovereign receives a crown. I could envisage my son mounting the throne in my own lifetime.[20]

Like Mao Zedong, Shah Mohammed Reza would not let the approach of death frustrate his quest for immortality, but in trying to consolidate his White Revolution for his son, he inadvertently paved the way for Khomeini's Islamic revolution. Consumed by urgency to accomplish his mission for Iran in the few years remaining to him, the shah in his headlong rush to glory ensured instead the failure of that mission.

Begin of Israel: Fighting for His Country
from a Hospital Bed

Before he yielded to terminal despair, Menachem Begin had fought with single-minded devotion for his nation, despite fragile health. His three coronaries and stroke were pointed reminders that his time was limited and that his lifelong dream of a Jewish homeland at peace would not be achieved in his lifetime. Like Moses, he would not enter that promised land. But if he could not achieve an Israel at peace, then in the time remaining he would fight to ensure a secure Jewish state. As each illness underlined the brevity of his remaining time, in the wake of serious illness came some of his most dramatic political moves. Two of Begin's most controversial political actions not only occurred in relation to his illness but were decided from his hospital bed.

In May 1980 the popular defense minister Ezer Weizman resigned, culminating a fractious dispute within Likud inner circles. Weizman had pushed for a more flexible and conciliatory posture toward the Palestinians, considering trading land for peace, but Begin had rigidly resisted, insisting on the integrity of the biblical land of Israel:

There are some people who suggest that there will be a Palestinian state ruled by that Mr. Arafat in the mountains of Samaria and Judaea overlooking the valley of the Mediterranean, in which two-thirds of our people are being concentrated, and from those mountains they will be able to reach every city and town—Tel Aviv, Jaffa, Rehovot, Giv'atayim, Bene Beraq—not only by the Soviet guns and tanks but even with machine guns, and the infamous Katyushas. They were very famous in the days of Stalingrad, but now they are infamous because they are being supplied by the communists to the murderous PLO in order to shed our blood in this generation, in which we have suffered so much and lost so many. Should we turn over this part of our land of our forefathers to those who want and swear that they would strike to liquidate the Zionist entity, to liquidate us, the Jewish state, the little state which brought in Jews from four corners of the world and moulded them into one renascent nation? I don't think that any man of good will, any man in his good sense would give such advice to us.[21]

In June 1980 Begin suffered a minor coronary occlusion. While recuperating in the hospital, he became obsessed with the need to declare unambiguously to the world his commitment to the integrity of the biblical land of Israel. To his doctor's dismay, he received political advisers daily. From his hospital bed he crafted a statement read to the press on July 6.[22] "It is the national consensus and the policy of the Government of Israel that Jerusalem, which has been reunited as a result of a successful legitimate self-defense, will remain forever united, forever indivisible, and forever the capital city of the State of Israel by virtue of right." This was a highly provocative and unnecessary statement, coming as it did during an American presidential campaign. It led to tension with the United States, Israel's strongest supporter. It also strengthened the hands of the Arab states that wished to perpetuate the state of hostility with Israel, for they could point to Israel's intransigence to justify their own. When Begin was released from the hospital on July 14, he endorsed the statement and spoke again of his vision of Jerusalem as Israel's capital. "If the Arab countries recognize the State of Israel and Jerusalem as its capital, 20 Arab flags would fly in Jerusalem, the capital of Israel, which would be recognized by all the Arab countries."[23]

On November 26, 1981, Begin tripped in the bathroom of his home and fell. He suffered a fractured hip, a frequent affliction of the aged, requiring surgical repair. The postoperative hospital stay was painful. During this hospitalization, too, he became preoccupied with Israel's security. On

December 14, the day of his discharge, Begin asked Ariel Sharon to cancel a planned trip to Jerusalem and called an emergency meeting of the Cabinet. Still in his hospital bathrobe, he announced the extension of Israeli law to the Golan Heights, the equivalent of annexation.[24] The Golan Heights, which had been captured from Syria in the 1967 war, had long been a source of menace to Israel, with nightly rocket bombardments of the helpless settlements to the south in northern Galilee. "Never again," vowed Begin, would Israel be exposed to that mortal danger. Once again, physical weakness had precipitated a politically "strong" response, an affirmation of Begin's lifelong creed, "I fight, therefore I am!"

Psychologically, Begin's aim was to establish an identity with an eternally secure Israel. Physically weak, he was demonstrating his strength as a leader. But politically, like the annexation of East Jerusalem, this provocative policy damaged Israel's standing in the West and Begin's ability to deal with moderate Arab governments.

Charles de Gaulle of France: Terminal Grandiosity

Charles de Gaulle, like Menachem Begin, identified himself with his country and devoted his entire life to it. And as was true of Begin, the waning of his physical health led him to exaggerated political actions. De Gaulle's absolute faith in his own greatness meant that he never doubted France's eventual victory over its many conquerors and would-be conquerors: the Germans, the Anglo-Saxons (as he called the Americans and the British), self-seeking French politicians, France's European partners, and even the radical French youth of the 1960s. De Gaulle would overcome them all.

De Gaulle's identification with France was shaped in his family home. His father, a schoolmaster, was such an ardent nationalist that he never permitted his children to learn English. With his encouragement, de Gaulle chose a military career, becoming an outstanding student at the military schools of Saint-Cyr and the Ecole de Guerre.

Throughout his life, de Gaulle set himself apart. He chose his few friends with care. His biographer, de Launay (1968), has attempted to explain de Gaulle's apparent aloof arrogance. It was, he observes, not so much that de Gaulle felt others to be his inferiors as that they were merely ordinary human begins, whereas de Gaulle believed himself to represent France. Indeed, he declared, "J'etais la France." This explanation, of course, confirms the lofty narcissistic pedestal from which de Gaulle viewed the world. His arrogant certainty conveyed strength to his followers but was the source of despair to other Allied leaders during World War II. Churchill once remarked that the heaviest cross the Allies had to bear was the Cross of Lorraine (the symbol of de Gaulle's Free French).[25]

This serene and stubborn grandeur not only supported de Gaulle after

France's defeat by Germany but was his armor against the maelstrom of French politics. As the political activist and intellectual Françoise Mauriac wrote,

As for those whose profession was politics, who constituted the fauna of committees and congresses, they discovered what was to be their tragedy. This meteoric general, the product of Saint-Cyr and the École de Guerre, seemed to them the incarnation of all that was most hateful: the absolute preponderance of the State, the cult of the nation, the indifference to ideologies, the mistrust of political parties, plus an antagonism to them personally and a determination to dominate, to defy, and if possible, to destroy them. The professional politicians understood on that day of the liberation of Paris that this man would be their tragedy. This staff of iron would not bend. They would have to take him or leave him, as we say, but the history that began that day, and that is still being made, would come down to this: each time they rejected him, they would be obliged to take him back, on pain of death. This insupportable man was an inevitable man.[26]

De Gaulle was sixty-seven in 1958 when he agreed to become something very close to dictator of France in order to put down the revolt of French army officers in Algeria and so avoid civil war. His leadership was strong and highly personal. During the next decade, the identification of France with de Gaulle was reaffirmed. But over this decade, his reactions were to become increasingly extreme.

Even the normal decline of once-powerful abilities foreshadowing death is likely to create overcompensation. Charles de Gaulle's inflammatory exhortations for an independent Quebec during the summer of 1967 were considered by his opponents to be the cries of a man on the edge of senility. One commentator quipped that "liberté, égalité, sénilité" was the motto of de Gaulle's government.

De Gaulle's actions, however, did not represent aberrational behavior in the face of senility. They were in continuity with his political style, attitudes, and behavior over the years, *only more so*. Le grand Charles was, if anything, grander than ever. He was beginning to parody himself.

Studies of the life cycle of political leaders do not support the notion that old age brings a mellowing.[27] In fact, especially for narcissistic individuals, as a man grows older, he becomes more like himself. The same drives and needs that impelled the individual throughout his life are still present, only now the time is short, and for some the inhibitory effect of judgment is reduced. De Gaulle's exaggerated behavior in the twilight of his political career is quite consistent with this pattern.

A careful review of his political behavior during his last years in office suggests a direct relation between his failing physical powers and his exaggerated political moves. At almost seventy-nine, de Gaulle's eyesight was progressively deteriorating. Three years earlier, in 1964, he had submitted to prostate surgery. Though he was by no means showing symptoms of senility, observers noted that he had lost his edge. Particularly when he was made aware of his diminished stature as a world leader or of his failing power as a physically healthy and mentally alert man, he tended to behave in an exaggerated fashion to reaffirm his mastery. He would not be ignored. The weaker he felt physically, the more secondary France seemed politically, the grander were de Gaulle's moves.

He was again in power in May 1968, when an intense student rebellion seemed for a time to threaten revolution. His supreme self-confidence, a reflection of his narcissistic personality, and his great political ability had permitted him to stand his ground until then. The student protest was particularly painful for de Gaulle; he thrived on public adulation. During the events of May his narcissistic belief in the indispensability of his own leadership came into conflict not only with his political perception but also with his grudging acknowledgment of his ill health. Should he remain a rod of iron and face down his opponents or should he defeat them by sacrificing his office?

De Gaulle chose the path of self-sacrifice in his nation's interest. He removed himself as an issue by resigning his office. Though some have seen this as genuine self-sacrifice, the act had a petulant quality. Always convinced of his own rectitude, de Gaulle, especially in his later years, felt contempt for anyone who disagreed with him and was impervious to constructive criticism. But he did remove himself as a focus of contention. He deflected the protests into peaceful and legitimate channels by calling for national elections. De Gaulle did what so few national leaders do when faced with illness and national revolt: he stepped aside, averting national disorder and perhaps even revolution and civil war.

The narcissistic identification of a leader with the nation often makes it impossible for that leader to step aside. In the case of de Gaulle, it was that very identification that permitted him to step down, for he recognized that the destiny of his nation, his France, required it. But to be turned out of office by the nation to which he had dedicated his life was painful, and he spent his remaining two years of life isolated and embittered. De Gaulle the private citizen died in the autumn of 1970.

The Soviet Gerontocracy: Terminal Paralysis

In a hierarchical, highly authoritarian system, the illness of the leader in effect decapitates the state. To be sure, in the Soviet Union, there was a tradition of consensual decision-making, but the Communist party chairman's role was an extremely powerful one. Before—and setting the stage for—the vigorous transformational leadership of Mikhail Gorbachev, the Soviet Union was virtually paralyzed by a succession of aged, ailing leaders.

Leonid Il'ich Brezhnev became head of state in 1960 at age fifty-three and was elevated to general secretary of the Communist party in 1964. He held this position for eighteen years, until his death just before his seventy-sixth birthday. But after a coronary in 1975, Brezhnev's health deteriorated and he was never the same. For several years before his death, he suffered from generalized arteriosclerosis, including involvement of the arteries of the brain. This led to a decline in his intellectual functioning and leadership. He was progressively infirm and had trouble speaking. His work load was significantly reduced, and for the last two years of his life he was essentially a figurehead.

Boris Yeltsin, who was to become Russia's first elected president, consistently criticized the inefficiency of the Soviet leadership. He has vividly described Brezhnev's style of leadership in his final years. This description contains an example par excellence of the syndrome of the captive king and his captive court:

Here's a typical example of how the country was run in those days. We needed to get a top-level decision on the construction of a subway system. Sverdlovsk was, after all, a city of 1,200,000 inhabitants. We needed permission from the Politburo, and I decided to go to Brezhnev. . . . I had been told how to handle him, so I prepared a text to which he had only to add his signature for approval. I went into his office and we talked for literally five or six minutes. . . . He was incapable of drafting the document himself. He said to me, "Just dictate what I should write." So of course I dictated it to him: "Instruction by the Politburo to prepare a draft decree authorizing the construction of a metro in Sverdlovsk." He wrote what I had said, signed it, and gave me the piece of paper. Knowing that even with Brezhnev's signature, some documents might be misplaced or disappear altogether, I told him, "No, you should call your aide." He summoned an assistant, and I said to Brezhnev, "Give him your instructions that he must first enter the documents in the registry and then take the necessary official steps to ensure that your instructions to distribute it to the Politburo members are carried out." He did all this; the aide collected the papers; and Brezhnev and I said goodbye.

The incident was typical and revealing. *In the last phase of his life, Brezhnev, in my opinion, had no idea what he was doing, signing, or saying. All the power was in the hands of his entourage.* He had signed the document authorizing the construction of the Sverdlovsk metro without giving any thought to the meaning of what I was dictating. Granted, as a result of that signature a good deed was done. . . . *But how many of the rogues and cheats, indeed plain criminals, who surrounded Brezhnev exploited him for their own dishonest purposes? How many treaties or decrees did he calmly, unthinkingly sign, bringing riches to a few and suffering to many?*[28]

While the circle around him made accommodations, there was a virtual paralysis of leadership in the face of Brezhnev's growing incapacity. He died in 1982 at age seventy-five. Brezhnev's terminal incapacity produced pressure for a more youthful successor. Factional disputes, however, led to the appointment of another aged ailing leader to succeed Brezhnev—Iaril (Yuri) Vladimiravitch Andropov, who had served as Brezhnev's KGB director for fifteen years.

At the time he was designated to succeed Brezhnev in November 1982, Andropov, sixty-eight, was already seriously ill with kidney disease. So the leadership paralysis characteristic of Brezhnev's last years continued during Andropov's brief reign, which was, for the most part, a death watch, punctuated by lengthy medical absences. Pallid and frail when elected CPSU chairman, Andropov was in power for only fifteen months and spent the last six of these in the hospital. The metabolic imbalance characteristic of serious kidney illness typically produces a clouded mental state and would have seriously impaired his decision-making. Andropov died of kidney failure at age sixty-nine.

The factional striving for his successor led to the appointment of yet another aged, ailing leader as a transitional figure, Konstantin Ustinovich Chernenko.

Konstantin Chernenko: Terminal Détente

We have earlier observed how the intolerable prospect of the end of life for Mao Zedong contributed to the convulsions of the Cultural Revolution and how the prospect of death accelerated the shah of Iran's attempt to consolidate his place in history. Chernenko had not made his mark in history when he was named general secretary of the Communist party. He, too, attempted to achieve an honored place in his nation's history. But unlike the dramatic efforts of Mao Zedong and the shah of Iran, Chernenko's were gentle, for the most part attempting to set a new tone and ultimately to no avail. Enfeebled when he took office, facing the end of his life clearly contributed to his endorsement of détente.

Well before 1984, Chernenko had developed emphysema, chronic obstructive pulmonary disease, and right-sided heart failure, conditions that could only be expected to become more severe and debilitating. Yet he was elected general secretary in 1984, not despite these major health problems but precisely because of them.

The struggle to succeed Andropov between supporters of the conservative Grigori Romanov and those of Mikhail Gorbachev was so fierce and the forces were so balanced that a deadlock resulted. The only other eligible candidate who was a member of both the Politburo and the Secretariat was the seventy-two-year-old Chernenko. Members of the old guard—Dimitri Ustinov (seventy-six), Nikolai Tikhonov (seventy-nine), and Andrei Gromyko (seventy-five)—were reluctant to accept a new generation of leadership and distrusted a leader as young as Gorbachev (fifty-two), yet they feared that Romanov would be insufficiently responsive to their collective authority. Accordingly, they pressed for a transitional chairmanship by Chernenko, believing that the previously undistinguished leader would at least continue the policies of Brezhnev. It was, after all, his commitment to communist ideology and a thirty-year association with Brezhnev that had brought him to the Kremlin. Both Gorbachev and Romanov also supported a Chernenko interregnum, for neither had had time to shore up sufficient support for himself.

Because Chernenko seemed most fulfilled in the role of follower, both the old and the new guard probably believed that they had nothing to fear from his leadership and would be able to manipulate him, especially in view of his failing health. The regime was well aware of Chernenko's medical problems; the day after Andropov's funeral, Dr. Yevgeny Chazov, director of the Kremlin medical clinic, ran a computer search seeking information concerning pulmonary disorders, especially emphysema and asthma, apparently specifically for Chernenko's disorders.

Before being elected to the Soviet Union's highest position, Chernenko was known as one of "the butchers of Stalin's great terror of 1937."[29] In Dnepropetrovsk, as deputy personnel chief of the NKVD, the Soviet secret police, Chernenko played a leading role with his comrade-in-arms Leonid Brezhnev. This surely was not a predictor of a commitment to détente on assuming the position of party chairman, yet this is exactly what Chernenko developed. We believe that the gravity of Chernenko's health problems and his recognition that his career had previously been undistinguished by notable achievements were major factors in Chernenko's decision to marshal his faltering energies in the service of détente.

In the year before his election as chairman, Chernenko was absent from official duties for three months because of bronchitis, pleurisy, and pneumonia. Also demonstrating that health was weighing on his mind and was influencing his political perspective were a book by Chernenko that appeared that year, *Establishing the Leninist Style in Party Work* (1983), and a major address he delivered to the CPSU Central Committee on June 14, 1983.[30] The texts are strewn with references to vigor, vitality, struggle, superiority, and well-being as well as wishes to enrich, strengthen, and succeed. Although these statements were made in a political context, the choice of words contrasts with the failing health of the author. Chernenko commented, "Human health, vitality and mood depend not on medicine alone" and recommended that individuals attend to their health, through, for example, participation in sports.[31] This may have reflected a rueful wish for Chernenko, for whom each breath was a struggle. Chernenko had begun smoking at age nine, and despite his emphysema, continued to smoke nonstop. At a Politburo meeting during the Andropov years, Andropov himself rebuked Chernenko for befouling the atmosphere.[32]

The regime was successful at first in concealing the gravity of Chernenko's health problems from the West, but soon a public preoccupation with Chernenko's health dominated his term in office, the third death watch in a row. His fragile health and diminished stamina were manifest in his public appearances shortly after he returned to Moscow in February 1984. In his inaugural speech, he spoke in short gasps, breathing very rapidly, and could barely raise his arms to salute Soviet troops marching past the reviewing stand. Foreign medical experts noted his shortness of breath, hunched shoulders, difficulty saluting, and irregular speech, all suggesting advanced pulmonary disease.[33]

Chernenko delivered a major speech in March 1984 on Soviet-U.S. relationship. But the effect of his words was overcome by his blatant difficulty in speaking. Not only was he breathing heavily throughout the speech, but a break in concentration was so confusing for Chernenko that he overlooked the most crucial page of the text. He failed to recognize his error and continued with the address.[34] A month later Chernenko was seen in the Kremlin hospital, although it was reported that he was there to visit an ailing comrade, Tikhonov, rather than for his own health.[35]

In May, during a meeting in Moscow with King Juan Carlos of Spain, Chernenko appeared frail and tired. He had to be helped from his limousine by two aides, had trouble buttoning his coat, and moved around "like an automaton or a bear, with arms dangling and an absent-minded air."[36] His hunched shoulders, uneasy breathing, and occasional difficulty in raising his arms confirmed the earlier impressions of advanced emphysema. In another speech from which he omitted the key passages, he stumbled and stuttered, frequently lost his place, and showed labored breathing. During the opening session of an important congress in June, he had two "sick spells" in close succession, causing him to break off his speech twice.[37] After that, his speeches were read by announcers.

The more serious Chernenko's condition, the more intense the efforts to cover it up. The emergency room visit and hospitalization were not initially reported. The official Moscow line was that the general secretary was on holiday, but he was out of sight for more than a month, extremely unusual considering his recent assumption of power. Belying Chernenko's "holiday," Chernenko's son returned from Greece to the Soviet Union, and an officially planned trip to France by Gorbachev was also canceled with no explanation.[38] In mid-February, Dr. Yevgeny Chazov, director general of the Soviet Cardiology Research Center, who had earlier claimed that his presence in the United States refuted the "rumors" of Chernenko's ill health, was recalled to Moscow.[39] Chernenko then developed heart irregularities, but the medical cover-up continued. A late February photo purportedly showing Chernenko voting in a polling place was shown on analysis to have been taken in Moscow's Kuntsev Hospital. In a public appearance at the end of February, Chernenko sat slumped in a chair, exhausted, and speaking with difficulty.

Konstantin Chernenko died on March 11, 1985. The autopsy showed chronic emphysema, an enlarged, damaged heart, congestive heart failure, and cirrhosis of the liver (which could have resulted either from alcoholism or from chronic heart failure).[40] A consequence of the emphysema and heart failure would have been chronic oxygen deprivation, which would have affected Chernenko's mental functioning and decision-making.

Chernenko's thirteen months in office were marked by advanced pulmonary and cardiac illness. Yet despite, or because of, his grave illness, the climate between the Soviet Union and the United States improved noticeably during his brief period of leadership. The chill of 1984 was epitomized by the Soviet boycott of the Olympics and the U.S. reaction to the Soviet banishment of the dissident scientist Andrei Sakharov. But Chernenko negotiated deals on trade and other exchanges and was ardent, if short of breath, in his speeches in calling for reduction of tensions between the superpowers. Chernenko was no Gorbachev; health, temperament, and the politics of the period prevented him from doing more, but he did push for a major improvement in U.S.-Soviet relations until his last gasp.

Sclerosis in the Eastern Bloc: Aging Autocrats

> Dictators ride to and fro upon tigers which they dare
> not dismount. And the tigers are getting hungry.
> —Sir Winston Churchill, *While Eagles Slept*

The remarkable story of the dramatic collapse of Eastern European socialist states is at one level the story of the refusal of aging autocratic communist leaders to give up power and their inability to respond flexibly to the tides of political change. An aging, sclerotic political system led to the selection of aging, sclerotic leaders. These leaders were unwilling to transform the system that so faithfully mirrored them.

The stagnation of leadership was even more pronounced in Eastern Europe than in the Soviet Union. In many cases, the same leader had been in place since socialist governments were established at the end of World War II. The actuarial statistics for this group are striking. The average age of the leaders of Eastern Europe was seventy-six years at the end of their rule, and the mean duration of their control of their countries was twenty-seven years. This is not a recipe for innovative response to rapidly changing unprecedented situations. These are the statistics not of stability but of stagnation.

For most of these leaders, how they came to power and exercised leadership inevitably linked them symbolically to totalitarian response in the minds of their citizens even if they were otherwise disposed. This was particularly true of Erich Honecker of East Germany, who erected the Berlin Wall; Gustav Husák of Czechoslovakia, who crushed the Prague spring; and János Kádár of Hungary, who invited Soviet troops to snuff out the nascent revolution in his country. The wisdom of the aged leader derives from having a long historical perspective from which to view events. The hazard is that with advancing age, leaders tend to see the present in terms of the past and to look to the past for solutions when the circumstances are actually quite different and call for new and innovative responses. At times of crisis in particular, aged leaders are apt to call on the leadership behaviors that brought them success in their prime. The exodus from East Berlin in 1988–89 reminded Erich Honecker of his success in stemming the westward flow of refugees in the late 1950s by building the Berlin Wall. Rather than respond with flexibility as the new winds of democracy swept across Eastern Europe, he responded with the rigidity of the aged and the repressiveness that had marked his career.

Honecker of the German Democratic Republic: Terminal Crisis

When serious illness suddenly strikes a controlling autocratic chief of state, the leadership of the nation is seriously impaired. When the illness coincides with a moment of political crisis, the consequences can be catastrophic. Such was the case in the German Democratic Republic during the summer of 1989.

Serious incapacitating illness struck the seventy-seven-year-old Communist party chairman Erich Honecker during a Warsaw Pact meeting in Bucharest on July 14, 1989. He did not return to the seat of government until September 25. During that long, hot summer of discontent, the pro-democracy virus sweeping through Eastern Europe spread to East Germany. His government, paralyzed by the medical absence of their autocratic leader, was unable to respond, and the Wall came tumbling down.

Honecker was a member of that generation of revolutionary Marxists who witnessed the rise and fall of European communism. To understand Honecker's resistance to liberalization, the crisis of 1989 must be viewed in the context of his life in the party. Honecker joined the Communist party at age seventeen, was sent to a party school in the Soviet Union, and returned as a party youth leader who went underground to fight the Nazis. Arrested by the Gestapo two years later, he was charged with high treason and sentenced to ten years' imprisonment in Brandenburg Prison. Freed just before the Nazis capitulated in 1945, Honecker returned to Berlin to organize the communist youth organization Free German Youth. He rose rapidly in the ranks, soon becoming a top member of the Socialist Unity party, which assumed power in 1949 when the Soviet Union converted its postwar zone of occupation into the East German state, the German Democratic Republic.

Honecker was promoted to the ruling Politburo in 1958 and placed in charge of East German security forces. Three years later, as thousands of East Germans streamed to the West in search of a better life, a search to be replayed twenty-eight years later, party leader Walter Ulbricht ordered Honecker to erect the Berlin Wall to stop the emigration. This act consolidated Honecker's reputation for taking firm action in the Stalinist mode. By 1970 Ulbricht's strident calls for austerity had led to social unrest and political discontent, and in the following year Ulbricht, who had ruled for eighteen years, was ousted in favor of Honecker, who was to reign for another eighteen years. The act that brought Honecker to the acme of power was erecting that monument to totalitarianism, the Berlin Wall. Thus Honecker had been devoted to a particularly repressive form of communism in East Germany. It was a devotion that had rewarded him well.

For Honecker to abandon communism would be to abandon an essential part of himself. Given his past commitments and actions, Honecker's natural reaction when challenged was to respond with uncompromising force. Honecker identified himself with East Germany, with communism, and with Stalinism. To destroy any one of this trinity would be to destroy all. And because his leadership was so personally controlling and autocratic, Honecker's absence was keenly felt during the summer of 1989. Bold moves were required to respond to the rapidly moving events, and Honecker's subordinates could not act decisively in his absence.

The illness that struck Honecker on July 14 during the Warsaw Pact meeting was an acute abdominal emergency. Initially hospitalized in Bucharest with a "severe gallstone attack," he was medically evacuated to a hospital in East Berlin for three days and released. There were hints that his condition was worse than was being reported, for his deputy, Egon

Krenz, canceled a planned visit to China.[41] On August 18, Honecker underwent gall bladder surgery. A routine cholecystectomy (gall bladder removal) typically requires one to two weeks of hospital care, but Honecker was slow to recover, for reasons that emerged only later. During the surgery, cancer involving the gall bladder and intestine apparently was found, and an extensive surgical resection was required. The gravity of Honecker's illness was concealed, although the length of his recuperation led to speculation that he would not return to office. When it became apparent that the surgery had not been curative and that Honecker remained seriously ill, Krenz began to mobilize forces to prepare the way for his accession to power.

That August, East Germans vacationing in Hungary discovered that they were able to cross the boundary between East and West without interference by the Hungarian border guards. After Honecker attempted to halt the exodus by refusing permission for East Germans to travel to Hungary, thousands drove to Prague, abandoned their cars, and jumped the back fence of the West German embassy. At least a thousand more sought sanctuary in the West German embassy in Warsaw. The East German leadership did nothing to stem this tide.

On September 10, a news report circulated that Honecker's surgery had been unsuccessful and that his health had worsened considerably. He was reported to "show no spiritual buoyancy or will to recover" and to be "having difficulty maintaining his concentration."[42] Rumors circulate that the discovery of cancer at the time of the first surgery had made it impossible to remove the gall bladder; instead, resection of the cancerous colon (large intestine) was carried out, and a second operation had been required (probably true, for resection of the colon is often done in two stages).

During his extended recovery Honecker was kept informed of the mass uncontrolled emigration but was accused by the Politburo of being rigid and of not understanding the significance and extent of the exodus. In Honecker's continuing absence, his government seemed unable to function. "It seems to be staring as if paralyzed at what is going on. Apparently the illness of the chairman plays a certain role there," said West German Minister for Internal Affairs Dorothee Wilms. "So far there have not even been indications the East German government is thinking about reforms."[43]

The leader's personality is especially likely to influence political behavior in a crisis, when followers look to the leader for strong and effective direction. The more autocratic the leader, the more his absence will be felt. So strong and controlling was Honecker's leadership that the state could not function in his absence.

Moreover, the strict hierarchy within the party apparatus and the leaders' desire to protect their positions in anticipation of a possible shake-up kept potential reformers from asserting themselves. Adding to the paralysis, several of Honecker's peers were ailing. The diabetes of Günter Mittag, minister of economic affairs, led to the amputation of a leg. Prime Minister Willi Stoph, also in his seventies, was suffering from a chronic stomach ailment. The conservative West German newspaper *Die Welt* editorialized: "A lot in East Berlin reminds one of the last months of Brezhnev and Chernenko. . . . State and party leadership is paralyzed."[44]

As Honecker slowly recovered, his followers looked to him to take charge in his characteristically firm manner. Six weeks after surgery, Honecker returned from his lengthy medical absence, but he appeared weak and fragile in his first public appearance, on September 26. His initial political moves were ineffectual. On October 1, for example, in an effort to reduce tensions, he permitted refugees to emigrate by train. But this was too little and too late. His weak appearance and performance magnified the crisis, strengthened the opposition, and imparted the feeling that events were going out of control.

In early October, violence broke out as East Germans desperate for freedom forced their way onto trains carrying their compatriots to West Germany. At this moment of crisis, the inspiration for reform in the Eastern Bloc, Soviet premier Mikhail Gorbachev, arrived on the scene, purportedly to help celebrate the fortieth anniversary of the founding of the German Democratic Republic. Honecker went to Schönfeld Airport to greet Gorbachev, "walking with a deliberate jauntiness to show that he was in good health."[45] According to party insiders, however, Honecker had no grasp on the situation. More than 100,000 East Germans had left for West Germany in the preceding twelve months to escape the grayness, oppression, and lack of opportunity within East Germany, but Honecker did not even acknowledge the exodus, which Egon Krenz later called "a great bloodletting."[46] Despite advice to reform from within and from outside the party, he stubbornly insisted that he was on the right course and would brook no leniency. He told a Chinese visitor that any attempt to change his course was "nothing more than Don Quixote's futile running against the steadily turning sails of a windmill."[47]

As Gorbachev stood on the podium next to Honecker, the contrast could not have been more vivid. The vital, self-confident Soviet leader, the symbol of hope and reform, stood beside the white-haired, obviously frail Honecker, the representative of Stalinist totalitarianism and resistance to change. In his speech, Honecker extolled the glorious past of the state, praised its achievements, indicated that it was on the right path, and criticized West Germany for fomenting disorder. Gorbachev, in contrast, spoke of the need to develop "beneficial" relations with West Germany, predicted a glowing future for Eastern Europe, and emphasized the need for "progressive" changes.[48] Praise for Honecker, which the situation required, was notable by its absence. Cheering crowds chanted, "Gorby, Gorby," leading one East German official to comment wryly, "It looks as if they wish you to liberate them again."[49]

During the three-hour meeting between Gorbachev and Honecker that followed, there were massive protests in Leipzig, Cologne, and Berlin. The West German newspaper *Bild* reported that the regime was planning large-scale expulsions.[50] Seeing the weakness of Honecker's position but also noting his unwillingness to respond to the crisis, Gorbachev decided to undermine Honecker's leadership and extend his support to Egon Krenz in whatever actions Krenz took to rescue the rapidly deteriorating situation.

More violence occurred in Leipzig on October 9. Police officers and secret police had been issued live ammunition and had written orders, signed by Honecker, to shoot if necessary. Markus Wolf, the retired head of East German's spy agencies, called this "a Chinese solution," adding, "It could have been worse than Beijing."[51] Honecker's order to shoot was the last straw for those who opposed his leadership. It demonstrated his willingness to shed blood to preserve his rigid Stalinist system and showed that he did not understand the situation and could not respond flexibly to the crisis and the widespread pent-up frustration it represented. The security chief, Erich Mielke, remonstrated, "We can't beat up hundreds of thousands of people!"[52] But the seventy-seven-year-old communist leader would not be swayed; he insisted that his plan to use force on the demonstrators was the proper solution and ordered that it be carried out.

This was the turning point. With Gorbachev's support, Egon Krenz canceled Honecker's orders for a "Chinese solution." Honecker reacted with impotent anger and befuddlement, a broken man. Within ten days, stripped of authority, the aging, ailing Honecker had resigned. Although official East German accounts said that he had asked to be relieved of his position for health reasons, clearly he had been forced from office. A proud, inflexible autocrat clinging to the world of his past—no more unsuitable blend of psychological ingredients could have been found to respond to a nation's crisis, when what was necessary was the ability to communicate empathy, openness to new ideas, creativity, a willingness to change directions and admit that past solutions were no longer effective, and a flexible adaptive response.

President Jafar Nimeiri of Sudan: Terminal Religiosity

The death-bed religious conversion is not an uncommon personal reaction to a confrontation with mortal illness. But when a chief of state belatedly turns to the deity and makes his terminal religiosity the basis of national policy, the consequences for the country can be painful. Such was the case with Jafar Nimeiri of Sudan.

In 1969, after years of an ineffective democratic government, thirty-nine-year-old Jafar Nimeiri led a group of military officers in a successful coup d'état and assumed the leadership of Sudan. As with all successful coups, specific circumstances determined its success. In this case, it is relevant that it occurred on the eve of Nimeiri's fortieth birthday. The press to action is a frequent reaction to the midlife transition (ages thirty-eight to forty-three); a disproportionate number of leaders who assumed power by military coup have acted during this period of psychological flux.

Although Nimeiri portrayed himself as a lifelong Muslim in his revisionist history, *The Islamic Way, Why?* he was not particularly devout. He describes in the book how he and his colleagues prayed to Allah before the coup, but in fact they were intoxicated that night. (The *shari'a,* the codified Islamic law that governs the conduct of everyday life for devout Muslims, specifically proscribes alcohol use.) In his initial speech on assuming power, there was no sense of mission, no mention of Allah, no description of Sudan as an Islamic republic. Rather, he described the new regime as neither Eastern nor Western but a democratic socialist regime working for Sudan's interests alone.

In the early years of his leadership, Nimeiri devoted his energies to dealing with Sudan's longstanding social, economical, and political problems. He met with considerable success and improved Sudan's position both domestically and internationally. His greatest accomplishment was the Addis Ababa agreement of 1972, which ended seventeen years of civil war between the Islamic north and the largely Christian south. This achievement alone would have assured Nimeiri a prominent place in Sudan's history.

By exerting his influence against the Islamic fundamentalists and clerics, Nimeiri, espousing the belief that the south could remain culturally and religiously distinct, crafted a constitutional formulation that recognized and protected the south's unique status within a unified Sudan.[53] Article 8 specified autonomy for the south, with its own governmental and administrative structure, but most important were the guarantees of religious freedom. Article 16 declared Islam the religion of the Democratic Republic of the Sudan but recognized that a large number of citizens professed belief in Christianity. The constitution guaranteed that "heavenly religions and the noble aspects of spiritual beliefs shall not be abused or held in contempt." It expressly forbade "the abuse of religious and noble spiritual beliefs for political exploitation. . . . The State shall treat followers of religion and noble spiritual belief without discrimination and . . . shall not impose any restrictions on citizens or communities on the grounds of religious faith."[54]

Yet such discrimination and restrictions were exactly what occurred when Nimeiri became obsessed with religion in the face of mortal illness. In the late 1970s, while still in his mid-forties, Nimeiri began to experience drowsiness and confusional episodes, described as temporary dementia, and collapsed in public on several occasions. At first his illness was undiagnosed, but ultimately Nimeiri traveled to the United States and underwent a thorough medical evaluation at the Walter Reed Army Medical Center in 1979. The evaluation revealed that Nimeiri's longstanding diabetes mellitus was under poor control and that he had developed widespread arteriosclerosis, which was affecting circulation to the heart and brain. In addition to involvement of the coronary arteries, arteriosclerotic plaque had led to obstruction of the internal carotid artery, which provides the main blood supply to the brain—the cause of the mental symptoms.

Nimeiri returned to Walter Reed in 1980 for a three-week checkup to treat his heart ailment and better regulate his diabetes. He again returned later that year for surgery to remove the clot obstructing the carotid artery. On returning from this procedure, he informed his aides that his maintenance medication sometimes affected his mental faculties and judgment. Early in 1981, he announced that he would retire in August 1982 because of illness. Nevertheless, by January 1982, he had reconsidered, claiming to be indispensable to Sudan's future, and declared himself President for Life.

It was this siege of serious illness that prompted Nimeiri's turn to Islam. But Nimeiri was not content to apply this epiphany to himself alone. As he explained in *The Islamic Way, Why?* the way of Allah was the way for all of Sudan, and if some did not see that way, they would be shown it and made to walk it.[55] Islamic law began to be forced on all Sudanese, regardless of their religion, and regardless of the constitution.

When Nimeiri's health problems had begun in the mid-1970s, his local physicians had strongly recommended that he stop drinking alcohol, which they felt was contributing to his medical condition. With the onset of serious illness, not only did Nimeiri abstain, but he sent a circular entitled *Guided Leadership* to cabinet ministers and other senior officials instructing them to swear an oath to him that they, too, would abstain from alcohol. At the same time, Nimeiri, a deeply superstitious man, fell under the sway of Sufi mystics and, to the dismay of his cabinet officials, began to rely on witch doctors to divine the future and guide his policies. One of the holy men gave him a ring and walking stick to assure him divine protection.

To compensate for his growing physical enfeeblement, he spoke of his total power, as if he were a law unto himself: "Beware, I am empowered by the Constitution to take any measures I deem necessary for the protection of the May revolution." Pointing to a guard, he said, "According to the Constitution, I can order this guard to shoot anybody and he would have to obey me."[56]

Nimeiri's assumption of religious leadership was not confined to Sudan. In August 1981, he sent sermonizing open letters to both Hafez Asad of Syria and Muammar Qaddafi of Libya, instructing them to leave Lebanon alone, to stop burning people, and to side with Iraq in the Iran-Iraq war. They did not respond. When earthquakes struck Syria in December 1981, Nimeiri sent a message to Asad, explaining the natural disasters as divine punishment.

> The news of the disaster which has afflicted Damascus has been conveyed to us. God gives reprieve but does not forget. What has happened in Damascus is the result of your disregard for God's law and your attempt to extinguish the fire of the Qu'ran and the Light of Islam. Justice is the only way for establishing peace and the first principle of justice which God has decreed is the sanctity of human life and the futility of manslaughter without good cause and genocide without just trials. All these are against Islamic law. God, our destiny is in your hands.[57]

Further demonstrating both his lack of international political sensitivity and his proselytizing zeal, during a trip to the People's Republic of China, he tried to convert the Chinese to Islam.

As Nimeiri's health declined, the manifestations of his public religiosity grew more intense as he violated the Addis Ababa accord, dividing his country, and destroying the greatest achievement of his presidency. His leadership became increasingly personal and less institutional, and his Machiavellian manipulation of the factions within the system led to a progressive disintegration of the fragile unity he had achieved. But he had not yet strongly institutionalized Islamic practices into law, and many of his exhortations were greeted with a wink and a nod. This changed abruptly in 1983, when Nimeiri again traveled to the United States for surgery. Before the trip he talked to his military commanders about funeral arrangements. This forcible encounter with his mortality led to a major escalation in the pace of the Islamization of Sudan.

In September 1983, without warning he declared the shari'a the law of the land, including the largely Christian south. He introduced the shari'a dramatically by pouring millions of gallons of alcohol into the Nile. The shari'a was to be rigorously enforced, including flogging for possession of alcohol, amputation of the hand for theft, and death by stoning for women who committed adultery. Adultery had rarely been punished in Sudan, for the shari'a requires four witnesses to the adulterous event. Nimeiri, however, invented a new offense, attempted adultery, which did not have the same witness stipulations.

He fell increasingly under the sway of his spiritual mentors and was increasingly isolated from his secular advisers. Nimeiri's rule became more and more idiosyncratic, and so certain was he of the righteousness of his ways that he would not tolerate criticism. Indeed, those who criticized his policies would find themselves not only out of a job but liable to be imprisoned.

Nimeiri became preoccupied with his own role as spiritual leader for his nation, and his speeches increasingly showed that he had identified himself as the spiritual leader of Sudan, as its Imam. Beginning all his speeches with verses from the Koran, he regularly referred to his mission for his country, making it clear that his goal was to "establish the religion [Islam] amongst your ranks."[58] He prayed for God's help in carrying out his divinely ordained mission. He spoke about his enemies and the rumors they spread that he was ill by again quoting the Koran in such a way as to make it clear he identified himself with the Prophet.

The declaration of the shari'a and Nimeiri's divisive policies propagated under the sway of his religious advisers led to great civil unrest, prompting him to declare martial law in April 1984. He indicated that those in the south who had risen against him were also enemies of God. Though he pledged to carry out the shari'a mercifully, the specifics of his policies suggested the opposite: "Although Islam is the religion of forgiveness, the religion of brotherliness and the religion of honor and integrity, we will flog people publicly, we shall publish names in papers . . . because the Muslim hates to hear his name. . . . We shall continue to publish . . . to flog . . . to amputate hands . . . until we establish a righteous Islamic community."[59]

Increasingly out of touch with his people and obsessed with his religious mission, Nimeiri continued to struggle with his health. In March 1985, he again traveled to Walter Reed for a thorough evaluation and treatment. While in Cairo en route to Khartoum, he learned that a coup d'état had occurred and he had lost his pulpit. Searching for the kingdom of God, he lost his kingdom on earth.

Deng Xiaopeng of Communist China:
Clinging to Power, Reliving the Past

"Xiaopeng, Xiaopeng, in his eighties!
Health okay, brain not sharp!
Go home quickly, go play bridge!"
—Poster in Tiananmen Square

We still have a large group of veterans who have
experienced many storms and have a thorough
understanding of things. They were on the side of
taking resolute action to counter the turmoil.
—Deng Xiaopeng, reflecting on the events in
Tiananmen Square

In our discussion of paranoia we noted that it is sometimes difficult to determine whether an act is an example of hard-headed prudence, simple overreaction, or a reflection of paranoia. In fact, in a conspiratorial environment such as the Kremlin, the boundary line between prudence and paranoia may be impossible to distinguish. The same sort of problem exists in determining whether an extreme action of an aging leader in a closed society springs from rational calculation or is an irrational defense of a private self-identity. This problem is exemplified by Communist party chief Deng Xiaopeng's treatment of the pro-democracy youth movement in the People's Republic of China that ended, at Deng's orders, in the bloody massacre at Tiananmen Square. By placing this event in the context of Deng's personal history and political psychology, we shall attempt to clarify his motivations.*

At the conclusion of the party's National Congress in November 1987, eighty-three-year-old Deng Xiaopeng won international praise and admiration for engineering the first stable succession in China's modern history. Deng's efforts to consolidate and institutionalize the revolution and to transcend Mao Zedong's charismatic and highly personalistic rule dated back thirty-four years. At the party congress of 1956, when Deng was appointed general secretary, he emphasized the primacy of law and institutions and sought to curb the personal power of Mao. In giving up his own formal power thirty-one years later, Deng was, through his selfless example, personifying the issues he had championed throughout his life, the primacy of the country and its institutions over any one man.

Premier Zhao Ziyang, who would now lead the forty-six-million-member party, indicated that even though Deng had given up his major positions of power, he would retain considerable influence: "I have a high respect for Comrade Deng Xiaopeng. I will often ask his advice so that I will be able to do things better."[60] Furthermore, Deng had not given up *all* his positions, having chosen to retain control over the People's Liberation Army and to remain head of the party's Military Affairs Commission. As the architect of the reforms and China's most revered revolutionary vet-

*The chronology for the events leading up to Tiananmen Square draws on a series of articles that appeared in the *Los Angeles Times* and a major article in the *New York Times Magazine*.

eran, Deng would continue to have ultimate decision-making power if he chose to exercise it.

In fact, despite his selfless public postures, Deng did not relinquish power. Just a year and a half later, he made the decisions that led to the bloody massacre in Tiananmen Square. It was Deng who rejected the anguished pleas of Zhao to negotiate with the demonstrators. It was Deng who threw his support to hardliner Premier Li Peng. It was Deng who was ultimately responsible for the decision to impose martial law, which led to the violence. And in the aftermath it was Deng who orchestrated the firing of his erstwhile protégé Zhao Ziyang as party chairman.

Deng was supported in his decisions by the party elders, especially by his fellow octogenarian and close political ally Yang Shangkun, China's president, a veteran of the Long March. On May 24, 1989, Yang made an important speech to the Military Affairs Commission explaining the decision to impose martial law, asserting that he and the other party elders "feel there is no way to retreat." This speech demonstrates how aged leaders tend to oversimplify their interpretation of the present in terms of the past. "Backstepping will be the end of us. It will be the end of the People's Republic of China. It will be the restoration of capitalism, the goal which was sought by [U.S. Secretary of State John Foster] Dulles. After several generations, our socialism would be turned into liberalism."[61] Yang's worldview was shaped and frozen in time forty years earlier. The generational succession struggle was epitomized in a joke circulating in China that the country's political crisis could be explained as "a bunch of eighty-year-olds telling a bunch of seventy-year-olds which sixty-year-olds should retire."

In the wake of Mao Zedong's disastrous policies, Deng had led the movement to bring economic reform—the introduction of a market economy—to China. But it was to be economic reform under the strict control of the Communist party, whose leadership was not to be challenged. The communiqué announcing Zhao's dismissal accused him of supporting the student "turmoils" and thus "splitting the party" and weakening the cardinal principles of Communist opposition to bourgeois liberalization.[62] For Deng and other members of the old guard, the student demonstrations and Zhao's support for them as well as his failure to submit to Central Committee discipline had threatened the primary role of the party and their own authority.

There were, however, more personal reasons as well. To comprehend fully the decision-making that led to the tragedy at Tiananmen Square, one must attempt to view the events from Deng's perspective. Deng feared political disorder even more than he desired economic liberalization, and for good reason. A loyal follower of Mao Zedong from the revolution's earliest days, Deng had nevertheless suffered greatly during the unchecked violence of the Cultural Revolution. During that period which seemed to pit young against old, Deng was stripped of his rank and forced to "confess his errors" in a public rite of humiliation. His son suffered a paralyzing spinal-cord injury when thrown from the second story of a building by Mao's young zealots, the Revolutionary Guards. While Deng emerged from the Cultural Revolution with the reputation of a hero, the emotional scars were deep.

The spectacle of the protesters in Tiananmen Square must have awakened painful memories of youth out of control violently rebelling against their seniors during the Cultural Revolution, in which Deng and his son had been humiliated and injured. Never again should rebelling youth be permitted to destroy the fabric of society, which depends so strongly on Confucian traditions and unquestioned respect for patriarchal authority. Never again should "turmoil" (the code word for the upheavals of the Cultural Revolution) sweep the nation. This fear was not irrational on Deng's part or on the part of his colleagues, some of whom had suffered even more severely in the Cultural Revolution at the hands of youth. Precisely because Confucian societies emphasize the subordination of youth to age, once that subordination is broken, the violence of youth against authority becomes extremely dangerous.

In 1988 and early 1989, there was a great deal of social unrest in China in response to the economic stress produced by Deng's market reforms. Inflation was running at 30 percent, higher than in any year since the Communist Revolution in 1949. Although Zhao had instituted the policies, they were clearly in response to Deng's leadership. Student demonstrations mounted and Deng, who for so long had been a hero to the youth of his nation, was now a target of blame. One placard read, "The Chinese people should not put their hope in a single, benevolent emperor."

The event that catalyzed the youthful protesters in the spring of 1989 was a coronary occlusion. On April 8, during a Politburo meeting, Hu Yaobang, the voice in the Politburo urging that the nation's youth succeed its aged leaders, was stricken with a heart attack. He died a week later. The previous summer Hu had gone so far as to suggest that all of China's elderly leaders, including Deng, should retire. He was soon forced out by an enlarged politburo stacked with elderly leaders. Hu replaced Deng as the great hero to the nation's youth and was extolled for his courage in confronting the generation of aging leaders holding onto power. His fatal heart attack, occurring under such dramatic circumstances, sparked powerful protests. Within hours of Hu's death, this poster appeared: "A great man has died, but false men still live." Hundreds, then thousands, of protesting students began to gather at Tiananmen Square and other places of assembly around the country.

As the protests mounted and the crowd in Tiananmen Square grew larger, Zhao argued for moderation and negotiation. But a hard-line editorial entitled "Take a Clear Stand against Turmoil" was drafted at the explicit instructions of Deng, condemning the student unrest and calling for a crackdown. Each time the term for "student movement" was used in the draft editorial, Deng scratched it out and substituted "turmoil," the pejorative used to describe the Cultural Revolution.

The threat to the primacy of the party and its maintenance of order was a threat to core values of Deng, values shared with his elderly colleagues. If the leadership of the party were defeated by these young demonstrators, a new Cultural Revolution would result. To Deng and his close associates, that would have to be prevented at any cost. Deng brought in troops from outside the Beijing military district and warned the students that violence was likely if they did not disperse. The students refused, the troops acted, and thousands of unarmed youth lost their lives in the violent confrontations that ensued. In the aftermath, Deng righteously reflected on the correctness of the regime's actions, emphasizing the need to avoid "turmoil" and celebrating the wisdom and experience of his aged comrades.

In fact, Deng himself seemed to be questioning his capacities and judgment. In a remarkable but little noticed speech on November 18, 1989, he warned a group of officials not to listen to him if he "starts to say crazy things as he gets older and becomes less clear-minded."[63] Could it be that he regretted the hard line that led to the tragedy at Tiananmen Square and wished that his subordinates had not listened to him, that he was recognizing that his age was affecting his capacities for leadership, and that his judgment was compromised and had already failed him and his nation? Perhaps, but in a discussion with Henry Kissinger at about the same time, he indicated that he was not yet ready to retire, that he had too much to do, and that his leadership remained important.

History should record the tragedy at Tiananmen Square as the expression of conflict between generations, of youth impatient for their place versus aged leaders holding on tightly to the reins of power lest everything they valued be destroyed. These leaders were trying to safeguard the accomplishments of their lifetimes, and given the behavior of youth during the Cultural Revolution, they had reason to fear the students in Tiananmen Square. But ironically, in their unwillingness to retire and pass on the torch of leadership, Deng Xiaopeng and his old guard were tarnishing the very historical legacy they were hoping to preserve. Rather than go down in history as the great reformer who helped bring China into the modern world, Deng is likely to be remembered as the leader responsible for the massacre in Tiananmen Square, the controlling old man who clung to power beyond his time.

Being faced with the end of life—whether because of the impact of mortal illness or the passage of years—inevitably requires a leader to assess his accomplishments. His assessment, and his reactions to the threatened loss of power, will depend significantly upon his personality and political psychology.

The controlling autocrat and the narcissist will have particular difficulty in yielding the throne of power. For the autocrat, such as Erich Honecker, the throne of leadership is the seat of power and control. To yield that throne is to lose control. Paradoxically, it is only by responding to pressure from below and yielding a greater degree of control to the people that the autocratic leader can hope to retain his position. But the very psychological and political forces that contributed to his controlling leadership make it impossible for him to yield even partially, and a powerful struggle for control ensues.

The narcissist is often successful in achieving power, in large part because he appears to be totally self-sufficient. But under the arrogant, self-confident facade he is consumed by self-doubt and feelings of inadequacy, which drive him in a never-ending quest for attention and approval. This insatiable drive for admiration makes the end of the heroic life unthinkable for the consummate narcissist. No amount of success can fill that inner void. And thus it was that even Mao Zedong, clearly to be immortalized in the pantheon of history's great leaders, and the shah of Iran, who brought his country to the edge of modernization, were still not fulfilled at the end of their lives. Whatever the evaluation of the outside world, their inner drive was undiminished, their vaulting ambition for immortal glory unrealized.

Whether the leader stays past his time and in terminally holding on to power destroys the achievements of his lifetime will depend significantly on the nature of the political system and the relation of the leader to it. This consideration takes us to the next chapter. For it is not simply the disease and the pre-existing personality pattern that determine how an ailing monarch leads. The institutions, formal and informal, in which the king operates will vitally affect how he may act and even whether he will be permitted to act at all.

6

The Rules of the
Kingdom

The secret malady of a statesman can
be as disastrous as his secret diplomacy.
—Arnold Rogow, *James Forrestal*

All societies, from the most primitive to the most
advanced, have a structure and procedures for gover-
nance. These procedures and the associated organizations—collectively referred to as the institutions—are
designed to transcend individual variability and to
lend predictability to human interactions. Whether an
ailing leader can hold onto power will depend upon
the structure of the kingdom. How much has power
become concentrated in the chief of state? Are there
institutionalized constraints? Are there systematic
procedures for succession?

The death or removal of an absolute monarch with
total control over the domain can produce a major
crisis for the kingdom as successors struggle for the
vacant throne. And, as we have seen, in his final days
the dying king with absolute powers can inflict great
damage on the kingdom. The more power is concentrated in the person of the leader, the greater is the
likelihood of a crisis for the kingdom. And the more
power is dispersed and succession institutionalized,
the greater the likelihood that the transition will be
smooth.

An institution is a set of stable human interactions.
These interactions need not be democratic. Indeed,
there is no necessary relation between modern and
traditional, democratic and authoritarian types of government and levels of institutionalization. The democratic United States and Great Britain have a high level
of political institutionalization, and most newborn authoritarian dictatorships do not. Conversely, the auto-

cratic Ottoman Empire was highly institutionalized, and the democratic Fourth Republic of France was not.

Consider, for example, one of the best institutionalized—and most pernicious—methods of ruling, one that fostered leader psychopathology as a policy, and one that operated with great stability for more than two centuries: the golden cages.

Sultans of the Golden Cages

Mehmed the Conqueror, the founder of the Ottoman Empire, wrested Constantinople from the Byzantines in 1453. After his accession, the sultan issued a statement "enjoining his descendants to mark their accession with a slaughter of their brothers."[1] This brutal practice—the law of fratricide, as it was called—had a perverse logic: the permissibility of plural marriage and the harem system meant that rulers had many children, sometimes scores. Factions would arise around one or another of these claimants, causing bloody court intrigues and civil disorder. Eliminating the claimants was the simplest method of removing the intrigues and the disorder. The practice offended morality and was also often difficult to carry out. But the law of fratricide was not discontinued until the sixteenth century; the last mass killings took place under Murad III in 1595.

After that time, a new practice was instituted, that of the *kafe,* or cage. Under this system, which varied over its two centuries of use, prospective rivals for power were imprisoned—some when as young as two years of age—in a luxurious pavilion within the palace ("the golden cage"), where they were instructed in the Koran, astrology, and official composition. Deaf mutes and a small group of concubines were their sole companions. One prince spent fifty years in confinement. Members of these harems were forbidden to have children; any offspring were immediately killed.[2]

The early seventeenth-century ruler Mustafa I was the first occupant of the golden cage to accede to the throne. He had spent ten years in this luxurious isolation. "By the time Mustafa I became Sultan, he was completely demented. He appointed two favorite pages—scarcely out of their infancy—to be governors of Cairo and Damascus."[3] Mustafa was ultimately dethroned, reinstated by the Janissaries, again deposed, and finally strangled.

This was not an auspicious beginning for the kafe system, yet it continued and even expanded. What began as a system to protect the sultan from rivals for the throne now became a requirement for succession. Every future monarch was obliged to spend some time in the kafe. The new system required that the succeeding monarch be the oldest surviving male member of the Imperial House. Occupants of the throne therefore tended to be men at least in middle age, which generally meant that they had spent many years in the golden cage.

This system hardly prepared the future ruler of the Ottoman Empire for the effective and responsible exercise of power.[4] Quite the opposite: it extinguished any capacity for leadership. Moreover, the enforced isolation of the kafe system engendered a gross distortion of character, even madness. While the prospective sultan lived in the kafe, not knowing whether he or another rival would be the oldest royal survivor at the time of the reigning sultan's death, he could exercise no power. Even those of strong character and mental balance would be ignorant and inexperienced in government. As he was presented with great power, his entire world suddenly changed, but he was often mentally incompetent to use it.

Was this system as irrational as it seems? For society as a whole, yes. For the inner circle, no. It was a means of *institutionalizing* a captive king pattern. The new sultan was free only in name and in form. In fact he was likely to be the puppet of those who constituted the court. The real power of the Ottoman Empire rested with the members of the palace. This system, a stable one, served them well. The problem of succession was minimized because the sultan did not in fact rule.

On the other hand, the death or removal of an absolute monarch with total control over his domain can produce a major crisis for the kingdom as successors struggle for the vacant throne. And, as we have seen, in his final days the dying king with absolute powers can inflict great damage on his kingdom. Such was the case with Habib Bourguiba of Tunisia.

Habib Bourguiba, President for Life of Tunisia: Creator, Evader, and Subject of the Constitution

The following is a medical statement which was issued at 0600 today, 7 November 1987:

We the undersigned hereby declare that the attorney general of the Republic has asked us to give a medical opinion on current developments in the mental and physical condition of Habib Bourguiba. After deliberation, discussion, and evaluation we note that his medical health no longer permits him to perform the duties entrusted to him.

Signed: Doctors Azzidine Guedich Mohamed BenIsmail, Haschemi Karaoui, Amarah Zeini, Mohamed Guedich, Sadak Ouachi, Abdelaziz Annabi

0700 7 November 1987

Citizens, the following is the official statement made this morning by Mr. Zine El Abidine Ben Ali, president of the Tunisian Republic and supreme commander of the Armed Forces.

In the name of God, the compassionate, the merciful. Citizens, the colossal sacrifices made by the leader Habib Bourguiba, first president of the Tunisian Republic, and his good companions for the sake of Tunisia and its development cannot be enumerated. We have loved and appreciated him and worked for many years with sincerity and devotion under his command at different levels in our people's Army and the government because of this.

However, because of his senility and lingering illness, national duty compels us to announce today that, on the basis of a medical report, he has become totally incapable of fulfilling the duties of the Presidency. As such, and in accordance with Article 57 of the Constitution, we assume, with God's help and guidance, the presidency and the supreme command of our Armed Forces.[5]

Constitutions can be weak or powerful instruments. A charismatic and skillful leader can sit atop a government and ignore even the most explicit laws. But if the autocrat's health, mental or physical, should fail, then the dry words on forgotten documents can become powerful weapons in the hands of those who know how to use them.

The medical communiqué quoted above, which legitimized Prime Minister Ben Ali's accession to power, bears a striking similarity to the document used to depose King Ludwig II of Bavaria. In both cases physicians cooperated (in these two cases, ethically) with frustrated courtiers and declared the ailing monarch incapable of carrying out the responsibilities of his office. But there the similarity ends. Mad King Ludwig had no interest in affairs of state, preferring to indulge his private passions, and it was only when the consequences of his mental illness affected the finances of his kingdom that his court felt impelled to act.

In contrast, the charismatic leader Habib Bourguiba was the very personification of Tunisia. Bourguiba had been the only president since the country gained independence from France in 1956 and had ruled it continuously—and imperiously—from its founding until he was deposed, a span of thirty-one years.

Like Mao Zedong, Bourguiba was a nation builder, a demigod. And like Mao Zedong, Bourguiba would not relinquish power, despite severe incapacity. At the end he was unable to provide effective leadership, yet he was able to muster enough resources to block attempts to prepare for his succession.

Ironically, in planning for his nation's future, Bourguiba had stressed the importance of institutionalization: "Revolts are not led essentially in the name of nationalism, but in the name of an overpowering desire for dignity. When the rebels can assuage this desire through institutions whose every detail has been organized by their leaders, success is bound to follow. When there are no institutions, there is chaos."[6]

Unfortunately for Tunisia, Bourguiba did not heed his own wise injunction. In a later interview, Bourguiba accurately—and pungently—characterized his own personalistic rule. "The system? I am the system."[7] His nation's fragile institutions were no match for Bourguiba's powerful personality. He repeatedly overrode them, running roughshod over the structures and procedures he had put in place. And, ironically, as he had predicted, the absence of effective institutions ultimately led to chaos.

Bourguiba's supreme confidence in his own abilities long preceded his assumption of his nation's leadership. It was at once the key to his charismatic appeal and his Achilles' heel. In *The Demigods,* Jean LaCouture cites powerful examples of Bourguiba's grandiose self-concept.

In 1952, while a prisoner of the French, he wrote: "If my life were taken, the people would suffer an irreparable loss in losing not so much their leader and moral counsellor as the fruit of all their past sacrifices. . . . As the creator of Tunisia, I have renewed her human substance." . . .

In 1962, asked if he felt an historical bond with Hannibal, Bourguiba likened himself instead to another heroic figure. "No, my ancestor was Jugurtha, who fought the foreign invaders . . . a patriot, like myself, not a conqueror. *Alive or dead, I am responsible for this nation's destiny.*" . . .

On the occasion of the tenth anniversary of independence, Bourguiba continued in the same self-exalting vein: "Having been the major artisan of Tunisian history for thirty-five years, I believe I should shed some light on the critical moments in our struggle. . . . Those events ought to be recalled so that the new generations may reflect upon this long journey of ours, this exalting epic which brought Tunisia to independence, whose origin was my work."[8]

Compounding the problem of replacing Bourguiba was his royal style of leadership, described as "presidential monarchy," at once highly personalistic and autocratic, yet relying on political institutions.[9] On the day the republic was founded, Bourguiba declared to the National Assembly, "I could, if I wished, install myself as monarch and found a dynasty. I prefer the Republic."[10]

But in fact he led as if he were the monarch, not the president, of the republic. Although a constitution had been proclaimed, the offices and processes it described were largely ignored. All decisions were centered on

Bourguiba, who was accorded unanimous legitimacy. Bourguiba led a single-party government, which he headed in a dual capacity—as president and as party leader. Despite the trappings of democracy, it was a benevolent dictatorship. All high-level appointments were made by Bourguiba and served at his pleasure. By the early 1960s, he had surrounded himself with a group of courtiers who had more influence than the official cabinet. He met with them over breakfast and reached decisions that he would then relay to his cabinet for implementation.

As his health declined, Bourguiba became increasingly unwilling to listen to criticism. As one minister explained, "There was no room for even the most cautiously worded disagreement with the leader, as it might enrage him to the point of endangering his health."[11] Bourguiba had been plagued by ill health for twenty-two years, since February 1967, when the sixty-four-year-old leader suffered his first heart attack. Within two months he had suffered a second, nearly fatal heart attack. Bourguiba took a six-month's leave for treatment in France. On his return in June 1970, he expressed his conviction that his popularity had not been diminished "in spite of what the people have gone through in my absence."[12] He then abruptly dismissed his prime minister, an example of an arbitrariness that increasingly bedeviled his senior officials. Bourguiba would be absent for prolonged periods because of illness, but to take action in his absence was to risk dismissal.

The diagnosis of advanced generalized arteriosclerosis became public knowledge in 1971, and succession became an open subject of discussion, with political figures jockeying for position. But Bourguiba was not ready to be counted out. At the party congress that year he dismissed one of his most outspoken critics and cautioned against too much liberalization. Offered the position of president for life, he refused, declaring that he would leave office at the end of his term in 1974, and should be replaced by Premier Nouria. Yet in an interview in *Le Monde* the same year, Bourguiba undercut any successor with the comment, "It will not be easy to replace a man like me."[13]

Actively directing his nation's foreign policy, in 1972 and again in 1974 Bourguiba suggested to Qaddafi a union between Libya and Tunisia.[14] Despite his poor health, and despite his earlier declaration that he would step down when his term expired in 1974, that September, Bourguiba reversed himself and in effect proclaimed himself president for life, accepting the title from his rubber-stamp parliament. How reminiscent of Deng Xiaopeng, declaring the need to turn the reins of government over to younger men but, when the time came, being unwilling to step aside.

In the winter of 1976, Bourguiba traveled to Switzerland for a restorative cure. On his return three months later, Tunisians were shocked to see that his face was ashen and haggard and that he spoke with difficulty. He was said to be suffering from circulatory, heart, and eye problems. In response to expressions of concern about Bourguiba's health, the secretary of state for information indicated that should President Bourguiba be prevented from carrying out his functions, the constitution stipulated that the prime minister would assume the presidency.

An illness in the summer of 1978 again required Bourguiba to leave Tunisia to enter the American Hospital in Paris for tests and evaluation.[15] His medical difficulties were sufficiently grave to require a month's postponement of the celebrations for his seventy-fifth birthday. In October, Bourguiba required further tests in Paris for a new symptom, a sleeping disturbance. While officially suffering from insomnia, Bourguiba was urgently transferred to a German medical clinic.[16] Lacking confidence in his own physicians, he sought out physicians in France, Switzerland, Germany, and the United States to review his diagnosis and treatment. Reviewing his treatment was a sensible decision, for Bourguiba often medicated himself and was a veritable walking drugstore between self-administered drugs and the medications his various physicians were prescribing. Many of his symptoms were almost certainly drug side effects.*

Canceled government meetings and public appearances for medical reasons were now more the rule than the exception. The medical bulletins would offer such reasons as "a chill," "an indisposition," "a cold," "exhaustion," "a minor illness," "a respiratory ailment," and "a slight deterioration in his health." In March 1979, Bourguiba entered the cardiac section of the military hospital for an evaluation; in May he spent several weeks in France for "dental treatment."[17]

Thus Bourguiba's health, ability to continue in office, and succession were of primary concern when the tenth Socialist party Congress was held in September. In his opening address, Bourguiba made it clear that his mortality was very much on his mind. The address had the tone of a valedictory.

---

*The elderly are particularly sensitive to medication. Bourguiba was taking so many pharmaceutical preparations for his various ailments that he was undoubtedly experiencing drug side effects. Several of the medications prescribed for his cardiac difficulties have stimulating side effects that could have produced insomnia. Moreover, some of the medications were probably prescribed to stimulate the seventy-five-year-old ruler, who frequently complained of "exhaustion" and drowsiness and became somnolent during government meetings; at one public appearance he fell three times, probably because of impaired cerebral circulation. If Bourguiba did take stimulants for these symptoms, such medications could have contributed to insomnia, especially if taken in large quantities. Rather than reduce his intake, Bourguiba was probably treating the side effects with yet other medications, which in turn produced side effects of their own.

In 1981, as rumors swirled concerning the serious illness of the seventy-eight-year-old leader, the problems of succession grew increasingly urgent. As president for life, Bourguiba had systematically blocked potential successors from gaining independent positions of prominence. Tunisia's drift continued, interrupted only by occasional spasms of repression, such as the military actions against the bread riots of 1984.

In that year, as popular criticism mounted and events seemed to be going out of control, Bourguiba suffered yet another heart attack. The government was largely paralyzed; unemployment had risen to 30 percent. Bourguiba was attending neither to the economy nor to the day-to-day affairs of government, but no one could act in his stead. Increasingly isolated, the autocrat at the end of his days was desperately holding on. He reacted with anger when newspapers mentioned succession, stressing that this was not imminent because he was in good health.

The only technique of leadership left in Bourguiba's impoverished repertoire was repression. In 1985 he ordered the arrest of several of his critics. When his family and closest supporters tried to blunt the excesses of his erratic decision-making, even they were not immune to his impetuous wrath: his son publicly opposed the wave of arrests, and Bourguiba responded by suspending him from his post as special adviser.

Bourguiba first undermined and then discharged his prime minister, seeing him as a threat to his power, and appointed Interior Minister Ben Ali in his stead. When his wife, Wassila, opposed Ben Ali's appointment, in August 1986, after twenty-five years of marriage, Bourguiba divorced her, further isolating himself.

By now the topic of succession was at the heart of all Tunisian conversation and political life, but when Le Monde published an article devoted to the succession of President Bourguiba, the newspaper was banned for a month in Tunisia.[18]

During 1987, Bourguiba's behavior became increasingly erratic. He would appoint ministers, revoke the appointments, announce decisions, and suddenly reverse himself. He would make multiple appointments to the same job; Tunisia briefly had two ambassadors to the United Nations. In perhaps the shortest tenure in history, an official was appointed minister of culture for thirty minutes.[19] Bourguiba signed a decree appointing several ministers, then the next day swore that he had not done so. No one could influence him, and to criticize a decision was to risk being discharged.

Ministers studied the constitution to determine how to terminate the rule of this now blatantly senile despot. They noted that Article 57 provided for the replacement of the president in the event of permanent inability. Bourguiba's decision to order the execution of several Muslim fundamentalist demonstrators (which might have led to a religious civil war) in combination with his decision to replace Prime Minister Ben Ali galvanized the inner circle, who called on a panel of physicians to certify Bourguiba's permanent inability.

As with Mad King Ludwig of Bavaria, the physicians made the determination of leader inability at the request of the inner circle without examining the ailing leader. Although the strength of Tunisia's constitution was not sufficient to control a healthy or even a failing despot, it was adequate to replace an eighty-four-year-old senile one, in what was, in effect, a constitutionally sanctioned, medically facilitated coup d'état.

The Rules of Succession

We have told the tale of Habib Bourguiba in detail because it epitomizes central themes of this study. It is the story of an aging, ailing leader holding onto power. It is the story of the complex relationship between a disabled king and his captive court. It is the story of weak institutions pushed aside by the personal force of a charismatic leader. And it is the story of those same institutions revived to depose a disabled leader.

In a highly institutionalized and legitimate society the procedures are well established, the members of the society agree on the need for them, and they are well observed. Such a society will have clear but flexible rules for deciding how a person becomes a leader, when the leader is replaced, and the scope and manner in which the leader can exercise authority. And these rules will be followed.

Old political systems tend to be better institutionalized than newer ones, for, as in Tunisia, newer systems tend to be dominated by the forceful personalities of their founders. When Bourguiba responded, "The system? I am the system," he was accurately describing the situation of Tunisia, a country dominated by a presidential monarch with unlimited powers. In effect, the succession crisis lasted for more than twenty years. Although Bourguiba became ill in 1966, there were no constitutional provisions for succession until 1975. And although these provisions ultimately formed the basis for Bourguiba's removal from power, they were designed to permit the president to choose his own successor. Moreover, the constitutional provisions were so weak and so susceptible to manipulation by the president that he was able to remain in office for many years beyond the time when objective criteria would have indicated that he was disabled and ineffective.

Because systems that have faced and overcome crises tend to be better institutionalized than those that have had a relatively serene history, Tunisia may in the long run benefit from the challenge Bourguiba's refusal to step down presented. In his initial address to the nation in 1987, Ben Ali, now president, announced pending changes to the constitution to eliminate governmental practices "in which the people are not involved." These included abolition of the position of president for life and of automatic succession. There would be a limit of three five-year terms, and succession would be determined by popular election. Declaring, "There is no room for repression and injustice," Ben Ali committed himself to strengthening democracy in Tunisia by opening the political system to other parties.[20] He stressed the importance of a government of law. In effect, he was saying, "As a consequence of the crises that have afflicted our nation, I am committed to strengthening our institutions so that never again will our nation be held hostage to the capricious rule of an aging tyrant."

Why Succession Is So Poorly Institutionalized

The kafe system of the Ottomans is best understood as a substitute for rather than a means of succession. Throughout the spectrum of political systems, procedures for dealing with impaired leaders are at best poorly institutionalized and more often than not, not even considered. As we have suggested earlier, one reason may lie in the universal wish for leaders to be all knowing, all wise, and all powerful; the possibility that the leader might be afflicted with disabling illness is unthinkable. Another reason for this institutional weakness is that impairment is the exception, not the rule, and is frequently so intermittent in its manifestation that anticipatory rules are difficult to codify. Moreover, there is a tendency for the system to conceal disability from public view, for in many nations military leaders have shown a proclivity to move against the government as soon as its leader falters.

Our studies do suggest that democratic constitutional states are better in dealing with succession problems than are dictatorships—not so much because of the democratic ethos as because of the institutions that accompany democracy. But even the most effective institutions operating in even the most democratic states are not fully protective against the dangers attendant upon an ailing leader.

For succession to proceed smoothly, several conditions are required: the rules of succession must be clearly established; a successor must be clearly designated by the constitutional process or by the ailing leader; the court must be satisfied that it will not be endangered and will share in the successor regime. The case of Habib Bourguiba illustrates how a mentally disabled and increasingly dangerous leader can be replaced even in a threatening environment if the inner circle acts with skill and can point to a legitimate procedure to defend its actions. A satisfactory alternative leader was present—Prime Minister Ben Ali—who had the legal and political resources to organize other members of the court to replace a ruler who seemed intent on bringing his country to religious civil war. Ben Ali's intent was not to overthrow the system but to ensure its stability and continuity. Not only was there a clearly designated constitutional successor, but, no less important, court members were satisfied that their interests would be preserved in the new regime. All the requirements were fulfilled for implementing succession procedures.

The political dynamics are quite different when there is a dangerous alternative. Such was the case in the Philippines in the last days of Ferdinand Marcos and in Iran in the last year of the shah's reign. Despite the close supervision of the election, the Marcos forces committed blatant fraud to retain the presidency. The conclusion that they must take whatever steps were necessary to maintain the seriously ailing Marcos in power was not irrational. To permit electoral succession to occur would lead not merely to a peaceful switch of ruling parties. They had every reason to believe that Corazon Aquino, if she succeeded in assuming the presidency, would reopen the investigation of her husband's assassination. They had every reason to believe there would be criminal investigations of the millions systematically looted from the Philippine treasury. The alternative to Marcos's remaining in power was likely to be prison or death for his supporters.

Similarly, there was no question about what Khomeini would do to the shah's court once he got into power. Those around the shah fought as long as they could to support their monarch, but in retrospect, the nation would have been better served had the shah's inner circle, like Bourguiba's, persuaded or forced him to step aside on medical grounds at a far earlier date and installed a vigorous regency. The opportunity to save the regime, if there was one, was brief indeed. Had the court broken ranks and informed the United States of the shah's mortal illness, suggesting an acceptable successor, perhaps the outcome could have been different. Ironically, the shah was destroyed by the fact that he had kept his court under such strict control and concealed the grave nature of his illness from all but those closest to him. Had the members of the shah's court been more independent and the nature of his illness been revealed earlier, his throne may well have been saved.

Delaying Succession

In closed and open societies alike, partial disability of the leader will often produce factional struggle, with the loyalists wishing him to remain in power, and rivals pressing for his removal. But when the immediate alternative, the constitutionally designated successor, poses a greater danger than the incumbent, the opposition party may wish to preserve the disabled leader in office in the hope that in time political circumstances may be more propitious.

Recall that President Eisenhower's stroke of November 25, 1957, affected his thinking and his ability to communicate. It was, moreover, well known that such strokes are often followed by others and that the situation might worsen. Eisenhower, who had already suffered a heart attack while in office, considered stepping down. Despite Richard Nixon's remark in *Six Crises* that at times of crisis leaders put their personal concerns aside and think only of the nation's interests, nothing could be further from the truth.[21] Times of crisis are times of opportunity. As leaders of both parties considered the complexities of this succession crisis, they naturally considered their own self-interest and the interests of their party as well as those of the nation. They probably rationalized that the two were identical.

What would happen if Eisenhower were to step down or be removed from office because of his medical disability? His vice president, the skilled politician Richard Nixon, would replace him. Presumably Nixon would run for the presidency in 1960 as an incumbent, a great political advantage. The two principal congressional leaders (both Democrats), Senate Majority Leader Lyndon Johnson and Speaker of the House Sam Rayburn, discussed the problem and concluded that they must do everything possible to retain the Republican Eisenhower in office, sick or well. They certainly would not suggest his removal. In the event, Eisenhower recovered fully from the stroke. But the calculations of Johnson and Rayburn were entirely partisan, and they were not inaccurate. Nixon lost to Kennedy by a hair in 1960. Had Nixon had the advantages of incumbency, he almost surely would have won.

This event illustrates the "better-the-devil-I-know" theory of support for an ailing incumbent. If the alternative is uncertain or dangerous, even those who oppose the incumbent will try to keep him in office and not press for his removal. In the case of Bourguiba, the alternative was safe. In the case of Eisenhower, the alternative was potentially more dangerous to the Democrats than the incumbent. Very often the alternative is unpredictable.

In the last days of his premiership of Israel, Menachem Begin was seriously depressed and apathetic, unable to provide effective leadership to Israel. He recognized that he lacked the mental and physical stamina required by the demanding position. This was an accurate judgment, shared by senior leaders of his Likud party as well as the Labor opposition. He wanted to step down. Israel was a thriving democracy, by no means a dictatorship, and had experienced peaceful transfers of prime ministerial power before. But this was a time of crisis for Israel (as is often the case for that beleaguered nation), Begin was a man of great stature, a symbol to his partisans of strength and resistance, and there was no one in his party of the stature to step in at that critical juncture. Begin was pressed to stay in office far longer than he desired or was good for his country. Only when Begin unequivocally stated that he could not go on did he leave the premiership.

The king in this case was held in a captivity not of his own making. This captivity was not due to institutional defects in the Israeli political system, but was generated by his followers' fear and uncertainty. His closest supporters believed it was dangerous to replace Begin. None of them was politically powerful enough to be certain he could maintain the coalition's fragile majority in the Knesset. To lose their leader was to risk losing control of the government. The king was kept captive, without a plan for his succession, because of the fear of the unknown and uncertain future.

The Twenty-fifth Amendment to the U.S. Constitution: Contradictions Unresolved, Provisions Evaded

The most detailed and best documented description of how a complex institution deals with the problem of executive disability is found in the history of the U.S. presidency. Beginning with concern over the health of James Madison in 1813, there has been continual discussion, and often action, regarding presidential disability. Given the nature of both the office and American society, these discussions and the actions associated with them have been especially well documented.

Practice and principle have been distilled in the Twenty-fifth Amendment to the Constitution (see appendix B), which deals with the specification of the succession procedure and the identification of disability. In the Twenty-fifth Amendment, the United States is considered by many international legal scholars to have one of the most advanced and best codified procedures for constitutional succession. The development and use of the amendment, however, demonstrate that no written procedure can ensure certain and legitimate succession. As we will see, there are inherent contradictions between the necessity for promptness and the requirement of due process, between clarity of procedure and flexibility. Understanding how the most carefully devised of all procedures for the removal of political leaders fails to solve (though it does mitigate) the problem of succession demonstrates that, even in the most advanced democracy, when illness strikes the leader, the system is jeopardized.

In spite of several deaths in office and many disabilities, few efforts were made before the mid-twentieth century to change the formal constitutional status of the succession process. In part this reluctance had to do with the American preference for precedent over legislation as well as the fact that previous problems had been surmounted without great harm. With John F. Kennedy's assassination, associated initially with fears that it was part of a coordinated effort to weaken the United States and render it vulnerable to a nuclear strike, demands grew for a clarifying amendment bearing on disability and succession. On February 10, 1967, the requisite thirty-eight states ratified the Twenty-fifth Amendment.

The Twenty-fifth Amendment provides for two major processes concerning the identification and determination of inability or disability. The president, *recognizing his disability* or approaching disability and *on his own initiative,* relinquishes the powers of his office to the vice president, who then becomes *acting president.* If, however, a disabled president is unable or unwilling to relinquish his powers, the Twenty-fifth Amendment provides for a procedure by which his powers may be taken from him.

In the first case, the president, recognizing his weakness or perhaps about to undergo a disabling medical procedure, may transmit in writing to the president pro tempore of the Senate his intention to relinquish the powers and duties of the office of president (though not the office itself) to the vice president, who becomes acting president. The president can then recover these powers and duties *upon his own initiative.*

This voluntary and presumptively temporary relinquishment of the powers of the presidency has never been carried out under the Twenty-fifth Amendment, though the circumstances it anticipates have occurred. President Ronald Reagan, for example, made no provision for the transfer of powers when he was seriously wounded, and his staff has acknowledged that in the press of the crisis it did not occur to them that this was exactly the sort of situation for which the Twenty-Fifth Amendment was designed. When Reagan later underwent an operation for cancer of the colon, instead of using the Twenty-fifth Amendment, he simply wrote out a statement that Vice President George Bush would exercise the powers of the office while he, the president, was disabled. White House representatives asserted specifically that the Twenty-fifth Amendment was not invoked, though they did not say why they used what was in effect the pre-amendment Eisenhower-Nixon system of private agreement. Demonstrating reluctance to yield the reins of power, even temporarily, they noted only that they believed the amendment was to be used for more serious and extended periods of disability. In his letter transferring power to Vice President Bush, Reagan said that he was "mindful of the provisions of Section 3 of the 25th Amendment to the Constitution and of the uncertainties of its application to such brief and temporary periods of incapacity. I do not believe that the drafters of this amendment intended its application to situations such as the instant one."

The counsel to the Commission on Presidential Disability and the Twenty-fifth Amendment suggests that in effect Reagan did use the provisions of the amendment, although the text of the letter to Vice President Bush was ambiguous. In contrast to the statements emanating from the White House, Reagan's attorneys aver that it was his intent to act in accordance with the temporary and voluntary transfer provisions of the amendment. If so, the conflicting statements from the White House aides weakened the intent of this part of the amendment—to give unambiguous evidence to the nation that an able leader is in charge.

When Reagan regained consciousness after the two-hour-and-fifty-three-minute procedure, he was disoriented. Members of the White House staff met with the surgeon to discuss the Twenty-fifth Amendment because of concern about whether Reagan was sufficiently clear-minded to carry out the duties of the presidency. Doctor Herbert Abrams, who has painstakingly researched the medical treatment of the president after the Hinckley assassination attempt and its aftermath,[22] describes the remarkable ad hoc manner in which the determination was made that Reagan was competent to regain office. The White House council, Fred Fielding, Chief of Staff Donald Regan, and White House Deputy Press Secretary Larry Speakes devised their own test. A letter had been drafted for the president to sign in order to regain his office:

> Following up on my letter to you of this date, please be advised I am able to resume the discharge of the constitutional powers and duties of the President of the United States. I have informed the Vice President of my determination and my resumption of those powers and duties.
> Sincerely,
> RONALD REAGAN

Fielding, Regan, and Speakes decided that if Reagan could read this two-sentence letter coherently, he was sufficiently lucid to reclaim the office. Fielding asked the attending surgeon to confirm that if Reagan could understand the letter, that would be evidence that he was lucid. The surgeon responded, "Yup." (A thoracic surgeon may be the best judge of respiratory capacity but is surely not the best judge of cognitive capacity.) The White House physician was not involved, nor was any consideration given to administering the most rudimentary tests of cognitive functioning. As Abrams notes, it was essentially Fielding's decision that Reagan should sign the letter. No one asked Reagan whether he felt up to resuming the presidency and wished to do so. There was concern about the public reaction, and it was believed that the sooner the president resumed the responsibilities of office, the sooner the public would be reassured. It was essentially a political decision.

Undergoing general surgery is not a minor procedure, and full recovery takes time. In fact, as we have argued, attempting to exercise the responsibilities of high office while recovering from a serious illness not only can be medically dangerous but can adversely affect leadership decision-making. A year later, when Irangate broke, President Reagan claimed he could not remember the decision to ship arms to Iran—a decision made while he was recovering from surgery. Attorney General Edwin Meese suggested during the Irangate hearings that Reagan might have approved the shipment while "recovering from a serious illness and that his memory could have been impaired as a result of post-operative medication." It was politically expedient to declare the president competent to regain the office immediately after surgery, and it was politically expedient a year later to suggest the president's medical inability to exculpate him from responsibility for the Iran-Contra controversy.

While the temporary relinquishment provision appears to fulfill the requirements for certainty, immediacy, and public acceptability, it is voluntary. That it was not employed under two suitable circumstances suggests that it will be honored more in the breach than in the observance. The White House statements that the situations were not serious enough to warrant use of the amendment do not stand up to scrutiny, for the government was effectively without an officially designated acting president during Reagan's period of incapacity. There was no public expression of concern that so serious a matter as the nation's leadership was worked out by private understanding without public scrutiny. In the event, of course, all went smoothly. If Reagan had entered a prolonged coma, however, Bush's status as an informally designated stand-in without official mandate would have compromised his authority.

Perhaps influenced by President Reagan's private understanding with him at the time of the colon cancer operation, President George Bush reportedly developed a private understanding with Vice President Dan Quayle concerning the circumstances under which Quayle will serve as acting president, again outside the provisions of the Twenty-fifth Amendment. Although this understanding has been applauded, it is not clear why a matter of utmost public concern should be a matter of private understanding. Because the agreement is secret, it does not have the legitimacy of a constitutional provision.

It appears that the Twenty-fifth Amendment—or any procedure involving a matter so close to presidential power—will not be employed so long as the president and inner circle can devise a procedure of their own, exactly fitting their perceptions and wishes. If, as with a sudden event like a stroke or an assassination attempt, there is no opportunity to devise a special instrument, the inner circle will prefer simply to deal with the matter on an ad hoc basis.

It is Section 4 of the amendment, which deals with the circumstances when the disabled president is to be removed involuntarily, that is the most problematic. This procedure, too, has never been implemented. The selection of Nelson Rockefeller to fill the vacancy created by Spiro Agnew's resignation as vice president prompted months of political turmoil and controversy. Imagine the controversy and political infighting that would ensue under the provisions of Section 4, requiring a two-thirds vote by both Houses to replace a president who challenged his own removal. This provision clearly subordinates certainty and immediacy to due process and legitimacy. Unless the situation is clear-cut there will be hearings and debates, lasting as many as twenty-one days. The provision specifies that if supporters of a resisting president can prevent a vote within that period, the president remains in office. Thus opponents of removal will have great incentive for delay.

Medicine is by no means a precise science. The criteria for evaluating and predicting disability will founder upon medicine's inherent uncertainty. One need only consider medical malpractice cases in which certified experts testify to opposite conclusions based on the same case histories and evidence. Psychiatric evaluations are likely to be especially problematic and controversial. In such cases, which in fact would be among the most difficult to resolve medically and the most dangerous for the nation, the psychiatrist's own political attitudes are most likely to contaminate his or her professional judgment.

In fact, nowhere in the Twenty-fifth Amendment are the words *medical* or *physician* used, even though the circumstances that presumably would trigger the provisions of Section 4 are serious medical illnesses. The vice president—surely not a disinterested party—and a majority of the Cabinet would initially determine the President's incapacity. Presumably they would turn to physicians for consultation and recommendations, but they are not required to do so, and whom they choose is left to their discretion.

That judgments concerning the president's competence tend to be made by political figures was again demonstrated in the aftermath of the Iran-

Contra controversy. The dispute precipitated Donald Regan's departure as White House chief of staff. Former Senator Howard Baker was appointed in his stead. He found a badly demoralized White House staff and widespread concern over Reagan's lack of attention to the duties of the presidency.[23] One of Baker's first acts was to ask an experienced aide, James Cannon, to assess systematically the structure and decision-making of the White House. Cannon interviewed a number of senior White House officials who described an inattentive, often distracted president who appeared uninterested in his job: "All he wanted to do was to watch movies and television at the residence."[24] Cannon became so concerned that in his report he recommended that Baker "consider the possibility that Section 4 of the Twenty-fifth Amendment should be applied" because he had concluded that the president "was at the brink of being physically and mentally incapable of carrying out his responsibilities." Baker took the report seriously; accompanied by Cannon, he met with Reagan the next day.[25] After interviewing the president he satisfied himself that there was no basis for such a consequential step, and the matter was closed.

However astute an observer Baker was, it is remarkable that the determination of whether Reagan was disabled and unable to carry out the responsibilities of the president as specified in the Constitution was made by someone who lacked any medical knowledge, with no involvement of medical personnel. Yet, as we have observed in discussing the fluctuating course of cerebral degenerations, early in such illnesses the degree of impairment is easily masked; it requires skilled specialists and sophisticated tests to determine whether there is significant impairment. That medical personnel were excluded from the evaluation makes it clear that the political considerations outweighed the objective medical considerations—as they always will. Once again the White House staff was making decisions that required medical expertise.

The Twenty-fifth Amendment leaves many questions unanswered. Could Congress require a physical or psychiatric examination? Probably not. If it could, who would conduct such an examination? Who would judge and approve the findings?

Now as in the past, obvious cases will present few problems. If the president is comatose as a consequence of a massive stroke and medical opinion is unanimous that he will never recover, the disability determination process will proceed smoothly. The Cabinet and the vice president will regretfully transmit their finding to Congress, and it will be rapidly approved. If instead the nature of the president's illness is not clear, the prognosis and the degree or permanence of the resultant disability are uncertain, or if Congress or the president's circle has reason to fear or dislike the vice president, the situation will be unsettling and marked by conflict.

Although a certain imprecision is useful in such an amendment, the degree of latitude here is so great as to promote political manipulation of the uncertainties. Drawing on the *Report of the Miller Center Commission on Presidential Disability and the Twenty-fifth Amendment* and on Kenneth Crispell and Canos Gomez's *Hidden Illness in the White House,* Herbert Abrams has recommended a number of circumstances that should reduce the discretionary aspects of the amendment and automatically trigger its implementation:[26]

- Any planned surgical procedure that requires general anesthesia.
- The use of psychoactive drugs in significant amounts.
- The perception by the president or his physician that an illness, injury, or emotional condition is interfering with his judgment or ability to govern.
- Any serious illness.
- Death or serious illness in the president's immediate family.
- The diagnosis of Alzheimer's disease or of any other progressive, mentally disabling condition.
- Significant alterations of the president's cognitive faculties or ability to communicate.

Abrams further suggests that the White House physician carry at all times a signed, undated letter from the president invoking the amendment in the event of certain circumstances—among them, any surgical procedure requiring general anesthesia and any serious illness such as a heart attack or stroke.

Even if such guidelines—which themselves raise severe constitutional and practical questions—were to narrow the area of discretion, partisan and factional politics would continue to play a role. This emphasizes another political consideration. Although the Constitution designates the vice president and "the principal officers of the executive departments or of such other body as Congress may by law provide"* to make the crucial determinations and set the constitutional processes in motion, in fact those closest politically and physically to the president are the members of the White House staff. In practice, they, not the Cabinet, stand to lose the most should the president be declared incapacitated and are likely to make the politically crucial decisions.

This fact is well recognized by the White House staff. When Nixon was asked to hold Cabinet meetings during Eisenhower's first illness, Secretary of State Dulles stated at one meeting, "The big question will be, who has access to the President?"[27]

---

*The phrase "principal officers of the executive departments" is apparently intended to denote the Cabinet.

Who has access is indeed the crucial question. And with the illnesses of Wilson, Roosevelt, Eisenhower, Reagan, and Bush, it has been principally the White House staff. Indeed, by not invoking the provisions of the Twenty-fifth Amendment, these assistants to the president—neither elected nor subject to congressional approval—will be involved in critical decisions in all areas of the disabled president's responsibilities.

By failing to invoke the Twenty-fifth Amendment when Ronald Reagan was incapacitated after John Hinckley's attempted assassination, the White House staff rather than Acting President Bush managed day-to-day decisions. It would not be hard to imagine a situation in which the vice president and the Cabinet were on one side and the White House staff and presidential loyalists in Congress were on the other. Again, many would prefer their man sick to someone else's well.

Some have suggested that a way to deal with the problems of constitutional ambiguity, medical uncertainty, and political aggression as well as political diffidence would be to establish a commission of physicians charged with giving their evaluation of the president's health to the responsible officials—the vice president, members of the Cabinet, and perhaps the Congress. Some have even proposed a medical body that would assist in medical screenings of presidential candidates.[28]

Objective medical advice would be helpful, in some cases essential, in determining the leader's competence and medical prognosis. The problem with these proposals is in the details. Quis custodiet custodes? Do Republican doctors make different decisions than Democratic ones? Who will choose the doctors—the president-elect? a bipartisan congressional or judicial committee? the national committee of the president's political party? Each possibility is riddled with land mines and uncertainties.

More troublesome is the question of confidentiality. Will the president be candid about his health with anyone he believes might betray him politically? If his medical files are open to a presidential commission, will he be candid even with his personal physician? A president may very well avoid treatment or even discussion of a problem for fear that it might become grist for rumor or controversy, or even the means to his political extinction. We have seen that some politicians will risk corporeal death to avoid political death.

The utility of a commission on presidential disability was considered in the deliberations that led to the Twenty-fifth Amendment. Because of the complexities concerning the choice and role of the physicians, the concept of a medical commission was rejected. In effect, rather than incorporate a flawed medical mechanism, it was decided to use none at all, with the unfortunate result that physicians' judgments are not systematically incorporated in a decision process that is based significantly on medical understandings.

There is, if not a remedy, a palliative for this dilemma. A designated group of physicians could have medical access to the president and presidential candidates and their medical records in order to advise them about the quality of the care they are receiving; the doctors would otherwise be sworn to secrecy.[29] Someone should have told Wilson that he was severely impaired and would never recover his physical vigor and mental acuity. Someone should have told Roosevelt that his health was failing and that he was not likely to live out his fourth term. Someone should have told Kennedy about the dangers of amphetamines. But these doctors would have to swallow their objections if the president chose to ignore them.

The Twenty-fifth Amendment clearly is by no means a certain bar to disorder and abuse in the event of presidential disability. Nor is it a certain facilitator of transition when disability occurs. At best, it will only imperfectly structure a conflict that is likely to exceed the bounds of legitimate politics.[30] But if the Twenty-fifth Amendment is significantly imprecise, it is a model of precision when contrasted to the disability provisions of other national constitutions, which typically are extremely ambiguous or even nonexistent.

Hindenburg, Hitler, and the Weimar Constitution

Containing elements of both presidential and parliamentary systems, Weimar Germany's government is a pointed example of institutional failure. The system was helpless to remove the decent but doddering President Hindenburg; nor could it prevent the rise of the vigorous but pathological leader Adolf Hitler, whose support was based in the parliament.

Paul Ludwig Hans Anton von Beneckendorff und von Hindenburg was a classic product of the Prussian aristocracy. Born in 1847, he entered military service as a cadet at age eleven and won a commission in the Prussian Foot Guards at sixteen. He was imposing in appearance and bearing. If he lacked imagination, he did not lack loyalty—to his king, his country, and his military colleagues. He gave the impression of calmness and strength. He was a man who could be relied on to act properly—indeed, bravely— as long as the situation did not require creative imagination.

From 1863 until the beginning of World War I, Hindenburg's service in the military was undistinguished, though solid. After Germany had suffered unexpected reversals in the east, however, Hindenburg, by then in his mid-sixties, was given command in that sector. Thanks to his brilliant commanders, Generals Erich Luddendorf and Max Hoffmann, success was achieved, and Hindenburg became a national hero.

When Germany fell to the Allies on the Western Front, Germany's chief military commander, General Wilhelm Groener, decided that "the myth of Hindenburg should be preserved. It was necessary that one great German figure would emerge from the war free from all blame that was attached to the German Staff."[31] So Hindenburg stood above all others as the hero of Germany, someone whom almost all sectors of the public could respect and honor.

At the end of World War I, the victorious allies imposed democracy on Germany. The constitution of the Weimar Republic was skillfully crafted. Yet despite the intelligence of its framers and the dedication of many Germans to democracy, the mid-1920s were years of increasing political chaos and economic ruin. The hero of the Prussian forests was called back in 1925 to serve as president of the republic. In accordance with constitutional provisions, he would share power with the chancellor. But given the political confusion and divisions within Germany, as well as Hindenburg's heroic status, he would in effect select the chancellor, though he could only choose someone who had substantial political support. He chose Heinrich Bruning for the position.

Germany's situation worsened with time, and the international depression hit the Weimar economy hard. By the early 1930s Germany had more than a dozen political parties. There was the Nazi party, the Communist party, the Social Democratic party, and others like them. The Social Democratic party was being ground to pieces between the two fanatical totalitarian parties, and it seemed to many that the victory of either the Nazis or the Communists was inevitable.

Hindenburg had no sympathy for any of these groupings—neither the crude Nazis, nor the internationalist Communists, nor the feckless Social Democrats. When Papen resigned as chancellor in 1932, Hindenburg met with representatives of all the parties to discuss the formation of a new government. This would be a difficult and challenging political task for any leader, but for a man of vigor, intellect, imagination, and determination, not an impossible one.

In 1932 Hindenburg was in his mid-eighties, and his mental powers had manifestly deteriorated: he was "no longer capable of prolonged concentration and often dozed off during lengthy conferences. His conversation, even when the audience was meeting with him on official business, would often wander off to the happier days of the Prussian-Austrian War of 1866. He could remember the names of noncoms who served under him then, although even the memory of his famous victory on the Eastern front at Tannenberg in 1914 was hazy."[32] In fact, evidence of Hindenburg's decline was apparent in 1930. "By then he was in his eighty-third year, physically and mentally exhausted, hardly able to grasp, still less to solve a political crisis for which he had neither training nor aptitude. He leaned increasingly on his advisors. . . . To most Germans Hindenburg with his square head and massive frame was the incarnation of steadfast-ness. . . . Yet his stolidity had for some time been indistinguishable from inertia; the inertia now became a senile torpor."[33]

The befuddled Hindenburg was easy prey for a fellow general with clear and self-promoting ideas for the future of Germany. General Kurt von Schliecher gained access to the aged ruler through his son, who was serving as Hindenburg's personal aide. Schliecher was able to persuade Hindenburg which officials to promote and which to fire, including several chancellors. Heinrich Bruning was dismissed in 1932, a victim of Schliecher's manipulation. He was replaced by the ambitious and irresponsible Franz von Papen, again at the suggestion of the manipulative Schliecher.

Once before, in the mid-1920s, the power of Nazism had blossomed and threatened before wilting. The signs were now again that Hitler's popularity, substantial in 1932, was on the decline. Hindenburg himself held Hitler in low regard. He remarked in mid-1932, "That man for a Chancellor? I'll make him a postmaster and he can lick the stamps with my head on them."[34]

A policy of delay, division, and disengagement was called for, but at Papen's suggestion, a ban on Nazi activity was rescinded. The Prussian premier, Otto Braun, attempted to persuade Hindenburg of the danger of this move but found the aged president uncomprehending. "Hindenburg seemed so terribly senile that my anger at his decree was outweighed by my sympathy for the old man who . . . was now being misled by unscrupulous men in such an infamous way."[35]

Maneuverings continued around the doddering Hindenburg, who was persuaded by the still influential Papen to make the most foolish and most catastrophic of all decisions: to control the Nazi movement by making Hitler chancellor in the expectation that Hindenburg, as president and chief of state, could control Hitler as chancellor and chief of government. This fatal combination of conceit, galloping senility, and cynical manipulation led to the appointment of Adolf Hitler as chancellor on January 18, 1933.

Hindenburg had been stripped of perception and comprehension by his dementing illness, but as president he had retained authority and theoretically ultimate power. Good constitutional arrangements, especially untried ones under the new Weimar constitution could not, however, compensate for a senile leader. Once Hitler came to power, he was able to abrogate or pervert the constitution. In the hands of a strong president, Germany's constitution would have been more than adequate to the task of preventing Hitler's rise to power. In the hands of a senile ruler, it was unable to prevent its own destruction.

Oversight and Disclosure

External observation is almost always a positive influence in the *political* management of leader impairment—that is, in avoiding the dangerous consequences of concealing illness and disability. Yet the *medical* management of the temporarily or partially impaired leader may be adversely affected if it is conducted in the bright glare of publicity. In an open society, the two primary sources of external observation are an independent and aggressive press and the political opposition.

The Role of the Press

A diligent press has a crucial role to play. Such a press is found only in open societies, where freedom of the press is well established and constitutionally protected. Even in open societies, however, appropriate scrutiny is sometimes impossible without the cooperation of the leader and inner circle, as the cases of Roosevelt, Cleveland, and Churchill make clear.

No society has a completely unfettered press. Legal restrictions range from questions of national security to rights of privacy. Moreover, each society has cultural patterns that strongly influence what the press reports. The sexual behavior of political leaders, for example, is generally not reported by the press except when it reaches scandalous proportions or interferes with the conduct of government. Andreas Papandreou's extramarital liaison with the Olympic airline stewardess Mimi Liani was well known to the press for years but was reported only when it became a political embarrassment to the government. Similarly, the extramarital liaisons of several past U.S. presidents—notably Franklin Roosevelt, Dwight Eisenhower, and John F. Kennedy—were known to the press but were considered private and not reported. This tradition of discretion in sexual matters has eroded significantly in the United States in recent years, being replaced by an attitude many media critics decry, so-called attack journalism.

Alcohol abuse is another potentially politically relevant pattern that typically goes unreported. We have already mentioned that the press ignored Senator Key Pittman's alcoholism even though it seriously compromised his performance as chairman of the Senate Foreign Affairs Committee. Thirty years later it ignored similar alcohol abuse by the House Ways and Means Committee chairman Wilbur Mills, until his name was placed on a police blotter.

Sometimes lifelong alcohol abuse goes completely unreported. John Curtin, Australia's prime minister during World War II, had a long history of heavy drinking. The press was aware of but chose not to report this politically relevant impairment.[36] Similarly, John F. Kennedy's apparent amphetamine abuse was not revealed until well after his death.[37]

Even in matters that do not involve sex or substance abuse, the press can be thwarted by a determined inner circle. Recall that in the case of President Cleveland's operation for cancer of the mouth the press broke through the deception, but the resolute denial of the president's staff killed the story. In the case of Woodrow Wilson's stroke, the press was inadequate to its role of monitor, uncritically accepting the reassuring press releases issued by the White House.

In authoritarian societies the lack of a free press means that the illness or impairment of a leader is rarely reported. During the later career of the Soviet leader Leonid Brezhnev and throughout the terms of Yuri Andropov and Konstantin Chernenko, severe diseases associated with old age effectively immobilized Soviet policy, domestic and foreign. This situation was reported at the time in the Western press and has since been acknowledged in the former Soviet Union, but the Soviet public was almost entirely shielded from such knowledge at the time. In a society such as Tunisia where there is strong one-party rule and weak institutions, the threat of government intervention will constrain editorial policy even though the press is in theory independent.

Because of their tradition of an independent press, free societies are better positioned to monitor and evaluate leadership capacity than are more closed systems. At least since the time of George III, until disclosure peaked under Eisenhower, the role of the press as monitor in democratic societies has steadily improved.

The Role of the Opposition

In a democratic society, the opposition maintains an interest in weakening the government led by an ailing leader, but not in weakening the system. It will make public statements (though its members must tread warily so as not to be seen as hitting a sick man when he is down) but it will mostly work through the press, encouraging queries and criticism. When, for example, de Gaulle began to show signs of age and his usually astute political judgment faltered, stories were passed to the press and jokes (an effective weapon of the opposition) were created.

In a democracy, the opposition's best tactic is to work through the press to embarrass the government. To the degree that an opposition can function in an authoritarian system, its only option may be to use the leader's impairment as a continuing demonstration of the government's incompetence and vulnerability. Even in societies with a controlled press and no legal opposition, there will always be opposition forces. As was dramatically demonstrated as the wave of pro-democracy forces swept through Eastern Europe in 1989, in the age of electronic media no society can be totally isolated from the outside world, no leadership totally insulated from scrutiny.

It is in this area of public monitoring and public persuasiveness that highly institutionalized and open systems of government are at their greatest advantage. Such systems tend to resolve substantive questions (Is the leader disabled?) by turning them into procedural questions (How should disability be determined?) and then letting the procedure determine the outcome.

Ailing Leaders in Democracies: Parliamentary and Presidential Systems

The Weimar constitution provided for a mixed system, with both parliamentary and presidential characteristics. Though the system was cleverly contrived, it was inadequate to cope with the disability of its president. But perhaps if it had been a parliamentary *or* a presidential system the story might have had a happier conclusion, despite the major social and historical disabilities Germany faced. And of the two, the parliamentary system, at first glance, would appear to be much more effective in removing disabled leaders than the presidential system.

In presidential systems the chief executive has a fixed term of office that can be changed only through a procedure that differs from system to system but is always awkward. We have seen in the cases of Woodrow Wilson, Franklin Roosevelt, and Georges Pompidou how difficult it can be in presidential systems to identify and remove an ailing leader, especially if he denies his disability and his inner circle is bent on concealing it from public view.

Parliamentary systems, by contrast, tend to have weaker chief executives than presidential (or dictatorial) systems and procedurally are better able to replace or compensate for an ailing chief executive. In a parliamentary system, the chief executive is dependent upon a majority in parliament. That majority can remove him or her from leadership and designate another prime minister without ending the government. The threat, if not the implementation, of this procedure has sometimes worked well, as in the case of Prime Minister Bonar Law of Great Britain and, more recently, the replacement of Margaret Thatcher by John Major as prime minister.

Yet even in a parliamentary system the process of removing a disabled leader is not uniformly effective. Recall that Winston Churchill, who suffered from progressive senile dementia in his final term, was extremely difficult to replace. His illness was well hidden, his country respected him, and he denied the extent of his disability, stubbornly resisting all efforts to replace him. Moreover, the favorite to succeed him, Anthony Eden, was himself temporarily disabled with gall bladder disease, so it was expedient for the leaders of Churchill's party to temporize. They were not disposed to force the issue of Churchill's disability and in fact helped cover up his incapacitation.

Thus even when the disability of the leader is clearly recognized, a parliamentary system may elect to perpetuate the disabled leader in office. Two other British prime ministers, Sir Henry Campbell-Bannerman and Ramsay MacDonald, were maintained in office despite clear signs of pre-senile dementia, a situation in which the afflicted individual is often the last to know.[38] Bert Park has argued that Ramsay MacDonald's mental incapacity contributed to his failure to grasp the seriousness of the threat Adolph Hitler posed and to take steps to impede Hitler's rise to power.[39]

In spite of the openness of Israeli society and the fierce partisan combat that characterizes politics in the Knesset, Prime Minister Menachem Begin's melancholic depression and diminished leadership left his government paralyzed. Begin's supporters denied the extent of his disability and attempted to keep him in office, until Begin himself finally said he could no longer go on. But the period of paralysis lasted more than six months, and this in an open parliamentary system.

Thus, even in parliamentary systems, which institutionally *should* be most effective in replacing impaired leaders, the examples to the contrary are numerous. The removal procedure is effective when the leader is seen to be *politically* impaired, but it may take some time before medical impairment leads to manifest political impairment because the inner circle can obscure the degree of the disability and rule from behind the throne.

Delegatory versus Hands-on Leadership

The power vested in the leader varies widely from system to system and from leader to leader in the same system. The more the king not only reigns but rules, the greater the effect of illness in the throne room. Prudent leaders can, however, moderate the political consequences of their inevitable disability or death. How leaders exercise power also of course varies widely. And although styles of leadership are many and varied, it is useful to consider two positions in terms of delegation and, from this point of view, two types of political system.

At one end of the delegatory continuum is the hands-on approach. Here the leader will not only closely supervise and constantly check on subordinates but, more important, will become actively involved in direct decision-making. Presidents Nixon and Carter fall into this pattern, as did the shah of Iran. Some leaders will become actively involved only in certain areas that interest them, for example foreign policy, while delegating significantly in other areas, such as the national economy.

At the other end of the delegatory spectrum are those leaders who delegate authority widely and whenever possible. Presidents Eisenhower and Reagan are good examples. Such a leader sees his role as setting the general agenda and overall policy goals, choosing subordinates well, and letting them get on with the job. He will not involve himself in details.

Either type of leadership style can be successful or disastrous. Obviously, however, the effect of illness or death of the leader on the political system will be greatest where the leader has been a hands-on administrator. And the consequences are far greater when an autocratic controlling leader who lets no one else make decisions is felled by illness than when a leader who delegates widely falls ill. We saw this in the case of the shah of Iran, whose leukemia prevented him from giving the direction, or even delegating the authority, that his country required.

In contrast, we saw in the case of Dwight Eisenhower how his experience and skill in the staff-oriented military world served him and his nation well in the aftermath of his three illnesses. His military background, in which death and disability are faced more honestly than in civilian life, also led him to formalize succession in the event of disability, which eventually resulted in the Twenty-fifth Amendment.

The designation of a successor when the leader is healthy represents a special case of delegation. As in the choice of a vice-presidential candidate, it is often made more for political purposes than with consideration whether the designee is the best choice to succeed. Moreover, the healthy leader is able to supervise his appointee and can reconsider his choice should circumstances warrant. If the leader subsequently falls ill, it may be too late to redelegate. One of the most tragic lapses of effective delegation of authority in terms of successor designation occurred in the communist leadership of the Soviet Union at a crucial point in its history.

Vladimir Lenin and Josef Stalin:
The Misdelegation of the Century

The Russian Revolution certainly did not establish democracy in what became the Soviet Union. But neither did it immediately establish a tyranny. That came later, with Stalin. Under Lenin there was a dictatorship of the Communist party, but within that circle of loyal Bolsheviks, criticism, both personal and programmatic, was vigorous.[40] Consensual decision-making was emphasized. Although criticism was permitted, and indeed encouraged, it had to be constructive and within certain parameters. Those who challenged the legitimacy of the revolution or of the party's role in it would find themselves treated with the same brutality their counterparts would have received under the czars. Criticism also had to remain within the family; it could not be broadcast publicly. But so long as one stayed within the pale of communist loyalty and did not try to incite outsiders against the party, criticism was permitted.

Lenin stood far above his fellows. Had he chosen to exercise his supreme power in a fully autocratic manner, he probably could have done so. Certainly no one could have stood against any of his decisions. Yet, following the pattern established in the period of revolutionary struggle, Lenin's rule was collegial. He exercised a delegatory style with considerable skill. Much of the political and military success of the early communist government, in the 1920s, is due to Lenin's ability to choose effective subordinates, who carried out their roles with intelligence and vigor.

Lenin had established a successful ruling style, one that had overcome the czar, internal revolts, and covert foreign invasions, as well as consolidating civil authority throughout the land. The impact on Lenin's leadership of the series of strokes that disabled and ultimately killed him at the height of his powers illustrates both the utility of his delegatory style and its limitations.

In spite of the stress of leadership, Lenin's general health appeared excellent. In fact, he was an exercise and general health enthusiast. It was a complete shock to his followers when at just fifty-two years of age, Lenin suffered a major stroke. He may also have suffered minor premonitory strokes in the winter of 1921 and in March 1922,[41] but the evidence is inconclusive. There is no question that he was so stricken in May 1922: "On May 26, 1922, Dr. Rozanov was asked to see Lenin because of abdominal pain and vomiting. The physician was less impressed with Lenin's gastrointestinal complaints than with the finding of some slurring of speech and with a mild right hemiparesis [paralysis of one half of the body]. This, then was the first of a series of strokes that was to result in Lenin's death 20 months later."[42]

Trotsky noted in his memoirs that Lenin had looked unnaturally tired for months before this stroke and had lost his intellectual edge and stamina.[43] Lenin soon also lost his ability to speak and write and had to re-learn those skills. He returned to work officially in October 1922 but soon suffered additional strokes. On January 21, 1924, a year and a half after his first disabling stroke, he died. Lenin's serious illness and death were heavy blows for the Bolsheviks, who had not counted on the incapacitation or death of their leader in addition to all the dangers facing their new regime.

Given his faith in the revolution and his delegatory style, Lenin had reason for optimism about the future of the new government. There was only one thing he feared, one crucial matter he had left undelegated: the selection of a successor. True, little more than a month before his illness, he had made Leon Trotsky deputy chairman of the Council of People's Commissars, interpreted by many as making him the heir presumptive. But he had also seen that Josef Stalin was made general secretary of the Central Committee, another important post. And though these were both significant positions, they were filled while Lenin was a vigorous man in his early fifties. He was trying to balance two different wings in the movement. His departure from the seat of power did not seem imminent.

As Lenin became increasingly ill, plots and counterplots began to swirl around him. The stroke did not affect his personality nor did it, except through fatigue, lessen his keen intelligence. Seeing his death or complete paralysis approach, Lenin sought to correct his one great error in delegation: the admission of Stalin to the inner circle. Lenin noted in a letter to his intimates, his "Testament," that to a Marxist, personality was a trifle in history.[44] History, after all, is determined by impersonal economic forces. But he added that the selection of Stalin would be a *decisive* (by which he meant a catastrophic) trifle.

Lenin sought to prevent this event. As early as seven months after his first serious stroke and just two months after his "recovery," he accused Stalin of being one of several "typical Russian bureaucrats, rascals and lovers of violence." The next month he wrote: "Stalin is too coarse, and this fault, though tolerable in dealings among us Communists, becomes unbearable in a General Secretary. Therefore, I propose to my comrades to find some way of removing Stalin from his position and appointing somebody else who differs in all other respects from Comrade Stalin in one characteristic—namely someone more tolerant, more loyal, more polite, and considerate to his comrades, less capricious, etc."[45] But it was too late. Though Lenin was a skillful delegator, he had made one grave mistake. His illness prevented this mistake from being corrected. The effect of this error and the illness that rendered him incapable of reversing it were to be of inestimably malign consequence.

The metaphor of sharks attacking when blood is in the water rarely holds when a strong leader is ill. In the eighteen months between Lenin's first stroke and his death, there was no impetus to replace him, although there was much maneuvering for position in anticipation of his death. The ailing leader is likely to remain in office, for those around him are reluctant to be seen as attacking, even when it is in their party's or the nation's interest that he step down. The seriously ailing leader may perceive efforts to remove him as a personal attack and retaliate against those seeking his removal. We saw this with Woodrow Wilson when Secretary of State Lansing suggested the president be declared disabled.

Obscuring Subtle Disability

With a progressive illness, when the onset is gradual and the symptoms are fluctuant, the leader is unlikely to present an obvious or consistent public image of disability, even though the disability is evident to the inner circle. In such a circumstance, if the leader and his inner circle ignore how much the illness is compromising his decision-making and effectiveness and carefully orchestrate his public appearances, the disability can be significantly obscured, and public support for a change in leadership will not emerge. Such a situation can present a conscientious court with a choice between being disloyal to what may be a temporarily ill leader and deceiving the public.

As we have seen, this was the case with Franklin Roosevelt during much of his third term—and increasingly at the end of the term. His serious hypertension, heart failure, and chronic pulmonary disease were seriously compromising his effectiveness. The demands on him as commander-in-chief were immense, and his physical weakening left him without the stamina for sustained leadership under the stress of directing a nation at war. Formal disability proceedings were not required, for the end of his third term provided a graceful opportunity for the ailing president to yield the White House to a younger, more vigorous leader. Yet he did not step aside nor did any responsible Democratic leader suggest he do so.

Many factors probably contributed to this unfortunate decision. People are typically reluctant to change leaders during a crisis. Moreover, the severity of Roosevelt's health problems had been concealed even from him, his family, and many in the inner circle by Dr. Ross McIntire, the White House physician. Further, the press throughout Roosevelt's presidency had been complicit in not revealing to the public the extent of his disability from polio, and sustained this posture concerning his far more serious health problems, a situation that would be less likely given today's aggressive media climate. Concern about his health, however, was sufficient that the convention rejected FDR's choice for vice president, Henry Wallace, for the "safe" candidate Harry Truman.

The Roosevelt case is an excellent example of the "self-blinded court." Turning a blind eye is a psychological practice in which a person sees an unpleasant phenomenon but does not fully acknowledge it because either nothing can be done or the cost of recognizing it would be too high. As we noted in quoting the observations of Churchill's doctor, Lord Moran, who was present at Yalta, everyone could see that Roosevelt was largely disconnected from what was occurring around him. Yet the court chose to accept Dr. McIntire's reassurances. To admit the obvious would have been too disruptive.

The Roosevelt example shows that even in an open society the circle around the chief of state has significant opportunity to conceal the fact or degree of the leader's disability, but such concealment goes against the grain of that society. The public's "right to know" is a value regularly voiced in open societies, especially in the United States, and the media receive great latitude in the service of this right.

This stands in vivid contrast to such closed societies as the People's Republic of China and the former Soviet Union under communism, where there has been a strong tradition of secret authoritarian leadership. We saw that the signs were clear that Mao Zedong and Josef Stalin were terminally disabled, and we described the tragic consequences of their disability for their closed societies. Mao's power was lessened (though he was not removed from office) only after he had caused tremendous harm. He was replaced by other high officials through bureaucratic maneuvering. Stalin died of a cerebral hemorrhage while in office, apparently on the verge of mounting another major purge. These societies lacked established means either for identifying disability or for removing a disabled leader. Nor was there a means for effective external observation and intervention. Indeed, one of the central differences between governments in open and closed societies is their accessibility to external scrutiny and influence.

The Sometime Necessity of External Rescue

The Weimar constitution made allowances for the replacement of the German chancellor. The political system of Germany in 1932–33 had a variety of coherent institutions—among them, labor unions, political parties, courts, a parliament, and a bureaucracy. The institutions may have been weak and were eventually pushed aside, but they did exist. Hitler was delayed in his accession to power by institutional means, and it is conceivable that his attempt at totalitarian control could have been frustrated by institutional measures, given adequate leadership.

The situation in newly independent states or in nations that have recently experienced revolution is much less structured, as Habib Bourguiba's Tunisia certainly showed. In such fragile circumstances, it is often difficult to replace an impaired leader because the society is so disorganized and its institutions are so new that they have not yet been consolidated, precedents have not been established, and a force against him cannot be legally sustained. Moreover, leaders will always have some organizations behind them, for the very position carries with it some institutionalized organizational power. In such circumstances leaders will stay in power unless they die, become completely disabled, or are overthrown by outside forces. However, though domestic institutions may be weak, the international system has institutional mechanisms that can be mobilized when rogue nations exceed international norms, despite an inherent reluctance to violate national sovereignty.

In chapter 2, we described how President Idi Amin of Uganda imposed a despotic and murderous rule on his country. More than a hundred thousand people were killed for political or politically related reasons under Amin's leadership. Internal efforts to overthrow Amin were useless. External coercion was needed. International pressure and the mass granting of asylum in 1978 narrowly averted the massacre of Uganda's Asian population.

Using external military force to solve the basic problem—removal of the tyrant himself—was more difficult. Recall that Hitler, though removed from power by external forces, was attacked only after Germany, under his leadership, had committed aggression against a neighboring state. In the case of Amin, though he was privately condemned, there was a reluctance, especially among African leaders, to make this criticism public lest it be seen as interfering in the internal affairs of an African state and encouraging racist attitudes.[46]

Amin's pathology, sadistic paranoia, is often not politically disabling.[47] As in Amin's case, it may be part of an effective and even stable method of rule. Internal institutions may be useless in controlling or removing the leader, as they were with Hitler and Stalin. Finally, it was evident that only concerted action from outside could terminate Amin's destructive rule. Approximately ten years after he took office, neighboring Zambia and Tanzania joined forces and invaded Uganda to end Amin's tyrannical rule. Ever the survivor, Amin escaped and eventually found sanctuary in Saudi Arabia.

There is also another form of external rescue, not from beyond the borders of the country but from beyond the borders of the political system. Recall how Earl Long of Louisiana was removed from the governorship (albeit temporarily) not through any political or constitutional process but simply by the normal civil procedure for psychiatric commitment. Presumably, a president or prime minister in a democracy could also be so replaced, although it is more likely that relatives would be able to prevail in inducing voluntary resignation. The denial often associated with severe mental illness, however, could place such concerned family members in the camp of the enemy, as happened with Bourguiba's wife and son, or as allies in denial, as happened with Wilson's wife Edith.

Disability in Periods of Calm and Crisis

When the chief of state becomes seriously ill, the nation's serenity and security are threatened. Illness during a national crisis compounds the difficulties. In crises that affect the society as a whole—threats of war, natural disasters, economic catastrophes—the nation looks to the leader as rescuer and is likely to give him enhanced power. To question his competence in times of emergency may appear to be—and may in fact be—an act of disloyalty, a vote of no confidence. The ruling elite as well as the public will demand vigorous leadership. There may even be good reasons for withholding information from the public concerning the leader's disability. To reveal the leader's illness in a crisis can produce panic. While effective leadership will be greatly rewarded, the spotlight of attention in the emergency will cast any incompetence in glaring relief.

Recall that Eisenhower's first heart attack had little consequence, in part because there were no urgent political pressures to be faced. Similarly, after the initial shock and once it was clear that Reagan would recover, there was only transient anxiety during Reagan's convalescence from his would-be assassin's attack, as well as during his later cancer surgery. Again, no pressing issues faced the nation. And both Eisenhower and Reagan delegated authority to their staffs, which increased the continuity of leadership during their illness.

In Eisenhower's case, a crisis did develop two years later, when he suffered a stroke before an important NATO meeting. This time the inner circle was much less candid. Similarly, Grover Cleveland's oral cancer surgery was disguised because disclosure that the president might be replaced by a free silver advocate would have caused a financial panic. The two cases demonstrate a general tendency during a national crisis, especially true when the leader is ill: secrecy is magnified, and the circle of individuals with full access to all information is reduced. Moreover, during crises otherwise outspoken persons may keep their own counsel—in Cleveland's case, an impending crisis certainly facilitated secrecy.

In any system in which the leader is expected to perform in public, some impairments are more difficult to hide, even when the times are relatively calm. Prime Minister Ramsay MacDonald of Great Britain became increasingly incoherent in Parliament toward the end of his premiership, in 1935; this behavior eventually helped lead to his being replaced.

Some political systems are so accustomed to a weak or absent ruler that the leader's impairment is hardly noticed if it occurs in a peaceful period. President Antonio Segni of Italy, for example, suffered a stroke in August 1964. The stroke was well reported, but because the illness was officially described as temporary, Italy's parliament could not be convened as an emergency measure. No substantial adverse consequence ensued. In the 1950s and 1960s Italy often had long interregnums, and the government adjusted to that state of affairs.

Thus, on the one hand, the public absence of the leader is less noticeable during a peaceful interlude, which makes it that much easier to mask an illness; on the other hand, however, a crisis can become the rationalization for keeping the infirmity of the leader secret. In other words, secrecy can be maintained when there is no pressure of events, and it can be maintained because there is.

Replacing Constitutional Monarchs

Throughout we have used the terms *king* and *monarch* as metaphors for principal leaders, but many of our examples have indeed been monarchs. It is well to distinguish two classes of monarchs: traditional monarchs, who both rule and reign, and constitutional monarchs.

The shah of Iran and King Talal of Jordan are examples of traditional monarchs. The same rules apply to them as to any other principal political leader—only more so, for the institutionalized constraints upon their exercise of power are few. The constitutional monarch, in contrast, principally serves a symbolic function; he or she reigns but does not rule. The distinction between traditional and constitutional monarchs, then, concerns the exercise of power. In theory, the ruling monarch can exercise power, and the constitutional monarch is powerless. In practice, the distinction is less clear.

The primary role of constitutional monarchs like the queen of England and the king of Sweden is to symbolize the state and the authority of the government. Yet all constitutional monarchs have substantive power as well; they have access to decision-makers, to information, to the media, and by long service and study can gain special competence in certain areas. In time of crisis their symbolic role will attract real power to them. At the same time, the limited nature of their authority means that they are subordinate to the elected civilian authority in the exercise of power. Their special status makes their removal problematic, particularly when they are disabled.

Constitutional monarchs generally enjoy wide latitude, sick or well, as long as they do not interfere in the political system. Yet this latitude is not unlimited. When they do try to interfere, as exemplified by Ludwig II of Bavaria, they are, however, likely to be replaced. In some cases, inappropriate behavior itself can lead to dethronement. Some societies will eliminate an otherwise inoffensive leader if mental illness makes him insufficiently dignified.

Taisho of Japan: The Silly Emperor

Meiji Japan experienced a remarkable revolution from above in the mid-nineteenth century, ending an isolation of more than two centuries and leading to Japan's entrance into the modern world. The revolution was carried on by several key clans, but the cry was "power to the emperor." The Japanese emperor—who represents the oldest continuing political institution in the world—was thus given enhanced importance, and he and his office became associated with Japan's modernization, though his actual role in government remained largely—though not totally—symbolic. The Meiji emperor, the first modern ruler of Japan, reigned from 1867 until his death in 1912 and was succeeded by his son, Taisho.

The Taisho emperor was at first an adequate ruler, but in the early 1920s he began to act eccentrically in a manner grossly inconsistent with Japanese expectations of regal dignity. On addressing the Diet of Japan, he rolled his speech into a cylinder and peered through it as if it were a telescope. As Edward Behr has put it, "Inevitably, as Emperor Taisho's condition (variously thought to have been due to a stroke or an undiagnosed cerebral hemorrhage, but probably stemming from the aftereffects of meningitis in childhood) deteriorated, the *genro* [political elders] assumed increasing power, and so did the empress, who like any loyal Japanese wife, rallied to her husband."[48]

The emperor not only symbolized a new and rapidly changing state but was considered a god by his people and was treated as such even by his closest associates in the royal household. He was a much-needed symbol of continuity and divine legitimacy for the new Japan. The response of the Japanese leadership was effectively to create two gods where there had only been one. The emperor's son Hirohito was made regent in 1921, and Taisho remained retired until his death on December 18, 1926.

The lives of Ludwig II, George III, and Taisho illustrate the problem of replacing a constitutional monarch disabled by mental illness. A constitutional monarch is a symbol, but one that walks, breathes, and sometimes misbehaves. If monarchs deliberately and excessively misbehave, they have forfeited their special position and may be replaced, as was Edward VIII of Great Britain in 1936 after he insisted on marrying the American divorcée Wallis Simpson. But if the leader's disturbing behavior is caused by an illness out of his control, he may be prevented from exercising the authority of office but not removed from it. In each of these instances a regency was established. A regent, of course, cannot fully assume the rights, privileges, and powers of the throne. He lacks the symbolic power that he can attain only when he ascends the throne on the monarch's death.

Replacing Ailing Subordinates

Subordinates are generally replaced with less difficulty than chief executives. Senior ministers found it very hard to remove Habib Bourguiba from office even though he was manifestly impaired, but when Bourguiba's prime minister and heir apparent, Hedi Nouira, suffered a stroke in February 1980, Bourguiba easily replaced him. When the onset of the disability is insidious, however, a subordinate can do great damage before the incapacity is fully recognized.

The cases of Lord Castlereagh in England and Secretary of Defense Forrestal in the United States indicate that captive-king syndromes are much less likely among subordinates than principals. Both men suffered from involutional paranoid reactions, with obvious symptoms of depression and paranoia. In both men, the dramatic change in their behavior led to reasonably prompt recognition, with eventual removal from responsibility. But a "captive baron" circumstance can develop if the onset of illness is less dramatic. To subordinates, a disabled minister denying any incapacity may still be viewed as holding absolute authority. The career consequences of confronting the minister directly may be serious. To go over the minister's head and inform the chief executive will be risky; it will be seen as gross disloyalty by the minister, and if it fails, woe unto the treasonous underling. Moreover, loyalists around the subordinate minister may fight for their boss's retention, and cover for him or her. The process of removing a subordinate from responsibility is far from automatic, especially if the disability is not clear-cut. It takes time before the disability is fully developed, before it is evident, and before the ruler can act upon it, especially if the staff participates in a cover-up.

The mental illness of James Forrestal caused no significant harm to the nation. Nevertheless, especially in the nuclear age, the prospect that a secretary of defense might be suffering from a subtle undiagnosed paranoid reaction is alarming to contemplate. But the Forrestal case also illustrates an important danger-reducing characteristic of some hierarchical systems. Close associates of the impaired leader often will accept only those orders that are proper, ignoring all improper commands. Further, they see that the necessary is done: they initiate actions that would ordinarily be called for. This response to a sick leader is not unique to democratic systems. In his *Psychology of Dictatorship*, G. M. Gilbert recounts how Hermann Göring's subordinates ignored and covered up for the medically impaired leader of the Luftwaffe in the final days of World War II.[49] But one cannot count on subordinates to ignore a paranoid leader's destructive orders, especially in an authoritarian hierarchy, and especially if the leader has punished those who disobeyed him in the past.

Replacing Ailing Judges

Most of the examples given in this book are of executives, generally chief executives. It is in these cases that disability is most obvious, best recorded, and perhaps most consequential. Disability among legislators (for example, Senator Key Pittman) has also been noted. We have observed that in the case of Senator Thomas Eagleton the history of an illness that was considered disqualifying for the vice presidency—in his case, severe depression requiring electroshock treatment—was not viewed by the voting public as disqualifying for the U.S. Senate.

Although all constitutions to various degrees attempt to set the judiciary outside politics, this is never fully possible. In all countries the judiciary is under some degree of political influence—and sometimes is under frank political control. Judges typically are selected through a political process and often have themselves been active politicians at some time in their career. Their decisions have major political consequences.

The president of the United States considers the nomination of justices to the Supreme Court one of his most important responsibilities—and one of his greatest political opportunities. Because these are lifetime appointments, the selection is an intensely political process; all parties to the selection—the president, the Senate, the president's political supporters and opponents, and the public at large—recognize that the confirmed Supreme Court justice will influence the social, political, and economic life of the nation for the rest of his or her life. The practice of appointing judges for life is designed to free them from political influence, but it is this very length of tenure that makes judicial selection so politically consequential. The practice has a major cost, making it possible for senile, alcoholic, or otherwise disabled judges to hold onto their gavels and judicial robes. This is potentially as dangerous to the political system as the disabled monarch clinging to the throne. The U.S. Constitution permits the removal of a judge from the bench despite a lifetime appointment if he or she departs from the standards of "good behavior," but this has not been interpreted to include medical competence.

Although disability on the bench is unquestionably a subject of great importance, scholarly material on the issue is scarce because of the tradition of confidentiality that surrounds all aspects of judicial decision-making.[50] This is especially true concerning the competence of judges. In otherwise open societies there are laws abridging the discussion and exposure of judicial incompetence, even when it is attributable to a medical condition.

The judicial cost associated with revealing an impairment could be high. If it were revealed that a judge was mentally incompetent (through arteriosclerosis, for example) or acting under the influence of psychoactive substances (alcohol or even prescribed medication), decisions reached in his or her court could be appealed on that basis.

But evidence of impaired functioning cannot be fully concealed. Rumors circulate among courtroom habitués, and attorneys and other judges will be aware of impaired sitting judges. Stories about Judge X being drunk every day after lunch or having a hangover every morning are not uncommon. Anecdotes about the aged Judge Y not being able to remember who is the defendant and who is the defending attorney are also told.

As with cases of medical impairment in other branches of government, the system usually copes well. Cases are simply not given to weakened judges, or their work load is cut back considerably. Retirement provisions may be so generous that a judge can leave the bench at any time without suffering a decrease in income. Such policies exist to facilitate not only independence but also easy departure from the bench for the disabled judge. Because the appointment is for life, judges who are permanently or temporarily disabled, who deny their disability, and who are unwilling to remove themselves from the bench pose great difficulties to the system, even though administrative mechanisms have been established to deal with such circumstances.

The most famous case of judicial disability is that of Judge Daniel Paul Schreber, upon whom Freud based his classic "Psycho-analytic Notes upon an Autobiographical Account of a Case of Paranoia."[51] There is unfortunately no discussion of the political process involved in Judge Schreber's removal for a paranoid delusional disorder, though several studies have been written on nonpolitical aspects of Schreber's background.[52] A more accessible case is that of U.S. District Judge John Pickering, which involved precedent-setting constitutional questions, as well as alcoholism, senility, and partisan conflict.

John Pickering: Better My Man Sick Than Yours Well

John Pickering of New Hampshire served as a federal district judge from 1795 to 1804. This was a time during which the provisions of the newly enacted Constitution, essentially the first of its kind in the world, were first being implemented. As in any new system, unexpected problems were springing up, and lack of precedent made them difficult to resolve. The new nation was politically divided in many ways. Most important was the division between the Democratic-Republicans and the Federalists, the former tending to be the more populistic. As always, matters of principle and personality became enmeshed with questions of political advantage.

There seems to be little doubt about Pickering's behavior. His son Jacob wrote to the Senate that his father was "insane." Other Senate testimony given by a member of Congress stated that Pickering would alternate between normality and incoherence.[53] Edward Livermore, an attorney who had appeared before Pickering, later swore to the Senate that the judge seemed to be drunk and actually admitted his intoxication.

Even before he assumed the federal judgeship, Pickering's behavior had suggested emotional disturbance. While a judge he told stories of having visited England, France, and Germany and of having been a cavalry captain in the British army. He even described his military uniform. But these stories, which Pickering apparently believed, had no basis in fact. Another witness noted that Pickering told these stories when sober as well as when intoxicated. The tales may have been the confabulations associated with end-stage alcoholism, which produces organic brain damage. Pickering also refused to ride any ferry across a river, which greatly inhibited his circuit responsibilities in rural New Hampshire. In 1801 he suffered a severe breakdown that involved prolonged self-imposed isolation.

The problem was not identifying the judge's malady—alcoholism and organic brain syndrome—but deciding how to remove him. The Constitution provided for the removal of federal judges only by impeachment. Pickering's sympathizers argued that impeachment was inappropriate in the case of mental illness and that Pickering should be permitted to remain in office but not to receive cases. Pickering was a Federalist, and Federalists supported this point of view. Those arguing for impeachment were Democratic-Republicans. In 1804, Pickering was removed on a straight party vote in the Senate by a two-thirds majority, nineteen to seven.

Pickering's case demonstrates that even where the facts and the ultimate remedy are not in question, the removal of a judicial officer is likely to be affected by political divisions. Whether removal procedures are invoked will depend upon the political consequences. As here, a conservative legislature may prefer its own ailing judge on the bench to a healthy replacement from the opposing party.

Without effective scrutiny, the inner circle may prevent the revelation of the fact or degree of the leader's illness. Without an institutionalized method of removal, again, the leader may never be removed. The inner circle or other partisans of the leader will be able to defeat or at least delay the removal. Without any major press of events, no change may ever take place, except in the most flagrant cases. And, finally, the degree of inner circle resistance will be heavily affected by the attitude of the likely successor toward the inner circle. A hostile alternative will harden the inner circle's will to resist.

In a political system with no definitive procedure for determining succession, if members of the inner circle are convinced that they will suffer individually and collectively in the event that their ailing leader is removed, they will fight to the bitter end. Such was the case with Ferdinand Marcos of the Philippines. In contrast, if an ailing leader's illness quickly becomes public and members of the inner circle are confident of their security under his successor, they not only will not impede but will even facilitate his removal, as the transition from Winston Churchill to Anthony Eden illustrates. But even in this most favorable case, transition is unlikely to be quick or easy. No matter how well institutionalized the political system, when the throne room becomes the sick room, the consequences are incalculable.

7

FINAL DIAGNOSIS

AND PRESCRIPTION

The effects of ailing leadership on the march of history have regularly been underestimated or ignored. In the twentieth century alone, examples of leaders afflicted by serious illness when they occupied the seat of power include Woodrow Wilson, Franklin Delano Roosevelt, Winston Churchill, Anthony Eden, Josef Stalin, Adolf Hitler, Dwight David Eisenhower, Mao Zedong, Mohammed Reza Shah, Georges Pompidou, Ferdinand Marcos, Menachem Begin, and many others. In each case, their leadership was influenced by their illness, but, as we have seen, how it was influenced depended on many circumstances.

The Nature of the Illness and Its Treatment

The nature of the illness is of primary importance. The disease enters a politically stable or predictably developing situation and changes it in an unexpected way. The assassin's bullet, the blockage of an artery, the appearance of a carcinoma may in hindsight be seen as the inevitable work of fate or nature, but when they appear suddenly, they appear to the surprise of all. Even the gradually failing stamina of an aging leader comes as a surprise to close associates.

How illness presents itself significantly influences both its political effects and how it is handled by the inner circle. When the onset is dramatic and undeniable, such as the coronary and stroke that befell Eisenhower during his presidency, the options of the leader and the inner circle are significantly circumscribed. An insidious onset, however, makes it possible to minimize the illness or conceal it from public view.

Whether the resultant impairment is total or partial will determine the political consequences. Moreover, a time-limited illness from which the leader will recover, such as the cancer of President Cleveland, will clearly have different effects from an illness that is episodic or chronic. Obviously, gravest of all is a pre-terminal illness that can only increase in severity, such as the leukemia that ultimately claimed the life of the shah of Iran and the chronic kidney disease that felled Ferdinand Marcos.

Because a leader's followers become psychologically invested in their leader's being wise, judicious, decisive, and in control, an illness that affects the leader mentally and impairs decision-making ability and intellectual acuity is particularly threatening. With the disabilities of old age, the victim of early symptoms of senility is characteristically the last to know or acknowledge his failing abilities. President Hindenburg's leadership was significantly compromised in this way in his last years; Hitler exploited Hindenburg's impaired understanding and judgment in his rise to power.

The declining capacity of the elderly can be masked even when well advanced because the elderly are generally able to draw on experience to maximize what capacities remain. In this endeavor, an inner circle intent on maintaining its power can prop up the ailing leader as a figurehead while it carries out official duties.

Functional psychiatric illnesses, including paranoid and depressive disorders, can profoundly affect leadership. Paradoxically, the subtle undiagnosed mental illness can be more destructive than the blatant full-blown illness. The undiagnosed paranoid can be particularly destructive, especially if he has charismatic qualities.

The expression "the cure is often worse than the disease" has special implications for an ailing leader. Although the illness itself may not affect the leader's mental acuity, the treatment may. This creates a tension between leader competence and patient comfort, which may impel leaders to refuse treatment, endangering their health in the service of furthering their political goals. Sometimes even treatment that will increase the leader's comfort and performance will be avoided out of fear that public knowledge of the leader's illness will weaken his authority. To submit to optimal medical care may thus be politically dangerous, but to avoid treatment to maintain the optimal political image may be fatal.

And in this age of mood-altering drugs, leaders are not immune to the temptations of substance abuse. Both prescribed and illicit drugs can distort decision-making, especially in a crisis. Of particular concern are alcohol abuse and reliance on narcotics and stimulants. Substance abuse is not a private matter. It affects every aspect of the leader's functioning: perceptions, judgment, decision-making, and most important, the balance between his needs and those of his followers.

The Leader's Reaction to Illness

How a leader reacts to illness is largely determined by his personality. This will influence how much he denies or acknowledges the extent of his illness, which in turn will affect his interaction with the inner circle. Obviously, illness has less effect on the leadership of a personally weak or constitutionally limited monarch than on a strong-willed dictator. Whether the leader has the self-confidence, courage, and insight to recognize the illness is important. A leader who can face the intermediate as well as the final consequences of a diagnosis of terminal cancer is apt to escape becoming a captive king.

When circumstances inescapably force a leader to recognize that death is approaching, how he confronts mortality is an expression of his character. Some psychologically mature and well-balanced individuals bear their terminal illnesses, as did Chou Enlai, with equanimity. But for those obsessed with dreams of glory, the end of the heroic life is unthinkable, the appetite for glory seems insatiable, and the end of life always comes too soon. As they face the ebbing of their lives, they may seek to force the pace of history in a frantic attempt to ensure their historic immortality. Such was the case with Mao Zedong and the shah of Iran, and the consequences for their nations were tragic.

In some cases, as we saw with Sudan's Nimeiri, a terminal turn to religiosity can occur, with destabilizing effects when played out on the national scene. Other leaders facing physical weakness act with exaggerated political strength. Menachem Begin, facing death and impelled by his dream of creating a secure Israel within biblical boundaries, made several provocative decisions from his hospital bed, damaging Israel's reputation and international position.

There is no mellowing with age. In fact, personality traits tend to flower in old age. The inevitable decrease in judgment and increased urgency to make one's mark can lead to exaggerated actions in the twilight of a political career. The aged autocrat holding onto power has profoundly affected history—witness Erich Honecker of East Germany and Deng Xiaopeng of the People's Republic of China. The autocratic dictator Honecker was unable to respond to the wave of democracy as it raced through Eastern Europe in the late 1980s. He rigidly maintained his repressive Stalinist style to maintain the regime he had built, despite its clear failure and opposition by his people. The elderly leader Deng Xiaopeng was unable to pass the torch of leadership to the next generation, with the tragic consequence of the massacre at Tiananmen Square.

The individual leader, then, is not merely the object on which the forces of disease and the demands of power impinge. The individual matters.

Three factors associated with the individual and illness determine the political consequences of the disease:

Personality and acceptance of mortality. Is the leader psychologically mature and able to accept and prepare for the approach of death, or is he driven by dreams of glory to accomplish a mission before he dies? If the king believes he has a destiny to fulfill, he may be unwilling to yield the throne. Facing the end of life, the dying king may attempt to achieve the impossible in what time remains.

Awareness or denial of illness. Are the nature of the illness and the leader's personality such that the ruler is aware of and psychologically able to accept the extent of impaired leadership? Or is he psychologically driven to deny it? Or is the nature of the illness such that he does not realize how much it impairs his leadership capabilities? If the leader does not realize or is unwilling to acknowledge that illness or impending death, his attempts to carry on as before will result in a great dislocation of the political system.

Political power. Has the leader exercised much power or little? The greater his power, the greater the effect of his disease. The political context is critical, and the death of a powerful king will especially wound the nation.

The Political Environment

Among the political factors we have examined are the system's level of institutionalization and how open or closed it is, with special emphasis on the role of an independent media and opposition party, the clarity of the succession process, and whether there is a suitable successor to the leader acceptable to the inner circle.

If the system has an institutionalized means of recognizing and coping with a leader's impairment, either by removing the ailing leader or by delegating authority, then the illness is not likely to be very consequential. However, if the system makes no provision for legitimate succession, and the inner circle as well as the leader fear the potential successor, then a circumstance of increasing danger will result. The inner circle will feel compelled to deny the leader's disability while ruling in his stead, the end stage of the captive king syndrome. A divided leadership circle, lacking the coherence for such rule, can simply let the government drift, perhaps to disaster.

The Political Diagnosis of Disability

While the term *diagnosis* has a medical connotation, and physicians are usually involved in the disability process, the determination of leader disability is profoundly political.* A successful *political* diagnosis must fulfill three criteria. Appropriately, two of the political rules of diagnosis are the same as two of the rules for a successful succession:

Certainty. Once the ruler has been "accused" of disability by the court, they must succeed in removing him. The old adage "If you move to strike a king, you must strike to kill" applies here. Once the process is begun, either the ruler or those who have attempted to have him declared disabled will be removed from power. In some countries, to be removed from power under these circumstances can be extremely dangerous. In his memoirs, Khrushchev recounts that he and many other members of Stalin's inner circle had decided that Stalin in the final days had become mad. But they recognized that any action against him would have fatal consequences for them.[1]

Even in a democratic society, it can be politically fatal, as witnessed by Secretary of State Robert Lansing's removal from office for even suggesting that the Cabinet discuss the consequences of President Woodrow Wilson's stroke. Considering the gravity of Wilson's condition, this was a highly sensible suggestion, one required for the nation's welfare. But

---

*It is important to distinguish between *impairment* and *disability*. The American Medical Association, in its *Guides to the Evaluation of Permanent Impairment,* stresses this distinction. *Impairment* is a medical determination that is "directly related to the health status of the individual," whereas "*disability* can be determined only within the context of the . . . occupational demands or statutory or regulatory requirements that the individual is unable to meet as a result of the impairment." Thus *disability* is a function of the occupational context in which the individual operates. It can only be established by relating the impairment to the requirements of the particular job. To illustrate, let us consider two physicians—a surgeon and a psychiatrist—who required amputation of their right arm because of an accident. Both physicians suffered the identical physical impairment, but only one—the surgeon—is disabled. In the political arena, Roosevelt had a permanent physical impairment as a consequence of poliomyelitis, but it did not materially affect his ability to carry out the responsibilities of the chief executive, and hence he was not disabled in that role. When his significant cardiovascular and pulmonary disease impaired his stamina and cognitive functioning, his ability to function with full effectiveness as president was compromised, and hence he was partially disabled.

Bert Park has stressed this distinction in his thoughtful article, "Presidential Disability." He observes that under the present requirements of the Twenty-fifth Amendment, questions of presidential impairment can be considered without drawing upon medical expertise. He emphasizes the need to incorporate medical experts, particularly those with expertise in neurological disease, in adjudicating presidential disability, and suggests a Presidential Disability Commission. Emphasizing the distinction between impairment and disability, he stresses that the role of the physician must be confined to the absolute determination of impairment, and that the degree to which that impairment affects the president's ability to carry out the responsibilities of the presidency necessarily should involve political officials.

Wilson, who denied the extent of his impairment and was supported in that denial by sycophantic members of the inner circle, including his physician, viewed Lansing's actions as disloyal.

Immediacy. Once the question of disability has been raised and the leader has been "accused" of being unable to provide effective leadership, the matter must be rapidly resolved by one of three courses: he must receive a clean bill of health, resign, or be forcibly removed. Until there is some resolution, the government will be paralyzed, lacking legitimate authority.

In revolutionary Iran, for example, because of the intense factional strife between the radical clerics and the pragmatists, it was widely predicted in the West that the death or incapacitation of the Ayatollah Khomeini would precipitate a bloodbath. In fact, Khomeini was significantly disabled in his last years, serving largely as a figurehead. But neither faction could claim a clear advantage. Recognizing the possibility of internecine violence, the rivals reached a tacit understanding not to remove the aged ayatollah, letting his symbolic presence preserve the fragile unity of what had become a drifting regime.

Because the determination of disability is fundamentally a political decision, the leader's adherents may gather around their man, sick or well, and force out the traitors who have so disloyally suggested that he is unfit. If the leader is in fact disabled, then the loyalists of the inner circle will rule in his name, a variant of the captive king syndrome. But if it turns out that the leader is only partially impaired, or recovers from his impairment, then he and his loyalists will continue to rule, and the loyalists' credentials and prospects for ultimate succession will have been strengthened.

An extended period of uncertainty when the leader is out of public view, however, will encourage the opposition to force the issue. Particularly in a closed society where the constraints against violence are minimal, the opposition is likely to go to great lengths to demonstrate that the leader is disabled. If they cannot do so legitimately, they may act to remove him, rationalizing the action as required by the nation's interest.

Plausibility. It will be crucial to the success of any efforts to replace the disabled leader that the allegations of disability are believable. Key actors outside the ruling circle, among them the public, must interpret the effort to remove the leader as motivated and required by the national interest, not by private purposes, or the successor will not be perceived as legitimate. In these cases, a skillful and unscrupulous inner circle may seek to manipulate the failing leader for selfish ends, rationalizing their actions as being for the country's benefit.

Four Principles Governing the Successful Removal of a Disabled Leader

Political systems with weak institutions give the greatest sway to the aberrant behavior of a disabled leader, while mature societies have structured the political environment to guard against individual variability. Four factors are most important in determining whether a disabled leader is likely to be removed:

Effective institutions to provide scrutiny. Are the ailing leader and the inner circle subject to scrutiny from an independent press and a vigorous political opposition?

Clear and respected legal procedures for the transfer of power. Are there well-established procedures for the transfer of power from an ailing leader?

Political demands. Is the nation facing a crisis requiring strong and visible leadership, or is the leader only needed to perform routine tasks?

An alternative leader who promises continuity. Is there a likely candidate who could take the ailing leader's place? If so, will the interests of the inner circle be served by that alternative, or does the alternate pose a danger to the regime?

The Medical Care of the VIP

The royal physician plays a crucial role in dealing with the medically disabled monarch. In most cases one physician will stand first in the leader's confidence and will dominate his health care. The doctor may or may not be a member of the inner circle, but he will obviously have a great influence on the political dynamics surrounding the ailing leader. Hazards abound in the treacherous terrain the royal physician must traverse.

Will the doctor ministering to the medical needs of the leader define his or her primary responsibility as treating a suffering human being as an ordinary private patient, or will the physician subordinate the leader's private needs to some political demand? Does the physician, for example, put the nation's well-being first? And if so, what is his or her view of the public interest? Or is the doctor aligned with some court faction, and does he or she put that faction's interest first?

Depending on where physicians place their loyalty and how they construe their ethical responsibilities, they can play a central role in masking the degree of the leader's illness and in facilitating denial or in removing the mask of health from the medically impaired leader.

Meeting the Dilemma of Patient versus Public Responsibility: Prescription for the Leader's Physician

The primary obligations of the physician are to relieve suffering, prevent untimely death, and improve the health of the patient while maintaining the patient's dignity. The presumption is that the patient's interests come first. Yet physicians, like everyone else, are members of society. When the leader is ill, they must consider the effects of their actions and decisions not only on the patient but on society as well.[2]

To permit a chief executive to abuse amphetamines, for example, would make the doctor a moral accomplice. The physician would in this circumstance bear partial responsibility for a war started while the patient was in an amphetamine-induced paranoid condition. Whether to provide a fatigued leader with stimulants in a crisis may not be so easy a decision, however.

There are no universally accepted rules of ethics by which physicians treat their patients—the Hippocratic oath has long since been rendered obsolete by the complexities of contemporary society and biotechnology. Modern principles, accepted by most physicians, have evolved as the contemporary equivalent of the Hippocratic oath.[3] Robins and Rothschild have suggested the following twelve principles:

- Minimize harm to the patient.
- Do what is medically best for the patient.
- Tell the truth.
- Be candid.
- Encourage maximal patient autonomy.
- Maintain or improve the patient's quality of life.
- Maintain patient confidentiality and respect for the patient's privacy.
- Practice economy.
- Consider the family's wishes if the patient is incapable of making decisions.
- Keep up with developments in medicine.
- Know your limitations; enlist appropriate support systems when indicated.
- Consider the implications for society of your treatment of the patient.[4]

These principles will not seem remarkable to any practicing physician. Several are consistent with the Hippocratic oath. The first requirement for the physician remains *primum non nocere,* to do no harm.

The need to resolve conflicts among competing ethical principles is familiar to all physicians who deal with life-and-death decisions. What is distinctive for the king's physician is the very great importance that he must assign to society's rights. For this the physician has had little experience. So it is that the physician to a major political leader will always operate on unfamiliar ethical grounds. There is no such thing as a purely objective medical decision in such circumstances, for inevitably each medical decision will have political consequences and those consequences will affect medical decision-making. The king's physician must not only balance familiar ethical demands, always a difficult matter, but also balance them on unfamiliar scales.

The central ethical dilemma is confidentiality. The principle of medical confidentiality persists, but even as addressed by Hippocrates it is not absolute. "Whatever I may see or hear in the lives of men *which ought not to be spoken aloud* I will not divulge." Indeed, privilege is generally considered to reside with the patient, not the physician. Moreover, when the patient's revelations in psychiatric treatment reveal danger to others, the physician is under an obligation to break medical confidentiality in response to the higher principle of preserving life. Indeed, the requirement of confidentiality being maintained in a legal framework is specified in the current Principles of Medical Ethics of the American Medical Association: "A physician shall safeguard patient confidences within the constraints of the law." In fact, the obligation of the doctor employing psychotherapeutic treatment to warn and protect endangered third parties has now been adopted into law after the Tarasoff case.*

When, if ever, should the court physician violate the presumptive duties of confidentiality and political loyalty and turn to others for counsel and action? There are no simple formulas, but there are three circumstances in which the normal presumption of confidentiality might be subordinated to that of disclosure: when the leader is not competent to decide his own fate, as for example in circumstances of dementia or severe functional psychiatric disorders, such as mania or severe depression; when the leader is about to commit a major act of illegality because of medical impairment; and when the leader is about to commit a grossly immoral act because of medical impairment.[5]

Such principles do not suggest that the physician can arbitrarily overstep rules of confidentiality or of constitutional role. The physician's ethical dilemmas spring from the fact that he or she must carry out these responsibilities as part of a larger group, as a citizen of the larger society. But this curse is also a salvation. Where responsibility to the patient and responsibility to society strongly conflict, the court physician may turn to others

*The *Tarasoff* case is described in appendix C.

for consultation and support. Robert Simon cites the axiom of the noted forensic psychiatrist Jonas Rappeport, "When in doubt, shout!"

For a court physician, the requirement that he or she first do no harm must apply to society as well as to the patient. This dual obligation of the court physician will pose a dilemma for the ailing royal patient. To the degree that the royal patient sees the boundary of confidentiality as not being absolute, his trust in his physician will be compromised, he may come to see the physician as an adversary, and he may choose to conceal symptoms of a serious illness.

It is difficult to consider the galaxy of world leaders we have encountered in this book who were exercising leadership while medically impaired or facing death, without concluding that illness in high places has often had a great impact on the course of events. It is not a rare aberration but a common occurrence. Moreover, as we have demonstrated, it is by no means confined to closed societies. Seriously ill presidents and prime ministers in modern Western democracies have occupied the seat of power both in times of crisis and in periods of calm.

Ailing leaders can cause great damage by their lack of attention to matters of crucial importance. Special hazards are posed by aging autocrats who hang onto power and by leaders who are consumed by dreams of glory and are struck by illness before they have fulfilled what they believe to be their destiny. Dreams of glory are responsible for some of civilization's greatest achievements, but the intemperate reactions of aging, ailing leaders to the ebbing of their power and the frustrated dreams of their youth have been responsible for some of history's most tragic excesses.

The issue of ailing leaders in the seat of power is not merely a matter of historic interest. Leaders are flesh and blood, subject to the vicissitudes of the life cycle, prone to illness, and inevitably subject to the passage of their years. How leaders and their political systems react to illness and aging will continue to have tremendous consequences for society. Should the leader and his inner circle conceal the illness, profound distortions in leadership dynamics and decision-making can occur as the captive king and his captive court become locked in a destructive and often fatal embrace.

APPENDIX A

"HOLY MADNESS"

LEGITIMATED

Is Saul among the Prophets?

"Holy madness" is one of the oldest forms of legitimation. In the Judeo-Christian tradition it first appears in the story of Saul. Though well liked and from a prominent family, Saul was an unexceptional young man; no one saw him as having any remarkable military or political ability. Moreover, he displayed no particular interest in religion. When Saul was a young man, there was a demand among the Hebrew tribes, however, for a leader, or at least someone who could command them in time of war. Samuel, their informal leader, was too old for this position, and his own son was unfit for the role. But Samuel desired to retain his preeminence, and the only way he saw to do this was to select a new leader he could then manipulate. Saul, with his likable manner and family connections, was the logical choice. Perhaps more important, Samuel must have sensed that Saul was essentially weak and suggestible.

Samuel laid his plans in secret, telling Saul but no one else that Saul would be king. Saul would receive no popular support for this role unless there were some extraordinary event, some apparently divine intervention. Samuel, old and cunning, would have to lay the groundwork carefully. Under Samuel's coaching and suggestion, Saul began to associate with bands of ecstatic prophets and to report having visions with them. At first his friends were surprised: "The people said to one another 'what has come over the son of Kish? Is Saul among the prophets?'" (I Sam. 10:10–11). The exhibition of this holy hysteria puzzled the Hebrews but also planted the idea in their minds that Saul might be someone special. Samuel of course cultivated this idea. And, as is often the case, Saul began himself to believe that he had been divinely selected, that he had a special role to play. Samuel then arranged a lottery of sorts to help the Hebrews select their next king. God's hand was assumed to be involved in the lottery, but, it seems clear, so was Samuel's. Saul won the lottery and, after some other events ascribed to divine intervention, became Israel's first king about 200 B.C.

The holy madness of Saul's youth was not seen as a premonitory sign of the disabling mental illness that ultimately overtook him, nor was it seen as disqualifying him for the throne. On the contrary, it was interpreted as a sign that Saul was divinely inspired and selected and particularly suited for the throne. Years later, when he was an old man, Saul's mental illness became severe, and finally he slipped into a terminal melancholia.

Hung Siu-Tshuen and the Taiping Rebellion

Saul's hysteria was limited in time and scope, though its consequences were great. The most remarkable example of legitimating madness, involving millions of people and the deaths of hundreds of thousands, occurred in southern China in the mid-nineteenth century.

Hung Siu-Tshuen was born near Canton in the early nineteenth century. Canton was one of the first treaty ports, and pressure for westernization and commercialization—for example, the Opium War of 1840–42—focused on that area. Internal disorder prevailed as well. Strong ethnic conflict was rife in neighboring Kwangsi, and the secret part-religious, part-political Triad societies were intensifying their anti-Manchu activities. Hung came from a well-off, prominent family. He showed strong academic promise as a child, and this led his kin to place great hope in him and to spend much money on his education. But Hung failed in repeated efforts to pass the all-important civil service examination in Canton.

In 1837, after yet another failure, he complained of illness, apologized to his family, claimed that his death was imminent, and seemed to go into a trance. He appeared to be dead, but on awakening recounted a vision in which he was brought to a grand place and honored by a large crowd. An old woman, however, said he was dirty, washed him, and took him to a place where an old man cut out his internal organs and replaced them with new ones. Another old man with a golden beard told Hung to exterminate demons to honor him (the old man) and showed Hung the world's present depravity. Such visions continued for forty days, during which Hung was frequently hyperactive and seeing "demons." A psychodynamic reconstruction of this episode would be that Hung's repeated failures on the civil service examinations were intolerable blows to his self-esteem. They precipitated a psychotic decompensation, and he developed restitutive messianic delusions of grandiosity.

Hung's family believed him to be insane and put him under restraint. He appeared to recover spontaneously, but his character was much changed from his prehallucinatory personality. He became more imposing in manner, still severe with those with whom he disagreed but much more self-confident. Probably the special self-concept of his psychotic state had now become a fixed part of his personality. Hung took the examinations once more, failed yet again, and returned to Canton to take up the career of an ordinary schoolteacher. But the messianic ideas that had been vividly expressed in his psychotic visions apparently continued to obsess him.

In 1843, after working six years as a schoolteacher, Hung reconceptualized his experiences, giving them a millenarian interpretation. Christian tracts, part of the influence of the West, were by now widespread in southwest China. One of these had a remarkable catalytic effect on Hung. Now the pieces all fit together, and his destiny was clear. He declared himself to be Jesus' younger brother, the secular as well as religious ruler of the earth. He had come to bring God's message and to lead all to a perfect future. The Holy Ghost, Hung said, spoke directly through him. "Secretly aided by heavenly troops," he and his followers would be invincible. A new organization, the Association of God Worshipers, would give spiritual guidance as well as, perhaps more important, economic and physical protection to his followers.

Hung was clear that what he proposed was different from the policies of other rulers. All those institutions that had hurt him, especially the Confucian system and the Manchu rulers, he set out to destroy. Unlike the long line of rebels, some successful and some not, who had tried to overthrow and then replace the ruling dynasty, Hung wanted to abolish the entire social system. This revolutionary mission made him at first an extremely appealing figure, especially to the poor, but it was eventually one of the main reasons for his defeat.

The Manchus were the demon enemy. Hung called out to his followers to "exterminate the [Manchu] slaves," by which he meant all those who supported the Manchus. He referred to Emperor Hsieng-feng as "the head of the demons" and his five-year-old son as "the demon suckling."

There were practical advantages in being a follower of Hung. Like all successful millenarians, Hung did not rely only on his visions and his claim to be Jesus' brother but also employed practical inducements and traditional appeals. Logically inconsistent with his millenarian appeal but nevertheless useful, he held out the promise of present and future material rewards for his followers and their descendants. In his Proclamation on the Extermination of Demons, he promised, "Your accomplishments shall be recorded forever and your names shall become immortal. Hereditary ranks shall be awarded your sons and honor granted your wives . . . you shall share in the glory of founding a new state" (Hung Siu-Tshuen, "Proclamation of the Extermination of Demons," 863).

Hung appeared insane to others, but, to his followers, the rewards he held out were most important:

> Hung's moments of mental instability appear to have persisted into the war years themselves. As his career drew to a close, his thinking became increasingly dominated by fixed ideas. However, he eventually appeared less a madman than a prophet to the alienated, resentful *lumpen* of South China. Entry into his "Heavenly Kingdom of great peace," with its promise of individual and communal renewal, took the follower from an old life of low status and impoverishment to assured position among the elect and, at least in promise, a life of plenty. (Barkun, *Disaster and the Millennium,* 14–15)

At first Hung's well-disciplined puritanical troops swept all before them. By 1853 they had conquered Nanking, China's second city. Hung promised that complete victory would be theirs within twelve months. But then things started to go badly. Hung was a superb agitator and propagandist but an inept politician and an even more incompetent military strategist. He left warfare and administration to his lieutenants, and they fought among themselves. Moreover, his organization was unable to absorb the many undisciplined recruits who joined his army after the first great victories. Similarly, the new territories he conquered were left almost unsupervised. His extreme radicalism frightened many and rapidly unified his opponents and everyone who had anything to lose. Western interests objected to the disorganization the revolt brought, and Christian missionaries objected to his unorthodox (and competitive) brand of Christianity.

In 1864, eleven years after his early victories, Hung's armies were defeated and he poisoned himself.

Why did Hung do so well at first, and why finally did he fail so badly? Hung had many societal factors in his favor; charismatic leadership is most apt to flourish in a wounded society. But Hung's messianic vision, which had such broad appeal, was a psychotic delusion. He owed his start to mass acceptance of the validity of his delusional ideation. His private madness had been transformed into a public cause. His followers could identify with him because his bizarre experience had the following components:

- It grew out of the fruitless struggle of a talented person to succeed in a decaying world.
- It rejected that decaying world.
- It introduced symbols from a new and strengthening culture.
- It gave its followers a new set of values that satisfied them personally.
- It resulted in military and political success.

When the last characteristic faded, the doctrine faded as well. All God's messages require human validation.

Hung was a seriously impaired leader. We cannot completely discount the possibility that he enhanced and perhaps even made up some of his hallucinatory experiences for political gain. Looking at his life as a whole, especially the early period of failed examinations and personal withdrawal, however, it is evident that Hung had a severe psychosis and persistent destructive delusions. Tragically, the very strength of his hallucinatory messianic ideas inspired his followers and led to bloody civil war.

Appendix B

The Twenty-fifth

Amendment

to the U.S.

Constitution

[1967]

SECTION 1. In case of the removal of the President from office or of his death or resignation, the Vice President shall become President.

SECTION 2. Whenever there is a vacancy in the office of the Vice President, the President shall nominate a Vice President who shall take office upon confirmation by a majority vote of both Houses of Congress.

SECTION 3. Whenever the President transmits to the President pro tempore of the Senate and the Speaker of the House of Representatives his written declaration that he is unable to discharge the powers and duties of his office, and until he transmits to them a written declaration to the contrary, such powers and duties shall be discharged by the Vice President as Acting President.

SECTION 4. Whenever the Vice President and a majority of either the principal officers of the executive departments or of such other body as Congress may by law provide, transmit to the President pro tempore of the Senate and the Speaker of the House of Representatives their written declaration that the President is unable to discharge the powers and duties of his office, the Vice President shall immediately assume the powers and duties of the office as Acting President.

Thereafter, when the President transmits to the President pro tempore of the Senate and the Speaker of the House of Representatives his written declaration that no inability exists, he shall resume the powers and duties of his office unless the Vice President and a majority of either the principal officers of the executive department or of such other body as Congress may by law provide, transmit within four days to the President pro tempore of the Senate and the Speaker of the House of Representatives their written declaration that the President is unable to discharge the powers and duties of his office. Thereupon Congress shall decide the issue, assembling within forty-eight hours for that purpose if not in session. If the Congress within twenty-one days after receipt of the latter written declaration, or, if Congress is not in session, within twenty-one days after Congress is required to assemble, determines by two-thirds vote of both Houses that the President is unable to discharge the powers and duties of his office, the Vice President shall continue to discharge the same as Acting President; otherwise, the President shall resume the powers and duties of his office.

Sections 1 and 2 concern the clarification of rules of succession for vacancies in the offices of president and vice president. The Tyler precedent—that the vice president succeeds in every respect to the office of the president—is confirmed in Section 1. Section 2 provides a means of appointing a vice president if that office falls vacant. Rather remarkably, that provision was used twice within a decade of the amendment's approval.

On October 10, 1973, Vice President Spiro Agnew, as part of a plea bargain, resigned from the vice presidency, leaving the office vacant, and the Twenty-fifth Amendment was put into operation. Political discussions and maneuverings began, and many senior Republicans, including Ronald Reagan, Richard Baker, Nelson Rockefeller, and John Connally, were considered for the post. The nod finally went to senior Representative Gerald Ford (Pritchett 1977). Although there were committee hearings, there was little controversy concerning Nixon's choice. But even so, Ford was not confirmed until December 6, 1973—almost two months after the post fell open. The process was orderly and legitimate, but it failed on two criteria specified earlier: the successor was not specifically designated and the process was not immediate.

About six months later the office of vice president again became vacant when President Nixon resigned under fire and Vice President Ford became president under the provisions of Section 1. Again a new vice president had to be appointed. This time, in a controversial recommendation, Nelson Rockefeller was chosen. It took from August 9, 1974, the date of Nixon's resignation, to December 19, 1974—four months of difficult hearings before Congress—until Rockefeller was sworn in.

The process again worked, but again it showed that the requirement that both houses of Congress approve the nomination of the vice president inevitably led to delay and could become embroiled in political in-fighting.

THE *TARASOFF* PRINCIPLE

The Tarasoff duty to protect when a patient has made a serious threat of physical violence against an identifiable victim derives from a controversial legal case, *Tarasoff v. Regents of the University of California* (1976).

The *Tarasoff* case was concerned with a University of California student who murdered his estranged girlfriend, Tatiana Tarasoff. The student had been under treatment by a university psychologist. In his therapy, he had discussed his stormy relationship and anger toward Tarasoff. The treating psychologist feared that the student posed a danger to his former girlfriend and informed the campus police, who briefly detained and then released him. The student broke off treatment and two months later stabbed Tarasoff to death.

Tarasoff's parents sued the university, claiming an obligation to protect their daughter, including the obligation to warn explicitly of the danger posed by the patient. The court found for the plaintiffs. It first affirmed that the responsibility to protect third parties was present only in those circumstances where a special relationship existed between the victim, the individual whose behavior endangered the victim, and the defendant. The court then asserted that a special relationship did exist in this case by virtue of the treatment relationship between the patient and the treating psychologist. In affirming the lower court's finding, the California Supreme Courted stated: "Once a therapist does in fact determine, or under applicable professional standards should have determined, that a patient poses a serious danger of violence to others, he bears a duty to exercise reasonable care to protect the foreseeable victim of danger."

In the years since this precedent was set, most courts have found that any duty to warn that requires the breaking of confidentiality exists only when there is reason to foresee danger to a specific identifiable individual. In the John Hinckley case (*Brady v. Hopper*), for example, the treating psychiatrist was found not liable because of an inability to foresee the danger to President Reagan and Press Secretary James Brady, given the absence of a specific threat and victim. Other courts, however, have broadened the concept, holding that there is an obligation to warn in cases where patients pose a foreseeable danger to unidentified individuals.

For psychotherapists, this issue has raised an important concern: the sanctity of the consulting room is crucial in establishing a relationship of trust between therapist and patient. Without this guarantee of confidentiality, trust cannot be established, and some disturbed individuals will not enter treatment. Others will not divulge charged material. (Mills, Sullivan, and Eth, "Protecting Third Parties"; Rosner and Weinstock, *Ethical Practice in Psychiatry and the Law,* 203–5; Simon, *Clinical Psychiatry and the Law,* 308–13.)

NOTES

Introduction

1. Flexner, *Washington*, 261.
2. Tyndale, *Rex Inutilis*, cited in Peters, *Shadow King*, 4.
3. Lifton, *Revolutionary Immortality*.

1: When the Throne Room Becomes the Sick Room

1. Dale, *Medical Biographies*, 224.
2. Brooks et al., "Final Diagnosis of President Cleveland's Lesion."
3. *Le Monde* (Paris), April 4, 1974.
4. Ibid.
5. Ibid.
6. Ibid.
7. Ibid.
8. *Agence France Presse* (Paris), March 31, 1975.
9. Woodward, *Veil*, 122–23.
10. Nixon, *Six Crises*, 161.
11. Ibid.
12. Adams, *Firsthand Report*, 162.
13. Post, "On Aging Leaders."
14. Cited by L'Etang, *Pathology of Leadership*, 149.
15. Moran, *Churchill*, 361.
16. L'Etang, *Pathology of Leadership*, 153.
17. Moran, *Churchill*, 437.
18. Ibid.
19. Ibid., 444–45.
20. Stone, review of Gilbert, *Never Despair*, in *Sunday Times Book Review Section*, May 29, 1988.
21. L'Etang, *Pathology of Leadership*, 153–55.
22. Fisher, *Harold Macmillan*, 146.
23. Moran, *Churchill*, 633, 643.
24. Fisher, *Harold Macmillan*, 146.
25. Perkins, *The Roosevelt I Knew*, 74.
26. Moran, *Churchill*, 218, 223, 226.
27. Gunther, *Roosevelt in Retrospect*, 31.
28. Bishop, *FDR's Last Year*, 270.
29. Bullitt, "How We Won the War and Lost the Peace," 86.
30. Burns, *Roosevelt*, 470–71.
31. McIntire, *White House Physician*, 24.
32. Roosevelt and Shallett, *Affectionately, F.D.R.*, 311, 313.

34. Bruenn, "Clinical Notes on the Illness and Death of Roosevelt," 579–91.
35. Park, *Impact of Illness on World Leaders*, 226.
36. Bishop, *FDR's Last Year*, 201–2.
37. Tully, *FDR: My Boss*, 274.
38. Flynn, *Roosevelt Myth*, 403.
39. Sherwood, *White House Papers of Hopkins*, 2:812.
40. Park, *Impact of Illness on World Leaders*, 228.
41. McIntire, *White House Physician*, 24.
42. Bishop, *FDR's Last Year*, 499.
43. Park, *Impact of Illness*, 223.

2: The Mad King

1. Rogow, *James Forrestal*, xii.
2. Richter, *Mad Monarch*, 12.
3. Chapman-Huston, *Bavarian Fantasy*, 103.
4. Ibid., 166–67.
5. Anderson, "Death Anxiety and Political Motivation"; Strozier, *Lincoln's Quest for Union*; Forgie, *Patricide in the House Divided*.
6. Henry, "Psychiatric Illness of Castlereagh," 320.
7. Bartlett, *Castlereagh*, 1, 2, 259.
8. Leigh, *Castlereagh*, 349.
9. Henry, "Psychiatric Illness of Castlereagh," 320.
10. Leigh, *Castlereagh*, 350.
11. Bartlett, *Castlereagh*, 262.
12. Leigh, *Castlereagh*, 351.
13. Ibid., 354.
14. Hyde, *Strange Death of Castlereagh*, 182–90.
15. Ibid., 23.
16. Leigh, *Castlereagh*, 351.
17. Moran, *Churchill*; Storr, "Churchill's Black Dog."
18. Storr, "Churchill's Black Dog."
19. Moran as quoted in ibid., 98.
20. Storr, "Churchill's Black Dog," 99.
21. Fraser, *Cromwell*, 36–37.
22. Henry, "Personality of Cromwell," 102–10.
23. Silver, *Begin*, 111.
24. Ibid., 16.
25. Ibid., 30.
26. Ibid., 143.
27. Ibid., 117.
28. Perlmutter, *Life and Times of Begin*, 365.
29. Ibid., 361.
30. Ibid., 19.
31. Silver, *Begin*, 251–52.
32. Lee as quoted in Porter, *Social History of Madness*, 3.
33. Toland, *Hitler*, 888.
34. Payne, *Life and Death of Hitler*, 545.
35. Maser, *Hitler*, 228.
36. Khrushchev, *Khrushchev Remembers*, 283, 307–11.

37. Tucker, *Stalin as Revolutionary*, 460.
38. Ibid., 461.
39. Conquest, *Great Terror*.
40. Robins, "Paranoid Ideation and Charismatic Leadership"; Robins and Post, "Paranoid Political Actor."
41. Khrushchev, *Khrushchev Remembers*.
42. Amnesty International, *Equatorial Guinea*, 3. This section on Macias draws on Decalo, *Psychoses of Power*, 31–76.
43. Liniger-Goumaz, *Historical Dictionary of Equatorial Guinea*, 189.
44. Melady, *Idi Amin Dada*, 167.
45. Ibid., 88.
46. Quoted in Kyemba, *State of Blood*, 7, 15.
47. Melady, *Idi Amin Dada*, 40.
48. Ibid., 61.
49. Kato, "Escape from Kampala," 79.
50. *Sunday Times* (London), October 22, 1978.
51. Melady, *Idi Amin Dada*, 17.
52. Robins, "Paranoid Ideation and Charismatic Leadership"; Robins and Post, "Paranoid Political Actor."

3: The Royal Treatment

1. L'Etang, "Effects of Drugs on Political Decisions," 15.
2. Nixon, *Six Crises*, 285.
3. Wiegele, "Presidential Physicians and Presidential Health Care," 83.
4. Johnson, *White House Diary*.
5. *Washington Post*, August 25, 1986.
6. Thomas, *Suez Affair*.
7. James, *Anthony Eden*.
8. L'Etang, *Fit to Lead?* 97.
9. Lord Evans, medical consultant to Eden, quoted in ibid., 96.
10. Manchester, *Glory and the Dream*, 763.
11. This section draws on Rensberger, "Amphetamines."
12. *John F. Kennedy: A Family Album*, cited in L'Etang, *Fit to Lead?* 94, 95.
13. Report of Miller Center Commission.
14. Irving, *Secret Diaries of Hitler's Doctor*, 304–10.
15. Ibid., 14–15.
16. Ibid.
17. L'Etang, *Fit to Lead?* 89.
18. L'Etang, "Effects of Drugs on Political Decision"; Dalton, *Fateful Years;* Gorlitz, *Memoirs of Keitel;* Moseley, *On Borrowed Time.*
19. Baker, *Good Times*, 304–5.
20. Remmick, "Alcohol Said to Fuel Coup."
21. Ibid.
22. Glad, *Key Pittman;* Glad, "Personality, Role Strains and Alcoholism."
23. *U.S. News and World Report*, February 26, 1934.
24. Cited in Glad, "Key Pittman and Roosevelt Administration."
25. *Washington Post*, January 21, 1990.
26. Ibid.

27. Ibid.
28. Ibid.
29. Baldwin, "High Anxiety."

4: The Royal Physician

1. Brooke, *King George III*, 324.
2. Macalpine and Hunter, *George III*, 19.
3. Brooke, *King George III*, 329.
4. Runyan, "Progress in Psychobiography."
5. Ibid.; Macalpine and Hunter, *George III*; Brooke, *King George III*.
6. Quoted in Macalpine and Hunter, *George III*, 25.
7. Warren, cited in Porter, *Social History of Madness*, 44.
8. Porter, *Social History of Madness*, 44.
9. Ibid., 50.
10. Dr. William Heberden the Younger, cited in ibid., 50.
11. Greville, cited in ibid., 45.
12. Rev. Dr. Francis Willis, cited in ibid., 47.
13. Greville, cited in ibid., 46, 47.
14. Porter, *Social History of Madness*, 45.
15. Ibid., 48.
16. Volkan and Itzkowitz, *Immortal Atatürk*, 331–43.
17. Tumulty, *Woodrow Wilson*, 434–35.
18. Smith, *When the Cheering Stopped*, 90.
19. Grayson, *Wilson: An Intimate Memoir*, 101.
20. Smith, *When the Cheering Stopped*, 89.
21. Ibid., 99.
22. Grayson, *Wilson: An Intimate Memoir*, 53.
23. Tumulty, *Woodrow Wilson*, 238.
24. Grayson, *Wilson: An Intimate Memoir*, 53.
25. Wilson, *My Memoir*, 290.
26. Tumulty, *Woodrow Wilson*, 443–44.
27. Silva, *Presidential Succession*.
28. Grayson, *Wilson: An Intimate Memoir*, 106–7.
29. Ibid., 114.
30. Link et al., eds., *Papers of Woodrow Wilson*, 362–63.
31. Weinstein, "Denial of Presidential Disability," 379.
32. Smith, *Thank You, Mr. President*, 134.
33. McIntire, *White House Physician*, 67.
34. Taylor, "Exclusive Interview," 37.
35. *Washington Post*, November 27, 1986.
36. Park, *Impact of Illness on World Leaders*, xx.
37. Wiegele, "Presidential Physicians and Presidential Health Care."
38. Wandycz, *United States and Poland*, 293.
39. Campomenosi, "Adverse Effect of Roosevelt's Deteriorating Health"; United States of America, *Foreign Relations of the U.S.*, 129; Brezinski, "Future of Yalta."
40. Brezinski, "Future of Yalta," 279.
41. Altman, "Unique Problems."
42. Weinstein, *Woodrow Wilson*.
43. Durusau, "Buddy's Buddy," 5.

44. Kucharski, "On Being Sick and Famous."
45. Tyler, "Kin Says Khomeini Had Cancer."
46. Shawcross, *Shah's Last Ride;* Breo, "Shah's Physician Relates Story of Intrigue."
47. *New York Times,* July 16, 1984.
48. Ibid., April 16, 1985.
49. Ibid., March 16, 1985.
50. *Veja* (Brazil) March 27, 1985.
51. *New York Times,* April 5, 1985.
52. *Veja* (Brazil) April 10, 1985.
53. *New York Times,* July 24, 1985.
54. *Washington Post,* April 22, 1985.
55. *New York Times,* April 16, 1985.
56. Ibid., January 3, 1946.
57. Rogow, *James Forrestal,* 239.
58. Ibid., 55–56.
59. Forrestal, *Forrestal Diaries.*
60. Rogow, *James Forrestal,* 6.
61. Ibid., 307.
62. Ibid., 9.
63. Henderson and Gillespie, *Textbook of Psychiatry,* 274.
64. Rogow, *James Forrestal,* 38–39.
65. Ibid., 1–48.
66. Ibid., 5.
67. Ibid., 7.
68. *New York Herald Tribune,* May 24, 1949, cited in ibid.
69. *New York Times,* April 13, 1949, cited in ibid., 11.
70. *Washington Post,* April 9, 1949, cited in ibid., 10.
71. Rogow, *James Forrestal,* 16, citing Rear Admiral Morton D. Willcutts, commanding officer of the Naval Medical Center.
72. Ibid.
73. Mark Smith, M.D., chairman, Department of Emergency Medicine, George Washington University Medical Center, personal communication, December 1990.
74. Ibid.
75. Trevor-Roper, "Medicine in Politics."
76. Speer, *Inside the Third Reich* and *Spandau;* Lifton, *Nazi Doctor.*
77. Johnson, *Borgias,* 187–88.
78. Lifton, *Nazi Doctors.*
79. *Observer* (London), September 8, 1985.
80. L'Etang, *Pathology of Leadership.*

5: Sitting Crowned upon the Grave

1. Moran, *Churchill,* 840.
2. Iremonger, *Fiery Chariot,* 228.
3. Lifton, *Revolutionary Immortality.*
4. Cody, "Papandreou Embroiled in Love, Money."
5. Ibid.
6. Ibid.
7. *Washington Post,* January 19, 1989.

8. *Macleans,* January 30, 1989, 20.
9. *Washington Post,* January 30, 1989.
10. Ibid., February 3, 1989.
11. *Los Angeles Times,* March 13, 1989.
12. *Macleans,* March 27, 1989, 30.
13. *Los Angeles Times,* March 13, 1989.
14. Ibid., August 15, 1989.
15. Ibid.
16. Ibid.
17. Ibid.
18. Ibid.
19. Zonis, "Fear of Flying," 154–55.
20. Ledeen and Lewis, *Debacle,* 119.
21. Middle East Report, Foreign Broadcast Information Service (hereinafter FBIS), June 25, 1980.
22. Ibid., July 7, 1980.
23. *Jerusalem Post,* July 15, 1980.
24. Ibid., December 15, 1981.
25. De Launay, *De Gaulle and His France;* Werth, *France, 1940–1945,* 203.
26. Françoise Mauriac, quoted in Isaak, *Individuals and World Politics,* 109.
27. Post, "On Aging Leaders"; Post, "Dreams of Glory."
28. Yeltsin, *Against the Grain,* 69–70.
29. Solovyov and Klepikova, *Behind the High Kremlin Walls,* 44–49.
30. Soviet Report, FBIS, June 14, 1986.
31. Ibid., June 15, 1983.
32. Solovyov and Klepikova, *Behind the High Kremlin Walls,* 44.
33. *New York Times,* February 16, 1984.
34. *Newsweek,* March 12, 1984.
35. Soviet Report, FBIS, April 2, 1984.
36. *New York Times,* May 12, 1984.
37. Soviet Report, FBIS, June 26, 1984.
38. Ibid., February 7, 1985.
39. Ibid., February 14, 1985.
40. *New York Times,* March 12, 1985.
41. Ibid., July 24, 1989.
42. Ibid., September 11, 1989.
43. *Washington Post,* September 14, 1989.
44. Ibid.
45. *New York Times,* November 11, 1989.
46. *Washington Post,* October 19, 1989.
47. *New York Times,* October 10, 1989.
48. *Washington Post,* October 8, 1989.
49. *New York Times,* November 19, 1989.
50. *Los Angeles Times,* October 8, 1989.
51. *New York Times,* November 19, 1989.
52. Ibid.
53. For biographical material concerning Nimeiri and analyses of his leadership of Sudan, see Baynard, "Nimeiri"; Bechtold, *Politics in the Sudan;* Khalid, *Nimeiri and the Revolution of Dis-May;* and Woodward, *Sudan, 1898–1989.*

54. Khalid, *Nimeiri and the Revolution of Dis-May*, 47.
55. Nimeiri, *The Islamic Way, Why?*
56. Khalid, *Nimeiri and the Revolution of Dis-May*, 212.
57. *Al Ayan*, December 4, 1981, cited in ibid., 351.
58. *Al Sahafa*, May 25, 1984, cited in ibid., 262.
59. Ibid., 269.
60. *Los Angles Times*, June 25, 1989.
61. Ibid.
62. Asian Report, FBIS, November 19, 1989.
63. *New York Times*, November 19, 1989.

6: The Rules of the Kingdom

1. Gibb and Bowen, *Islamic Society and the West*, 36.
2. Barber, *Sultans*, 79ff.
3. Ibid., 80.
4. Gibb and Bowen, *Islamic Society and the West*, 37.
5. Arab Africa Report, FBIS, November 9, 1987.
6. Bourguiba, interview in *L'Expres*, September 1, 1960, in LaCouture, *Demigods*, 150.
7. LaCouture, *Demigods*.
8. Ibid.
9. Moore, *Tunisia since Independence*, 71.
10. LaCouture, *Demigods*, 171.
11. Ibid., 168.
12. *New York Times*, June 2, 1970.
13. Habeeb, "Zine el Abidine Ben Ali," 82.
14. *Newsweek*, January 28, 1974.
15. North Africa Report, FBIS, August 1, 1978.
16. Ibid., October 30, 1978.
17. Ibid., intermittent reports from 1967 to 1986, March 28, May 7, 1979.
18. Ibid., November 24, 1986.
19. *Independent* (London), November 10, 1987.
20. Habeeb, "Zine el Abidine Ben Ali," quoting from an interview in *Le Monde*, November 8, 1987.
21. Nixon, *Six Crises*, xvi–xvii.
22. Abrams, *"The President Has Been Shot,"* 202–5.
23. Ibid.
24. Mayer and McManus, *Landslide*, ix.
25. Abrams, *"The President Has Been Shot,"* 218–19.
26. Ibid., 221–27, 234–36.
27. Ambrose, *Nixon*, 375.
28. Park, "Doctors for the President"; Robins and Rothschild, "Doctors for the President"; Schattman, "National Press."
29. Robins and Rothschild, "Doctors for the President."
30. Ibid.
31. Quoted in Friedlander, "About Three Old Men," 467–73.
32. Ibid., 471.
33. Ryder as quoted in Park, *Impact of Illness on World Leaders*, 79.
34. Eyck as quoted in ibid., 85.
35. Braun as quoted in ibid., 84.

36. Ross, *John Curtain for Labour and Australia.*
37. Rensberger, "Amphetamines."
38. L'Etang, *Pathology of Leadership,* 57–60, 70–72.
39. Park, *Impact of Illness on World Leaders,* 93–116.
40. Tucker, *Stalin as Revolutionary.*
41. Friedlander, "About Three Old Men," 471–72.
42. Ibid., 472.
43. Trotsky, *My Life,* 489–508.
44. Tucker, *Stalin as Revolutionary,* 471.
45. Friedlander, "About Three Old Men," 472.
46. Ulman, "Human Rights and Economic Power," 528–43.
47. Robins "Paranoid Ideation and Charismatic Leadership"; Robins and Post, "Paranoid Political Actor."
48. Behr, *Hirohito,* 24–25.
49. Gilbert, *Psychology of Dictatorship.*
50. Handberg, "Talking about the Unspeakable," 70–73.
51. Schreber, *Memoirs of My Nervous Illness;* Freud, "Psycho-analytic notes."
52. Shattman, *Paranoia or Persecution: The Case of Schreber;* Kantor and Herron, "Paranoia and High Office," 507–11.
53. U.S. Congress, Senate, *Debates and Proceedings,* March 3–12, 1803.

7: Final Diagnosis and Prescription

1. Khrushchev, *Khrushchev Remembers.*
2. Kucharski, "On Being Sick and Famous"; L'Etang, *Fit to Lead?* Post and Robins, "Captive King"; Robins and Rothschild, "Doctors for the President"; Wiegele, "Presidential Physicians."
3. Englehardt, *Foundations of Bioethics;* Jonsen, Siegler, and Winslade, *Clinical Ethics.*
4. Robins and Rothschild, "Ethical Dilemmas."
5. Ibid.

BIBLIOGRAPHY

Abrams, H. *"The President Has Been Shot."* New York: W. W. Norton, 1991.

Adams, S. *Firsthand Report.* New York: Harper, 1961.

Alexander, L. "The Commitment and Suicide of King Ludwig II of Bavaria." *American Journal of Psychiatry* 3 (1954): 100.

Altheide, D. L. "Mental Illness and the Law: The Eagleton Story." *Sociology and Social Research* 61 (1977): 138–55.

Altman, L. K. "Unique Problems for a Physician Who Makes (White) House Calls." *New York Times,* February 21, 1989, 19.

Ambrose, S. E. *Nixon: The Education of a Politician, 1913–1962.* New York: Simon and Schuster, 1987.

American Medical Association. *Guides to the Evaluation of Permanent Impairment.* 2d ed. Chicago: American Medical Association, 1984.

Amnesty International. *Equatorial Guinea: Torture.* New York: Amnesty International, 1990.

Anderson, D. G. "Death Anxiety and Political Motivation: The Psychology of Abraham Lincoln." Paper presented at the annual meeting of the International Society of Political Psychology, July 20, 1983.

Baker, R. *The Good Times.* New York: Morrow, 1989.

Baldwin, D. "High Anxiety." *Common Cause Magazine* (July–August 1989): 35–38.

Barber, N. *The Sultans.* New York: Simon and Schuster, 1973.

Barkun, M. *Disaster and the Millennium.* New Haven and London: Yale University Press, 1974.

Bartlett, C. J. *Castlereagh.* New York: Scribner's, 1966.

Baynard, S. A. "Jafar Mohammed Nimeiri." In B. Reich, ed., *Political Leaders of the Contemporary Middle East and North Africa: A Biographical Dictionary.* New York: Greenwood Press, 1990.

Bechtold, P. *Politics in the Sudan: Parliamentary and Military Rule in an Emerging African Nation.* New York: Praeger, 1976.

Behr, E. *Hirohito.* New York: Vintage, 1989.

Bishop, J. *FDR's Last Year, April 1944–1945.* New York: William Morrow, 1974.

Blake, R. *The Unknown Prime Minister: The Life and Times of Andrew Bonar Law.* London: Eyre and Spottiswoode, 1955.

"Bourguiba's Demand for Crackdown Led to Coup." *Independent* (London), November 10, 1987.

Breo, D. L. "Shah's Physician Relates Story of Intrigue, Duplicity." *American Medical News,* August 7, 1981, 3–22.

Brezinski, Z. "The Future of Yalta." *Foreign Affairs* 63 (Winter 1984–85): 279–302.

Brooke, J. *King George III.* New York: McGraw-Hill, 1972.

Brooks, J. J., et al. "The Final Diagnosis of President Cleveland's Lesion." *Transactions and Studies of the College of Physicians of Philadelphia* 2 (1980): 1–26.

Bruenn, H. "Clinical Notes on the Illness and Death of President Franklin D. Roosevelt." *Annals of Internal Medicine* 72 (1970): 579–91.

Bullitt, W. "How We Won the War and Lost the Peace," *Life Magazine,* September 6, 1948.

"Burnham Death Puzzle." *London Observer,* September 8, 1985, 6.

Burns, J. M. *Leadership.* New York: Harper and Row, 1978.

———. *Roosevelt: The Lion and the Fox.* New York: Harcourt, Brace and World, 1956.

Butler, Lord. *The Art of the Possible.* London: Hamish Hamilton, 1971.

Camic, C. "Charisma: Its Varieties, Preconditions, and Consequences." *Sociological Inquiry* 50 (1980): 5–24.

Campomenosi, L. "The Adverse Effect of Roosevelt's Deteriorating Health on the Outcome of the Negotiations on Poland at the Yalta Conference." Unpublished paper, 1982.

Chapman-Huston, D. *Bavarian Fantasy: The Story of Ludwig II.* London: John Murray, 1955.

Chernenko, K. *Establishing the Leninist Style of Party Work.* Moscow: Political Literature Publishing House, 1983.

"Churchill's Stroke Kept Secret." *New Orleans Times-Picayune,* January 2, 1984.

Cocks, G. "The Hitler Controversy." *Political Psychology* 1 (1979): 67–81.

Cody, E. "Papandreou Embroiled in Love, Money." *Washington Post,* December 2, 1988.

Connel, P. H. *Amphetamine Psychosis.* London: Maudsley Monographs, no. 5, 1958.

Conquest, R. *The Great Terror: Stalin's Purge of the Thirties.* New York: Macmillan, 1973.

Cornell, C. S., and M. P. Leffler. "James Forrestal: The Tragic End of a Successful Entrepreneur." In J. W. Doig and E. C. Hargrove, eds., *Leadership and Innovation.* Baltimore: Johns Hopkins University Press, 1987, 369–406.

Crispell, K., and C. Gomez. *Hidden Illness in the White House.* Durham, N.C.: Duke University Press, 1988.

Curwen, C. A. *Taiping Rebel: The Deposition of Li Hsiu-Ch'eng.* Cambridge: Cambridge University Press, 1977.

Dale, P. M. *Medical Biographies.* Norman: University of Oklahoma Press, 1952.

Dalton, H. *The Fateful Years, 1931–45.* London: Frederick Muller, 1957.

Deaver, M. "The Reagan Legacy." C-SPAN television interview, January 3, 1989.

Decalo, S. *Psychoses of Power.* Boulder, Colo.: Westview, 1989.

de Launay, J. *De Gaulle and His France: A Psychopolitical and Historical Portrait.* New York: Julian Press, 1968.

"Did Ronald Reagan Get Bad Medical Advice about His Polyps?" *Johns Hopkins Magazine,* October 1985, 55.

Durusau, M. "Buddy's Buddy." *Baton Rouge Sunday Advocate Magazine,* July 10, 1988, 3–6.

Englehardt, H. T., Jr. *The Foundations of Bioethics.* New York: Oxford University Press, 1986.

Feerick, J. D. *From Failing Hands: The Story of Presidential Succession.* New York: Fordham University Press, 1965.

————. *The Twenty-fifth Amendment.* New York: Fordham University Press, 1976.

Finifter, A. W., ed. *Political Science: The State of the Discipline.* Washington, D.C.: American Political Science Association, 1983.

Fishborne, E. G. "Impressions of China and the Present Revolution, 1855." In P. Clarke and J. S. Gregory, eds., *Western Reports on the Taiping Rebellion.* London: Croom Helm, 1982, 55–61.

Fisher, N. *Harold Macmillan.* London: Weidenfeld and Nicolson, 1982.

Flexner, J. T. *Washington: The Indispensable Man.* London: Collins, 1976.

Flynn, J. *The Roosevelt Myth.* New York: Devin-Adair, 1948.

Forgie, G. B. *Patricide in the House Divided.* New York: Norton, 1979.

Forrestal, J. *The Forrestal Diaries.* New York: Viking Press, 1951.

Fraser, A. *Cromwell.* London: Weidenfeld and Nicolson, 1973.

Freud, S. "Psycho-analytic Notes on an Autobiographical Account of a Case of Paranoia [1903]." *Standard Edition,* 12:9–82. Trans. and ed. J. Strachey. London: Hogarth Press, 1958.

Friedlander, W. J. "About Three Old Men: An Inquiry into How Cerebral Arteriosclerosis Has Altered World Politics; A Neurologist's View." *Stroke* 3 (1972): 467–73.

Gallagher, H. G. *FDR's Splendid Deception.* New York: Dodd, Mead, 1985.

George, A. L. "Problems of Crisis Management and Crisis Avoidance in U.S.-Soviet Relations." Paper presented to the Nobel Institute Symposium on War and Peace Research, Oslo, June 1985.

George, A. L., and J. L. George. *Woodrow Wilson and Colonel House.* New York: John Day, 1956.

————. "Woodrow Wilson and Colonel House: A Reply to Weinstein, Anderson, and Link." Paper presented at the fourth annual meeting of the International Society of Political Psychology, Mannheim, June 1981.

Gibb, H., and H. Bowen. *Islamic Society and the West,* vol. 1: *Islamic Society in the Eighteenth Century.* New York: Oxford University Press, 1950.

Gilbert, G. M. *Psychology of Dictatorship.* New York: Ronald Press, 1950.

Gilbert, R. E. "Disability, Illness, and the Presidency." *Politics and the Life Sciences* 7 (1988): 33–49.

————. "Personality, Stress, and Achievement: Keys to Presidential Longevity." *Presidential Studies Quarterly* 15 (1985): 33–50.

————. "Psychological Pain and the Presidency: The Case of Calvin Coolidge." *Political Psychology* 9 (1988): 75–100.

Glad, B. *Key Pittman.* New York: Columbia University Press, 1986.

————. "Key Pittman and the Roosevelt Administration." Paper presented at annual meeting, International Society of Political Psychology, Oxford, July 20, 1983.

————. "Personality, Role Strains, and Alcoholism: Key Pittman as Chairman of the Senate Foreign Relations Committee." *Politics and the Life Sciences* 7 (1988): 18–32.

Goldberg, R. T. *The Making of Franklin D. Roosevelt: Triumph over Disability.* Cambridge, Mass.: Abt Books, 1981.

Gooddy, W. "Brain Failure in Private and Public Life." *British Medical Journal,* March 3, 1979, 591–93.

Gorlitz, W. *The Memoirs of Field Marshal Keitel.* London: William Kimber, 1965.

Grayson, C. *Woodrow Wilson: An Intimate Memoir.* New York: Holt, Rinehart, and Winston, 1960.

Greenstein, F. *The Hidden-Hand Presidency: Eisenhower as Leader*. New York: Basic Books, 1982.

Grey, I. *Ivan the Terrible*. New York: Lippincott, 1964.

Gunther, J. *Roosevelt in Retrospect*. New York: Harper, 1950.

Habeeb, W. M. "Zine el Abidine Ben Ali." In B. Reich, ed., *Political Leaders of the Contemporary Middle East and North Africa: A Biographical Dictionary*. New York: Greenwood, 1990.

Handberg, R. B. "Talking about the Unspeakable in a Secretive Institution: Health and Disability among Supreme Court Justices." *Politics and the Life Sciences* 8 (August 1989): 70–73.

Harriman, W. A., and E. Abel. *Special Envoy to Churchill and Stalin, 1941–1946*. New York: Random House, 1975.

Heaton, L. D., et al. "President Eisenhower's Operation for Regional Enteritis." *Annals of Surgery* 159 (1965): 661–66.

Henderson, D., and P. Gillespie. *A Textbook of Psychiatry for Students and Practitioners*. London: Oxford University Press, 1956.

Henry, W. D. "The Personality of Oliver Cromwell." *Practitioner* 215 (1975): 102–10.

———. "The Psychiatric Illness of Lord Castlereagh." *Practitioner* 204 (1970): 318–23.

Herman, C. F., ed. *International Crises: Insights from Behavioral Research*. New York: Free Press, 1972.

Heston, L. L., and R. Heston. *The Medical Casebook of Adolph Hitler*. London: William Kimber, 1976.

Hinder, W. *Castlereagh*. London: Collins, 1981.

Holsti, O. *Crisis, Escalation, War*. Montreal: McGill-Queens University Press, 1972.

Holsti, O., and A. L. George. "The Effects of Stress on the Performance of Foreign Policy Makers." In C. P. Cotter, ed., *Political Science Annual*, vol. 6. Indianapolis: Bobbs-Merrill, 1974, 255–319.

———. "Crisis Management: Proclivities for Tunnel Vision and Misperception." Paper presented at the ninth annual scientific meeting of the International Society of Political Psychology, Amsterdam, June 29–July 3, 1986.

"How Amin Chooses His Victims." *Sunday Times* (London), October 22, 1978, 10.

Hughes, C. W., et al. "A Review of the Late General Eisenhower's Operations." *Annals of Surgery* 173 (1971): 793–99.

Hung, Siu-Tshuen. "Proclamation of the Extermination of Demons." In F. Michael, ed., *The Taiping Rebellion*. Vol. 3. Seattle: University of Washington Press, 1971, 859–64.

Hyde, H. M. *The Rise of Castlereagh*. London: Macmillan, 1933.

———. *The Strange Death of Lord Castlereagh*. London: Icon, 1959.

Iremonger, L. *The Fiery Chariot: A Study of British Prime Ministers and the Search for Love*. London: Secker and Warburg, 1970.

Irving, D. *Adolph Hitler: The Medical Diaries*. London: Sidgwick and Jackson, 1983.

———. *The Secret Diaries of Hitler's Doctor*. New York: Macmillan, 1983.

Isaak, R. *Individuals and World Politics*. 2d ed. Monterey, Calif.: Duxbury, 1981.

James, R. R. *Anthony Eden: A Biography*. New York: McGraw-Hill, 1987.

Johnson, A., Jr. "Governor Earl K. Long: Political and Medical Disabilities in Office." Unpublished paper, 1982.

Johnson, L. B. *A White House Diary*. New York: Dell, 1970.

Johnson, M. *The Borgias*. London: Macdonald, 1981.

Jonsen, A. R., M. Siegler, and W. J. Winslade. *Clinical Ethics*. New York: Macmillan, 1986.

Kantor, R. E., and W. G. Herron. "Paranoia and High Office." *Mental Hygiene* 52 (1968): 507–11.

Karlen, A. *Napoleon's Glands: And Other Essays in Biohistory*. Boston: Little, Brown, 1984.

Kato, W. "An Escape from Kampala." *Granta* (Winter 1987–88): 77–128.

Khalid, M. *Nimeiri and the Revolution of Dis-May*. London: KPI, 1985.

Khrushchev, N. *Khrushchev Remembers*. Boston: Little, Brown, 1970.

Kucharski, A. "On Being Sick and Famous." *Political Psychology* 5 (1984): 69–82.

———. "Medical Management of Political Patients: The Case of Dwight D. Eisenhower." *Perspectives in Biology and Medicine* (1978): 115–26.

Kyemba, H. *A State of Blood*. New York: Ace, 1977.

LaCouture, J. *The Demigods*. New York: Alfred A. Knopf, 1970.

Lasswell, H. *Psychopathology and Politics*. Chicago: University of Chicago Press, 1930.

Lawrence, J. "Depression No Political Death Knell." *New Orleans Times-Picayune*, April 30, 1990, A-2.

Ledeen, M., and W. Lewis. *Debacle: The American Failure in Iran*. New York: Vintage, 1982.

L'Etang, H. *Fit to Lead?* London: Heinemann, 1980.

———. "The Effects of Drugs on Political Decisions." *Politics and the Life Sciences* 7 (1988): 12–17.

———. "The Health of Statesmen and Affairs of Nations." *Practitioner* 180 (1958): 113–18.

———. *The Pathology of Leadership*. London: Heinemann, 1970.

Leigh, I. *Castlereagh*. London: Collins, 1951.

Lifton, R. *The Nazi Doctors: Medical Killing and the Psychology of Genocide*. New York: Basic Books, 1986.

———. *Revolutionary Immortality: Mao Tse-tung and the Cultural Revolution*. New York: Norton, 1968.

Liniger-Goumaz, M. *Historical Dictionary of Equatorial Guinea*. 2d ed. London: Scarecrow, 1988.

Link, Arthur, et al., eds. *The Papers of Woodrow Wilson*. Vol. 64. Princeton: Princeton University Press, 1991.

Littlewood, R. "The Imitation of Madness: The Influence of Psychopathology upon Culture." *Social Science and Medicine* 19 (1984): 705–15.

Lule, G. Foreword to H. Kyemba, *A State of Blood*. New York: Ace, 1977.

Macalpine, I., and R. Hunter. *George III and the Mad-Business*. New York: Pantheon, 1969.

McIntire, R. T. *White House Physician*. New York: G. P. Putnam's Sons, 1946.

McIntosh, C. *The Swan King: Ludwig II of Bavaria*. London: Allen Lane, 1982.

McIntyre, A. "The Aging Narcissistic Leader: The Case of Sir Oswald Mosley at Mid-Life." *Political Psychology* 4 (1983): 483–500.

Magnor, T. "Yugoslavia and Tito: The Long Farewell." *Current History* 74 (19787): 154–58.

Manchester, W. *The Glory and the Dream*. Boston: Little, Brown, 1973.

Marmor, M. F. "Wilson, Strokes and Zebras." *New England Journal of Medicine* 307 (1982): 528–35.

Maser, W. *Hitler*. Trans. P. and B. Ross. New York: Harper, 1961.

Mayer, J., and D. McManus. *Landslide*. Boston: Houghton-Mifflin, 1988.

Mazrui, A. "Boxer Muhammad Ali and Soldier Idi Amin as International Political Symbols." *Comparative Studies in Society and History* 19 (1977): 189–215.

Melady, Thomas P. *Idi Amin Dada: Hitler in Africa*. Kansas City: Sheed, Andrews & McMeel, 1977.

Michael, F. *The Taiping Rebellion*. Volume 1. Seattle: University of Washington Press, 1966.

Mills, M., G. Sullivan, and S. Eth. "Protecting Third Parties: A Decade after Tarasoff." *American Journal of Psychiatry* 144 (January 1987): 68–74.

Moore, C. *Tunisia since Independence*. Berkeley: University of California Press, 1965.

Moran, C. *Churchill Taken from the Diaries of Lord Moran: The Struggle for Survival, 1940–1965*. Boston: Houghton Mifflin, 1966.

Moravee, F. *Master of Spies*. Garden City: Doubleday, 1975.

Morreels, C. L., Jr. "New Historical Information on the Cleveland Operations." *Surgery* 62 (1967): 542–51.

Moseley, L. *On Borrowed Time*. London: Weidenfeld and Nicolson, 1969.

Nimeiri, J. *The Islamic Way, Why?* Khartoum: Government Press, 1978.

Nichols, J. "President Kennedy's Adrenals." *Journal of the American Medical Association* 201 (1967): 115–16.

Nixon, R. M. *Six Crises*. London: Allen, 1962.

Pahlavi, M. R. *Mission for My Country*. New York: McGraw-Hill, 1961.

Paige, G. *The Scientific Study of Political Leadership*. New York: Free Press, 1977.

Park, B. E. *The Impact of Illness on World Leaders*. Philadelphia: University of Pennsylvania Press, 1986.

———. "Presidential Disability: Past Experiences and Future Implications." *Politics and the Life Sciences* 7 (August 1988): .

Payne, R. *The Dream and the Tomb*. New York: Stein and Day, 1984.

———. *The Life and Death of Adolf Hitler*. New York: Popular Library, 1973.

Perkins, F. *The Roosevelt I Knew*. New York: Viking, 1946.

Perlmutter, A. *The Life and Times of Menachem Begin*. New York: Doubleday, 1987.

Peters, E. *The Shadow King: Rex Inutilis in Medieval Law and Literature, 751–1327*. New Haven and London: Yale University Press, 1970.

Porter, R. *A Social History of Madness: The World through the Eyes of the Insane*. London: Weidenfeld and Nicolson, 1987.

Post, J. M. "Dreams of Glory and the Life Cycle." *Journal of Political and Military Sociology* 12 (1984): 49–60.

———. "Narcissism and the Charismatic Leader-Follower Relationship." *Political Psychology* 7 (1986): 675–88.

———. "On Aging Leaders: Possible Effects of the Aging Process on the Conduct of Leadership." *Journal of Geriatric Psychiatry* 6 (1973): 109–16.

———. "The Seasons of a Leader's Life." *Political Psychology* 2 (1980): 36–49.

———. "Woodrow Wilson Re-Examined: The Mind-Body Controversy Redux and Other Disputations." *Political Psychology* 4 (1983): 289–331.

Post, J. M., and R. S. Robins. "The Captive King and His Captive Court: The Psychological Dynamics of the Disabled Leader and His Inner Circle." *Political Psychology* 11 (1990): 331–51.

"Rehnquist Shared East's Doctor." *Washington Post National Weekly Edition*, August 25, 1986, 38.

Reich, B. *Political Leaders of the Contemporary Middle East and North Africa: A Biographical Dictionary.* New York: Greenwood, 1990.

Remmick, D. "Alcohol Said to Fuel Coup by Gang of Eight." *Washington Post,* August 30, 1991.

Rensberger, B. "Amphetamines Used by a Physician to Lift Moods of Famous Patients." *New York Times,* December 4, 1972.

Report of the Miller Center Commission on Presidential Disability and the Twenty-fifth Amendment. White Burkett Miller Center of Public Affairs at the University of Virginia. Latham, Md.: University Press of America, 1988.

Rhodes-James, R. *Anthony Eden.* London: Weidenfeld and Nicolson, 1986.

Riccards, M. P. "The Presidency: In Sickness and in Health." *Presidential Studies Quarterly* 7 (1977): 215–30.

Richter, W. *The Mad Monarch: The Life and Times of Ludwig II.* Trans. W. S. Schlamm. Chicago: Regnery, 1954.

Rigby, T. H. "Was Stalin a Disloyal Patron?" *Soviet Studies* 38 (1986): 311–24.

Robins, R. S. "Introduction." In R. S. Robins, ed., *Psychopathology and Political Leadership,* 1–33. New Orleans: Tulane Studies in Political Science, 1977.

———. "Paranoid Ideation and Charismatic Leadership." *Psychohistory Review* 5 (1986): 15–55.

———. *Political Institutionalization and the Integration of Elites.* Beverly Hills, Calif.: Sage, 1976.

———. "Recruitment of Pathological Deviants into Political Leadership." In R. S. Robins, ed., *Psychopathology and Political Leadership,* 53–78. New Orleans: Tulane Studies in Political Science, 1977.

Robins, R. S., and R. M. Dorn. "Stress and Political Leadership." Unpublished paper, 1991.

Robins, R. S., and J. M. Post. "The Paranoid Political Actor." *Biography* 10 (1987): 1–19.

Robins, R. S., and H. Rothschild. "Doctors for the President." *New York Times,* April 7, 1981, 25.

———. "Ethical Dilemmas of the President's Physician." *Politics and the Life Sciences* 7 (1988): 3–11.

———. "Hidden Health Disabilities and the Presidency: Medical Management and Political Considerations." *Perspectives in Biology and Medicine* 24 (1981): 240–66.

Rogow, A. A. *James Forrestal.* New York: Macmillan, 1964.

———. "Private Illness and Public Policy: The Case of James Forrestal and John Winant." *American Journal of Psychiatry* 125 (1969): 1093–98.

Rogow, A. A., and H. D. Lasswell. *Power, Corruption, and Rectitude.* Englewood Cliffs, N.J.: Prentice-Hall, 1963.

Roosevelt, J., and S. Shalett. *Affectionately, FDR.* London: Harrap, 1960.

Rosen, G. *Madness in Society.* London: Routledge and Kegan Paul, 1968.

Rosenhan, D. L. "On Being Sane in Insane Places." *Science* 179 (1973): 250–58.

Rosner, R., and R. Weinstock, eds. *Ethical Practice in Psychiatry and the Law.* New York: Plenum Press, 1990.

Ross, L. *John Curtin for Labour and Australia.* Canberra: Australian National University Press, 1971.

Runyan, W. McK. "Progress in Psychobiography." *Journal of Personality* 56 (1988): 295–326.

Schattman, P. "Health Screening for Political Candidacy." *Perspectives in Biology and Medicine* 33 (Autumn 1989): 45–49.

Schreber, D. P. *Memoirs of My Nervous Illness.* Trans. I. Macalpine and R. A. Hunter. London: Dawson, 1955.

Seagrave, S. *The Marcos Dynasty.* New York: Fawcett-Columbine, 1988.

Seton, M. *Panditji.* London: Denis Dobson, 1967.

Shapiro, J. "Aging and Political Leadership." Unpublished paper, 1981.

Shattman, M. "Paranoia or Persecution: The Case of Schreber." *Family Process* 10 (1971): 177–207.

Shaw, M. *The John F. Kennedys: A Family Album.* New York: Farrar Straus, 1964.

Shawcross, W. *The Shah's Last Ride.* New York: Simon and Schuster, 1988.

Sherwood, R. *The White House Papers of Harry L. Hopkins.* Vol. 2. London: Eyre and Spottiswoode, 1949.

Shuckburgh, E. *Descent to Suez: Diaries, 1951–56.* London: Weidenfeld and Nicolson, 1986.

Silva, R. D. *Presidential Succession.* New York: Greenwood Press, 1968.

Silver, E. *Begin.* London: Weidenfeld and Nicolson, 1984.

Simon, R. I. *Clinical Psychiatry and the Law.* Washington, D.C.: American Psychiatric Press, 1987.

Smith, A. M. *Thank You, Mr. President.* New York: Harper, 1949.

Smith, G. *When the Cheering Stopped: The Last Years of Woodrow Wilson.* New York: Time, 1964.

Soames, M. *Clementine Churchill.* Boston: Houghton-Mifflin, 1979.

Solovyov, V., and E. Klepikova. *Behind the High Kremlin Walls.* New York: Dodd, Mead, 1986.

Speer, A. *Inside the Third Reich.* Trans. R. and C. Winston. New York: Macmillan, 1970.

———. *Spandau: The Secret Diaries.* Trans. R. and C. Winston. New York: Macmillan, 1976.

Stepan, A. "Political Leadership and Regime Breakdown: Brazil." In J. J. Linz and A. Stepan, eds., *The Breakdown of Democratic Regimes: Brazil,* 110–27. Baltimore: Johns Hopkins University Press, 1978.

Stevens, R. A. "A President's Assassination." *Journal of the American Medical Association* 246 (1981): 1673–74.

Stone, N. Review of M. Gilbert, *Never Despair: Winston Churchill, 1945–1965.* In *Sunday Times* (London) *Book Review,* May 29, 1988, 1.

Storr, A. "Winston Churchill's Black Dog." *Esquire,* January 1969, 95.

Strozier, C. *Lincoln's Quest for Union.* New York: Basic Books, 1982.

Taylor, A. J. P. *Churchill Revised.* New York: Dial, 1969.

Taylor, B. "An Exclusive Interview with William M. Lukash, M.D., Personal Physician to the President of the United States." *Maryland State Medical Journal* (November 1977).

Thomas, H. *The Suez Affair.* London: Weidenfeld and Nicolson, 1967.

Thomas, L. *The First President Johnson.* New York: William Morrow, 1968.

Toland, J. *Adolf Hitler.* New York: Doubleday, 1976.

Torre, M. "Psychopathology and Political Leadership." *American Journal of Psychotherapy* 24 (1970): 611–26.

Trevor-Roper, H. "Medicine in Politics." *American Scholar* 51 (1981–82): 23–42.

Trotsky, L. *My Life.* New York: Pathfinder Press, 1970.

Tucker, R. C. "The Rise of Stalin's Personality Cult." *American Historical Review* 84 (1979): 347–66.

————. *Stalin in Power, 1929–1941.* New York: Norton, 1990.

————. *Stalin as Revolutionary, 1879–1929.* New York: Norton, 1973.

Tugwell, R. *The Democratic Roosevelt.* Baltimore: Penguin, 1957.

Tully, G. *FDR: My Boss.* Chicago: People's Book Club, 1949.

Tumulty, J. *Woodrow Wilson as I Knew Him.* New York: Doubleday, Page, 1921.

Turner, L. W. *William Plumer of New Hampshire, 1759–1850.* Chapel Hill: University of North Carolina Press, 1962.

Tyler, P. E. "Kin says Khomeini Had Cancer." *Washington Post,* June 12, 1989.

Ulman, R. H. "Human Rights and Economic Power: The United States versus Idi Amin." *Foreign Affairs* 56 (1978): 528–43.

United States Congress. Senate. *Debates and Proceedings.* 8th Cong., 1st sess., 1803–4, 10:13. March 3–12, 1803, pp. 315–68.

United States of America. *Foreign Relations of the U.S.: The Conference at Malta and Yalta.* Washington, D.C.: Government Printing Office, 1955.

Volkan, V., and N. Itzkowitz. *The Immortal Atatürk.* Chicago: University of Chicago Press, 1984.

Wallace, A. F. C. "Stress and Rapid Personality Changes." *International Record of Medicine* 169 (1956): 761–74.

Wandycz, P. S. *Soviet-Polish Relations, 1917–1921.* Cambridge: Harvard University Press, 1969.

Weinstein, E. "Denial of Presidential Disability: A Case Study of Woodrow Wilson." *Psychiatry* 30 (1967): 376–91.

————. *Woodrow Wilson: A Medical and Psychological Biography.* Princeton: Princeton University Press, 1981.

Werth, A. *France, 1940–1945.* London: Beacon, 1966.

Wharton, B. K. "Nasal Decongestion and Paranoid Psychosis." *British Journal of Psychiatry* 117 (1970): 439.

Wiegele, T. "Decision Making in an International Crisis." *International Studies Quarterly* 17 (1973): 295–335.

————. "Models of Stress and Disturbance in Elite Political Behaviors: Psychological Variables and Political Decision Making." In R. S. Robins, ed., *Psychopathology and Political Leadership,* 79–112. New Orleans: Tulane Studies in Political Science, 1977.

————. "Presidential Physicians and Presidential Health Care." *Presidential Studies Quarterly* 20 (1990): 71–89.

Wiegele, T., et al. *Leaders under Stress.* Durham, N.C.: Duke University Press, 1985.

Wilson, E. *My Memoir.* New York: Bobbs-Merrill, 1939.

Woodward, B. *Veil.* New York: Simon and Schuster, 1987.

Woodward, P. *Sudan, 1898–1989: The Unstable State.* Boulder, Colo.: Lynne-Rienner, 1990.

Yap, P. M. "The Mental Illness of Hung Hsiu-ch'uan." In Chun-Tu Hsueh, ed., *Revolutionary Leaders of Modern China.* New York: Oxford University Press, 1971, 32–54.

Yeltsin, Boris. *Against the Grain.* New York: Summit Books, 1990.

Zonis, M. *Majestic Failure: The Fall of the Shah.* Chicago: University of Chicago Press, 1991.

————. "Fear of Flying and Phallic Narcissism." In M. J. Fischer et al., *Psychological Approaches to Middle East Studies.* Chicago: University of Chicago Press, 1985.

INDEX